Joystick Nation

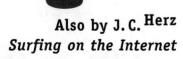

Also by J. C. Herz

Surfing on the Internet

Joystick Nation

J.C. HERZ

How Videogames Ate Our Quarters, Won Our Hearts, and Rewired Our Minds

Little, Brown and Company
Boston New York Toronto London

First Edition

The author is grateful for permission to include the following previously
copyrighted material:

Excerpt from "Nintendo and New World Travel Writing: A Dialogue,"
by Mary Fuller and Henry Jenkins, from *Cybersociety: Computer-Mediated
Communication and Community*, edited by Steve Jones.
Copyright © 1995. Published by Sage Publications Ltd.
Reprinted by permission.

Herz, J. C.
Joystick nation : how videogames ate our quarters, won our
hearts, and rewired our minds / J. C. Herz. — 1st ed.
p.   cm.
ISBN 0-316-36007-4
1. Computer games — History.   2. Videogames — History.   I. Title.
GV1469.15.H47   1997   97-434
794.8 — dc21

10   9   8   7   6   5   4   3   2   1

MV — NY

Published simultaneously in Canada by
Little, Brown & Company (Canada) Limited
Printed in the United States of America

To Mark Herz, my vidkid little brother.
YOWIE MOOEY!!!!!

Con_{tents}

Joystick Nation

Prologue

I was born the same year as the first coin-operated videogame, the same year that Intel stamped out its first microprocessor. I have no memory of a world devoid of colored dots chasing each other across a screen. I was toggling a joystick before I learned to read, mastered *Breakout* stratagems before memorizing the multiplication table, conquered *Asteroids* before solving the mystery of long division. Videogames have become a fixture of American childhood, and like most fixtures of childhood, they have a way of lodging and burrowing into the crevices of your mind. If *Citizen Kane* took place in the twenty-first century, Orson Wells would be sighing, "Mario!" instead of "Rosebud."

As this book is published, two generations of kids have grown up on five generations of videogames. This is not a small group of people. This is not a subculture. This is 50 million adults whose memory and imagination have been colored by Atari, Nintendo, and Sega, the same way that the memory and imagination of previous generations were tinted by television, cinema, and vinyl records. If your memories have pop soundtracks or big-screen kisses, if you've ever told an anecdote with instant replays or a coda of stadium applause, it's because you've been brought up with media that furnish those conven-

1

tions. Videogames provide a new set of conventions, which are being rapidly assimilated, as you read this, by a legion of six-year-olds. Their mental grammar is going to reflect that, just as the baby boomers' worldview echoes the impact of television.

But whereas TV turned kids of the fifties and sixties into a nation of screen watchers, videogames have created a cadre of screen *manipulators*. When you grow up playing *Missile Command*, you come to expect some kind of causal relationship between the choices you make and images on a screen. The kids that wiled away endless hours playing *Galaxian* are the same ones who'll walk six blocks to an ATM rather than wait for a bank teller. Why wait in line to confront some snarling drone when the whole process is just a pantomime of human interaction. At the Department of Motor Vehicles, you're not dealing with desk clerks, you're dealing with their computers. See how suddenly useless they become when the system goes down. So why not save yourself the aggravation and deal with the computer directly? If you can handle *Virtua Fighter 2*, you can handle computer banking, electronic tax returns, and the American Airlines online reservation system. You may even be able to hack the competing services of your local phone company, long distance carrier, cable service, satellite broadcast network, and World Wide Web browser.

Videogames are perfect training for life in fin de siècle America, where daily existence demands the ability to parse sixteen kinds of information being fired at you simultaneously from telephones, televisions, fax machines, pagers, personal digital assistants, voice messaging systems, postal delivery, office e-mail, and the Internet. International news is updated every thirty minutes, and the workplace has one foot in cyberspace. And you have to process all of this at once. You have to recognize patterns in this whirl of data, and you have to do it fast. Those to the joystick born have a built-in advantage. Neo-Luddite polemics to the contrary, kids weaned on videogames are not attention-deficient, morally stunted, illiterate little zombies who massacre people en masse after playing too much *Mortal Kombat*. They're simply acclimated to a world that increasingly resembles some kind of arcade experience. From computer-generated weather reports to interactive kiosks at the local megamart, from Hollywood to the Pentagon, we are swimming in animated icons, special effects, and computer simulations. Hand-wringing social critics argue this is a Bad Thing. Techno-cheerleaders counter that "interactive entertainment" is a $6 billion industry, and therefore it is a profoundly Good Thing. That determination, like the relative morality of credit cards, is beside the point. This is where we are now. And this is our late-model version of the future.

But as I discovered, digging through the attic for old Atari cartridges, arcade tokens, and handheld electronic football games, it's also the past. This is my childhood. And so my goals here are twofold: to trace the evolution of videogames from blips to behemoths, and to trace their radiation into our patterns of thought. And so here I stand with a Geiger counter to my head and a stack of old videogames. After twenty-five years, it's time to stop—no, pause—and scroll back for clues.

Chapter 1
Primitive
Blips

In the fall of 1961, a large, rectangular box landed on MIT's doorstep. It came from the Digital Equipment Corporation. The box contained DEC's new model computer, the PDP-1, and its manufacturers hoped that MIT's electrical engineering department would do something interesting with it — win the space race, breed artificially intelligent robots, or at least revolutionize information processing for the greater glory of corporate America. Within a year, the computing pioneers at MIT had done none of these things.

But one of them had written the world's first videogame.

It was a two-player game of dueling spaceships firing photon torpedoes against a field of electronic stars. Steve Russell, the Promethean figure in videogame lore, wrote it. And in the spirit of the Atomic Age, he dubbed it *Spacewar*. This was the ur-videogame, programmed on the first computer to use a real screen and a typewriter instead of endless stacks of paper punch cards.

Thirty-five years have gone by. Computer power has increased by a factor of thousands. Punch cards have given way to magnetic tape, floppy disks, and CD-ROMs. Steve Russell has gotten older and gruffer and now manages programmers in

Silicon Valley instead of tinkering with artificial intelligence code in Cambridge, Massachusetts. But he recalls the PDP-1 with the brio of a young grad student.

"It was the size of about three refrigerators, and it had an old-fashioned computer console with a whole bunch of switches and lights," he says, like he's describing a superdeluxe toy that just arrived on Christmas morning. "And it had a cathode ray tube, and it had a typewriter. I thought this was a great thing, and I was itching to get my fingers on it and try it. And so a bunch of us — some people who'd worked on the debugger and some friends of mine from Harvard — we started talking about how you could really do a lot more with the computer and the display. Space was very hot at the time — it was just when satellites were getting up and we were talking about putting a man on the moon. So we said, gee, space is fun, and most people don't appreciate how to maneuver things in space. And so I wrote a demo program that had two spaceships that were controlled by the switches on the computer. They were different shapes. They could fire torpedoes at one another, and they could navigate around the screen with the sort of physics you find in space. And then Pete Samson wrote a program called Expensive Planetarium." There were, he explains, a whole family of "Expensive" programs on the PDP-1, at a time when even the most rudimentary computer tasks required massive outlays of manpower and federal grant money. "There was Expensive Typewriter, which did just what a typewriter did, except it was much more expensive, and there was Expensive Desk Calculator, which was something similar. Expensive Planetarium displayed the star map sort of as you'd see it looking out the window, and I incorporated that as a background. And then Dan Edwards looked at my code for displaying outlines and figured out a way to speed it up by a factor of two or three, which gave him enough time to compute the effect of gravity on the two spaceships. And that made it a much better game, because with the stars in the background, you could estimate the motion of the ships much better than when they were just on a dead black background. And with the spaceships affected by gravity, it made it a bit of a challenge, and you got to try to do orbital mechanics — there was the star in the center of the screen, and it attracted them just as the sun would."

At first, Russell and his band of console cosmonauts used the PDP's row of tabletop toggle switches as game controllers. "You had four controls," Russell recalls, "rotate counterclockwise, rotate clockwise, turn on your rocket thrust, which caused a little tail of rocket exhaust to show on the screen, and torpedo. The torpedoes were proximity-fused, so that when they got close to something they blew up. If it was another torpedo, they both blew up, and if it was another spaceship, they both blew up. So it would work as a defensive weapon, because you could blow other torpedoes out of the sky if they were coming at you. But we very quickly found that your elbows got tired, because the table was hard and not quite at a convenient height. So we and many other people hooked up controllers which were basically four buttons in a row that you could control your spaceship with." The ur-joypad.

Working on *Spacewar* on study breaks, Russell and his friends polished up and completed the game in the spring of 1962. He remembers wondering whether maybe there might be some way to commercialize this thing and make some money. After thinking hard for about a week, he concluded that no one would pay for it. So he left the program on all the nearby computers so that anyone could play it or copy it. A few people did. And if anyone asked, Russell and his friends gave out the source code.

Of course, the handful of people that copied *Spacewar* off MIT's PDP-1 gave it to their colleagues, who shared it with their students, who spread it among their fellow programmers, until, by the mid-sixties, there was a copy of *Spacewar* on every research computer in America, as well as hundreds of personal variations on the source code and millions of dollars of lost-time cost to academia and the military-industrial complex. In this way, *Spacewar* foreshadowed the virulent spread of *Doom* across computer networks thirty years later. *Spacewar* was so pervasive that it's hard to overestimate its impact upon the computer culture of the time. Virtually every young programmer in the sixties played it. For some, *Spacewar* was their very first glimpse of a computer. "What happened," says Russell, "was that most of the people who had access to the PDP-1 would show their family and friends what they were doing and they would demonstrate with *Spacewar*, because it was more interesting than watching someone debug a program with DDT.

"Actually," he muses, "I think the thing I take the most pride in about *Spacewar* is that it got so many people hooked on computer programming. It caught a lot of eyes and got a lot of interesting people asking, 'How do you do that?' "

Thus initiated, a good number of those people went on to become software barons. And looking back, it wasn't powerful algorithms or lines of data-crunching code that lured them into computing. It was a primitive yet strangely compelling game, two little spaceships on a screen shooting bullets at each other — electronic dodgeball. It was the human drive to play, even on a hulking PDP-1. Russell, now revered as the granddaddy of videogames, was the first into the lake. But, he admits, "If I hadn't done it, someone would've done something equally exciting if not better in the next six months. I just happened to get there first." The advent of computer games was foretold in the stars of Expensive Planetarium. They were inescapable, because the impulse to convert million-dollar calculators into intellectual jungle gyms was simply too great.

And so as early computers propagated, so did the binary code that turned them into hugely expensive game machines. By the early seventies, a handful of antediluvian videogames were competing for precious computer processing cycles on academic mainframes. These proto-games were tiny and simple; they were to *Wing Commander V* what dinoflagellates are to a humpback whale. But in these primeval scraps of game code, you could catch a glimpse of much more powerful, complicated videogames to come.

Lunar Lander, for example, was an early mainframe game that challenged you to land a rocket pod on the surface of the moon. There were no game controllers. There wasn't even a screen. All this game did was print out successive lines of text in time-sequence turns. Each turn would tell you what your velocity was, how far above the lunar surface you were, and how much fuel you had left. You then had to choose the amount of rocket thrust for the next turn. The more thrust you used, the slower you descended—and the more fuel you used. If you decelerated too quickly, using too much thrust too early, you would run out of fuel and drop the rest of the way. If you waited too long to slow down, you couldn't decelerate in time to make a safe landing and crashed to bits on the lunar surface. Basically, you had to jigger it so that your distance to the surface fell to zero while your velocity was very low. All of this was calculated on a PDP computer using simple physics equations. That was it. That was the game. But *Lunar Lander* was, arguably, the first recreational aircraft simulator.

Another early game, sometimes called *Hammurabi*, sometimes called *Kingdom*, was fifty lines of BASIC code that crudely simulated a feudal domain. The game ran in yearlong cycles, and for each year you would tell it how many acres of grain you wanted to plant, what your tax rate was going to be, and a few authoritarian central planning fiats. The computer would run through its calculations like the imperious processors in a Douglas Adams novel and, after much humming and spinning, spit out the consequences for your digital terrarium. If your tax rate was low and there was excess food, for instance, then more people would come into the kingdom and the population would increase. But if the population was too high and there wasn't enough food, there'd be famine and people would die or move out. The object was to build up the kingdom and increase the population. Basically, *Hammurabi* is a distant ancestor of all the kingdom-building strategy games that involve infrastructure and political trade-offs, *SimCity* being the most illustrious descendant.

The wriggling protoplasm of dungeons-and-dragons tunnel adventure games was the legendary *Hunt the Wumpus*, a mainframe program so antique that just confirming its existence was a challenge. This program is the Loch Ness Monster of videogames, always receding into the mists of hacker history before it can be properly identified. Dozens of videogame designers had heard of *Hunt the Wumpus* but mumbled when I pressed for specifics. None actually knew what it was about. After countless dead ends and false leads, the trail of the elusive Wumpus led finally to Walt Freitag, a human Baedeker of videogame lore who now designs CD-ROMs for Byron Preiss Multimedia and lectures, with a Victorian professor's stamina and in Dickensian detail, about videogame theory and apocrypha.

"Ah yes," he says. "*Hunt the Wumpus. Hunt the Wumpus* was another one of these fifty-line BASIC programs, although this one was more like two hundred lines. It was a network of tunnels and nodes. And I believe the actual geometry of the network was a dodecahedron. So there were twenty vertices with three tunnels coming to each node. You had to choose a tunnel and go down it—this was all done in text—and it would print out: 'You are at node three. Move or shoot.' And you could shoot down a tunnel to any of the adjacent nodes, and if the Wumpus was there, you would kill it. But if you moved down the tunnel to where the Wumpus was, the Wumpus would kill you. There was also a warning if you were in a node adjacent to the Wumpus. It would print a little message that said: 'You are in node 5. I smell a Wumpus. Move or shoot.' And you had some limited number of shots, and if you ran out of shots, you would lose. There were also some bats, and if you were adjacent to where there were bats, it would say: 'I smell bats.' And the bats would randomly carry you to another node."*

Hunt the Wumpus flickered briefly as a computer game phenomenon, then faded. Like some australopithecine also-ran, it was superseded by a more robust contemporary, the legendary *Adventure* mainframe game of 1967. Originally known as AD-VENT (file names maxed out at six letters), *Adventure* was the

---

* Atari's *Adventure,* a dragon-slaying tunnel game released in 1980 for the venerable VCS home system, also featured a bat, which would swoop down, carry off valuable objects you had acquired in the course of the game, and deposit them in some random part of the maze. Whether this chiropteron free radical derives from *Hunt the Wumpus* is a matter of some debate among amateur videogame historians.

ur–sword-and-sorcery game, just as *Spacewar* was the ur-shooter. The object: explore subterranean caves, fight monsters, plunder storerooms for treasure, et cetera. *Adventure* was a logical extension of the fantasy role-playing games that suffused hackerdom, spawning cultish extracurricular organizations like the Society for Creative Anachronism. A high percentage of computer programmers were and are, not surprisingly, *Dungeons & Dragons* aficionados. There's an affinity between computer programming and games that require reams of graph paper and twenty-sided dice. Both are artificial universes governed by quantifiable rules, probability, and obsessive mapping. Charting out subterranean passages and dead ends is pretty much analogous to mapping out a circuit or debugging a piece of code. So a combination of computers and dragon-slashing games was begging to happen. *Adventure* not only took care of the scorekeeping and referee chores, but its bone-dry humor and exploratory conventions influenced a generation of game programmers.* In *Adventure* and its descendants, the emphasis was on puzzle solving and getting to some mysterious end at a slow, novelistic pace. In terms of genre and gameplay, it was a straight shot to *Myst*.

But then, most of the videogames we love trace their roots back to these cloistered computer games. If you look at *Asteroids*, it's hard not to catch a whiff of *Spacewar.* The resemblance is obvious. What was not obvious at the time was how or if these games would ever escape the rarefied atmosphere of electrical engineering departments. When these programs were written, computers were incredibly large and expensive. Even a game that resided on every PDP-1 on earth would still only be seen by a few thousand people. Everyone agreed that *Spacewar* and *Lunar Lander* and *Adventure* were incredibly cool. But no one could imagine computers cheap enough to make them a mass phenomenon.

---

* "[*Adventure*] defined the terse, dryly humorous style now expected in text adventure games, and popularized several taglines that have become fixtures of hacker-speak: 'A huge green fierce snake bars the way!' 'I see no X here' (for some noun X). 'You are in a maze of twisty little passages, all alike.' 'You are in a little maze of twisty passages, all different.' " (Eric Raymond, ed., *The New Hacker Dictionary* [Cambridge, Mass.: The MIT Press, 1991], 33.)

It took a long time for the computing power to get cheap enough. Not a long time in the normal historical scale. But ten years, in the computer universe, is a geologic era riven by massive earthquakes, volcanic explosions, and tectonic shifts. "I haven't done a precise back-of-the-envelope calculation on this," says Russell, "but when we do our games now, you don't consider things that work on a computer with less than 20 million instructions per second. Well, the PDP-1 was 30,000 instructions per second, and they sold fifty of them, so that's more than all the PDP-1s in the world. And that's the standard consumer product."

But even given the massive leaps in technology, when he programmed *Spacewar*, did he have any idea what he had done? That he'd invented, you know, *videogames?*

"No. Not until years later, when I was working at Stanford. We had a PDP-1, and as was customary for PDP-1s there was a copy of *Spacewar* on the console. One day, we had been working late, and we went up the street to the local bar, had some hamburgers and beer and sat around and talked. And I had to go back and get something from the computer lab, so I went back after they closed. And lo and behold, here were a couple of Stanford students who had been playing pinball back at the Oasis, and they had gone in and were playing *Spacewar* on the PDP-1. And I said, 'Aw, I guess it *is* sort of a pinball machine.' That was the first time I really was conscious that *that* was what I had done."

Chapter 2
A Natural History
of Videogames

I. COSMOLOGY

Billions and billions of bits ago, tiny strands of computer code rose up from the central processors of primordial computers, replicated, and evolved into the elaborate spectacles we see today. If the history of videogames were a twenty-four-hour day, *Pong* would arise at 6:37 A.M. The Atari 2600 bursts into existence late in the morning, at 10:17, and the Nintendo Entertainment System (NES) rolls onto American shores at 4:27 in the afternoon. Sega Genesis and Nintendo's Game Boy show up for happy hour at 6:30. And the most advanced home videogame system to date, the Nintendo 64, clocks in at twenty minutes to midnight.

The Pre-Pong Era

The Pong Era

Pong. The ur-arcade game,
Pong had only two instructions:
DEPOSIT QUARTER and
AVOID MISSING BALL FOR
HIGH SCORE. Pong was a
monolithic paddle game—and
curious bar patrons responded like
the awestruck apes in 2001.
Thus was born the arcade
revolution.

1962	*Spacewar.*
1966	First experimental TV/computer interface sends two blips skidding across a television screen. *"Also sprach Zarathustra"* chimes inaudibly through the antennae.
1967	Original *Adventure* mainframe maze game.
1971	*Computer Space,* the first coin-op arcade game.
1972	Nolan Bushnell founds Atari. *Pong* becomes the first arcade hit.
	Magnavox Odyssey, the world's first commercial home videogame. Paddle hockey. Black and white. No sound.
1974	Atari's Home *Pong.*
1975	Magnavox Odyssey 200 adds sound and scoring to the thrill of video badminton.
1976	Fairchild's Channel F, the first cartridge home videogame system. Goodbye, paddle hockey. Hello, tic-tac-toe.
	Atari sold to Warner for $28 million.

The Atari Era

Space Invaders. The original slide-and-shoot title, *Space Invaders* was the first videogame to go mega in the United States and the first to really exploit the medium rather than hark back to older games like Ping Pong, pinball, or hockey. *Space Invaders'* sci-fi aliens were the first animated characters in an arcade game. Forty-eight of them, arrayed in six horizontal rows, marched across and down like intergalactic redcoats firing laser bullets. The more you hit, the faster they advanced. When you finally eliminated them all, a new squadron appeared, starting one row lower, ad infinitum. There was no fixed ending, just an escalating degree of difficulty. Ultimately, this was an unwinnable life-or-death struggle, a definitive break from the sportsmanlike tennis idiom of *Pong.* And when you weren't dodging alien laser fire, you could always glance up at the high score—this was the first game to provide a continuous high-score display—for inspiration. In Japan, *Space Invaders* converted a nation of pachinko players into arcade fans. In America, it sparked videomania, spurring sales of a new electronic television toy called the Atari 2600.

1977 First Videogame Crash (The Hardware Plague)

Store shelves become soggy with Home *Pong* clones, which are summarily dumped at fire sale prices. Fairchild and RCA become extinct as home console manufacturers. Clone manufacturers die off. Atari survives.

1978 Atari's VCS (2600). Comes with paddle and joystick controllers and the venerable *Combat* cartridge. A hundred thousand living rooms echo the tinkling arpeggios of *Breakout.*

Magnavox releases the Odyssey2 to compete with Atari's VCS.

Atari 400 and Atari 800 computers released to a lukewarm public.

1979 Four ex–Atari programmers found Activision, the first videogame software house. Activision makes no hardware—only cartridges—and thrives as a symbiotic parasite of the Atari 2600 and subsequent platforms.

Asteroids. The original space ace flying shooter, and the last great black-and-white game. *Asteroids'* laser-thin vector graphics drew a wedge-shaped spaceship floating amid a storm of abstract space boulders, all of which had to be repeatedly blasted into smaller and smaller chunks. From its fluid game play to its *Jaws*-like drone, *Asteroids* had a minimalist elegance unmatched until the advent of *Tetris. Asteroids* was also the first arcade game with an electronic scoreboard, which let high-scoring players tap their initials onto a trophy screen at the end of a record-beating game. Suddenly, lunchtime executives could compete against after-school teenagers. Quarters flew out of gray flannel pockets and nylon backpacks in record numbers.

Battlezone. Atari's hulking 3D vector graphics tank game, *Battlezone* ushered in the arcade game as a ticket to virtual military jockdom. It was also built into a deluxe training toy for the U.S. Army.

Defender. The archetypal side-scrolling shooter, *Defender* was also the first dual-window-display game—it showed you a small map of the oncoming territory in the corner, warning of the intergalactic beasties that lay ahead. So before even reaching a new stretch of space turf, you knew when to brace yourself for the onslaught.

Missile Command. A true game for the Reagan era—nuclear attack from outer space—*Missile Command* used ground-based antiballistic missile-to-missile defense when SDI was a mere twinkle in the Gipper's eye. *Missile Command* had three left-hand fire buttons, furnishing a trio of launch bases where one would have functioned perfectly (thus proving that pork barrel military funding operates even in the videogame universe) and a trackball for guiding the

Annual rate of new cartridge releases begins to double, from a few dozen this year to over five hundred in 1983.

1980 Mattel's Intellivision.

missiles. To this day, *Missile Command* is still the only game to use a separate sighting device for aiming.

Pac-Man. The über arcade game. *Pac-Man's* blue maze is what flashes into the minds of the arcade generation when you say the word "videogame." *Pac-Man* epitomized the early-eighties kindergarten arcade aesthetic: a single-action control stick, bright colors, animation breaks between levels, and characters with no extremities and cute nicknames; *Pac-Man's* ghostly pursuers, Shadow (red), Speedy (pink), Bashful (blue), and Pokey (orange), were known, respectively, as Blinky, Pinky, Inky, and Clyde. When you turned the tables by gulping a power pellet and running them down, they just went floating home to recuperate—a far cry from the arcade abattoirs of the nineties.

Tempest. The final descendant in a proud and ill-fated line of vector graphics games, *Tempest's* blindingly fast action consisted of skirting a yellow, crablike creature around the edges of a vector tunnel while firing at Flippers, Quarks, and other intergalactic vermin that hurtled toward you. Freudian semioticians would later have a field day with this.

Frogger. One bullfrog's quest to avoid becoming roadkill. Run across a highway, hop from log to log across a river, and avoid poisonous snakes to reach your froggy little nest at the top of the screen. Not epic stuff, but it made for great game play. *Frogger* had more ways to die than any other videogame before or since and some of the best sound effects of its time—the ting of a new coin, the squitch of safety once you reached the nest, the forlorn descending tones of frog requiem, and three harpsichordian musical themes that drove players to near madness by lodging permanently in the brain.

1981

Nintendo and Sega begin exporting arcade games to the United States.

The *New England Journal of Medicine* reports "Space Invaders Wrist."

Centipede. Another slide-and-shoot game, *Centipede's* quantum leap from *Space Invaders* was a trackball and the ability to float up and down (rather than just slide from right to left), as well as unlimited firepower. Like *Space Invaders*, *Centipede* harked back to the movie monsters of the atomic age. But this time the menace was not intergalactic storm troopers but rather a swarm of terrestrial insects—fleas, spiders, scorpions, and centipedes, one of which graced the cabinet as a giant, red-eyed, scabrous, yellow-bellied monster drooling venom from a set of two-inch fangs. As bugs slithered down the screen, you shot at them through a thicket of fungi that only thickened as centipede segments you hit metamorphosed into mushrooms (detritivores unite).

Donkey Kong. Nintendo's first American hit, *Donkey Kong* turned the timeworn simian-kidnaps-damsel libretto into a blockbuster climbing platform game whose joystick-and-jump controls prefigured the martial arts games' leap-and-strike format. *Donkey Kong* was arcadia's introduction to a swarthy, overweight, mustachioed plumber named Mario. Fifteen years and twenty games later, he's still springing through the *Donkey Kong* dynasty.

*Q*Bert.* A jumping puzzle game featuring another cute, limbless character who bounces up and down a pyramid dodging a cascade of ugly/cute enemies while his snake nemesis, Coily, springs in hot pursuit.

Dig Dug. A maze game with a subterranean theme: dig your own underground maze while being chased by deadly fire-breathing dragons and lesser underground beasties. *Dig Dug* gave you two novel ways to destroy the enemy—pump them up with air until they explode, using the pump button, or dig strategically to create a timely underground cave-in.

1982

Colecovision debuts with superior graphics, an Atari cartridge adapter, *Zaxxon,* and *Donkey Kong.*

Atari 5200 (an Atari 400 minus the keyboard) ships, unable to play Atari 2600 cartridges.

Milton Bradley's Vectrex, an *Asteroids*-style tabletop mini-arcade.

Bally Astrocade.

Based on flimsy Christmas forecasts, Wall Street traders scurry off the sinking ship of videogame-related investments.

Tron. A videogame based on a movie based on a computer game based on a videogame. Cheesy on the silver screen, great as an arcade cabinet with movie music. *Tron* was really several games in one, using scenes from the movie as springboards for game play—the Light Cycles, a Tank Battle, and the final showdown with the MCP Complex interpreted as a variation of *Breakout.* It was the first game without printed instructions on the cabinet—to read them on the screen, you fired the trigger of *Tron's* oversized, ultraviolet, clear plastic joystick.

Zaxxon. The first 3D isometric game to use raster graphics. The isometric perspective was not quite across, not quite straight down, but somewhere in between, oblique in a vaguely Cubist way. This was a concession to the raster monitor, which painted the graphics one frame at a time (like a TV), as opposed to vector games like *Battlezone,* which outlined objects' precise position relative to each other but lacked any texture. *Zaxxon's* raster graphics gave the arcade detailed 3D terrain that could sustain animated 3D explosions (and it was Good).

Joust. Four words: ostrich-mounted lance combat.

Pole Position. The first hit driving game, *Pole Position* let arcade mavens play *Speed Racer* with a Formula One steering wheel, gas pedal, and nonstop stereo revving noises, preparing tens of thousands of preteen boys for the highway portion of their driver's license exam.

Punch-out. Foreshadowing fighting games to come, *Punch-out* matched the player against a gallery of troglodyte gladiators. These contenders lacked the lithe precision of their polygon descendants, but

1983

Second Videogame Crash (The Software Plague)

Awash in third-party cartridges, consumers become unable to distinguish the pearls from the dross and head straight for the sale bins, forcing even high-quality games into a vicious cycle of discounting and loss.

you got to see them from a first-person perspective—through the glowing green outline of your own fighter—as they threw punches toward you.

Dragon's Lair. The first and only successful laser disc game. Upside: Dirk the Daring's quest to save the nubile Princess Daphne looked just like a Disney animated adventure. Downside: you had to follow a highly scripted set of linear moves or die. As a game, *Dragon's Lair* was beautiful, yet stupid, not unlike Daphne, whose pneumatic blond giggle was your chunk of cheese at the end of the animated rat maze.

The 8-Bit Era

Gauntlet. The first arcade role-playing game, *Guantlet*'s sword-and-sorcery controls (joystick, fire, magic) could accommodate up to four players: Questor the Elf, Merlin the Wizard, Thor the Warrior (shirtless blond he-man with an ax), and his sword-wielding female counterpart, Thyra the Valkyrie, whose green chain-mail bustier shielded a 36DD bosom from the attacks of malignant orcs. Rumbling sonic cues announced important information like "Treasure, 100 points," and "Wizard, your life force is running out!" as *Gauntlet* prompted you to feed it quarters for extra strength.

Scores of software houses go bankrupt, and videogame R&D is frozen in cryogenic suspension.

1984 Mattel sells off its electronics division. Warner breaks up Atari.

Nintendo introduces the 8-bit Famicom in Japan.

1985 The U.S. home videogame industry is virtually nonexistent.

1986 The Nintendo Entertainment System (NES) and *Super Mario Bros.* take America by storm.

Sega's Master System follows on the heels of the NES.

1987 Acclaim, the first U.S. software house to manufacture games for Nintendo, becomes a successful symbiotic parasite of the NES and subsequent platforms.

1988 Nintendo's NES is the best-selling toy in North America.

The 16-Bit Era

Tetris. Designed by a Soviet math researcher, Alexi Pajitnov, and programmed by a student of computer infomatics at the University of Moscow, *Tetris* is the puzzle game that roared. The game was originally programmed on an IBM-PC, but the *Tetris* meme soon infected every hardware format on earth, from arcade cabinets and home consoles to CD-ROM players and Game Boys. It is possibly the most addictive videogame of all time, inducing a trancelike state with sufficient practice. Not many things are taken for granted in the videogame industry, but one article of faith is that *Tetris* will be available on every platform until the end of time.

Street Fighter II. The first megahit fighting game, featuring ten characters, each with his or her own fighting style, special moves, and combinations. *Street Fighter II* was the first step down the slippery slope to *Ultimate Mortal Kombat*.

1989 | The Sega Genesis.

NEC's Turbo-Grafx 16.

Nintendo's Game Boy and *Tetris* change family car trips forever.

The Atari Lynx and NEC TurboExpress portable units compete unsuccessfully with Nintendo's cheaper, less sophisticated Game Boy.

1990 | Nintendo's *Super Mario Bros. 3*, the best-selling game of all time, grosses $500 million.

Videogame cartridge rental becomes a reality, to manufacturers' chagrin.

1991 | Sega introduces charismatic mascot, *Sonic the Hedgehog*. Sales soar.

Super NES marks Nintendo's entry into the 16-bit arena.

Game Gear marks Sega's entry into the portable arena.

Mortal Kombat. Street Fighter squared. Not only did *Mortal Kombat* have an astounding array of strikes, kicks, and balletic combination moves, but it added the frisson of Fatality Moves, which allowed you to kick your opponent while he was down. "Finish him!" was your cue to put the loser out of his misery by, say, tearing out his heart or ripping off his head and holding the severed cranium, spinal cord dangling, aloft. *Mortal Kombat* gave players not only the primal thrill of vanquishing an opponent but also the theatrical chest-beating aftermath. Subsequent controversy only fueled enthusiasm for the game and a spate of sequels.

NBA Jam. The most successful arcade game of 1993, *NBA Jam* burned the phrase "Boom Shaka-laka-laka" into tens of thousands of silicon microchips and launched the next generation of celebrity-athlete-studded, major league blockbuster arcade games.

1992 Sega CD introduces videogamers to the optical disc.

Nintendo dominates the 16-bit jungle with *Street Fighter II*.

1993 Sega (and its blood-soaked version of *Mortal Kombat*) dominates Nintendo, sparking a Kontroversy in Kongress.

3DO's sophisticated REAL Multiplayer debuts. At $700, it rots on its pedestal.

The Atari Jaguar skulks around the edges of the videogame market, starving for decent games.

1994 PC CD-ROM becomes a viable medium.

Sega's 32X peripheral, designed to speed up the Genesis and Sega CD, flounders and asphyxiates in the absence of software support.

Virtua Fighter 2. Triumph of the polygon warriors. *VF2*'s 3D-rendered fighters looked and moved like human aliens, resplendently comfortable in their glossy virtual skins. For the first time in a fighting game, characters spun, kicked, leaped, and dodged like real people. You could see torque in the joints as they shifted from foot to foot. Their knees flexed as they transferred weight throughout a low strike or leaping combination kick, as the virtual camera swerved from one side of the arena to the other. *VF2* transcended the gore of *Mortal Kombat* with the brutal ballet of Hong Kong cinema.

The "Next Generation" Era

1995 Nintendo dominates the holiday season with SNES and *Donkey Kong Country 2*, the swan song of 16-bit videogames.

Sony Playstation.

Sega Saturn.

1996 Nintendo 64.

II. PHYLOGENY

The early 1980s were the Cambrian Age of videogames, when new species proliferated like so many marine algae. By the middle of the decade, distinct genres had evolved from archetypes like *Asteroids, Space Invaders,* and *Missile Command* into a whole menagerie of side-scrollers, maze games, driving games, and martial arts contests. Of course, there was some overlap, but arcade game genres were at least as distinct as summer Hollywood blockbusters, which could be neatly divided into explosion movies, Big Chill maturity sagas, and high school melodramas starring Molly Ringwald. At home, there was a neat divide between computer floppy disk games, which involved puzzle-wielding trolls, and console cartridges, which involved shooting crudely rendered projectiles at anything that moved. Arcade games (and their home console translations) came out of the pinball world. They were about fast action, visual pizzazz, and rapid wrist action. PC games sprang from the arcane realm of mainframe computers and the hacker *Dungeons & Dragons* sci-fi culture. They were slower and less visual and came with thick manuals and complicated back stories.

With the advent of CD-ROMs, all these tidy delineations went away. Storing games on optical disc boosted the visual dimension of computer sagas and introduced long-form adventures to the joystick crowd. Now you can play *Myst* on the Sega CD and Sid Meier's *Civilization* on Nintendo and *SimCity* on every platform under the sun. You can play retro Atari games on a PowerPC between blast runs on *Wing Commander.* Hardware no longer dictates genre. In terms of the games themselves, categories have also blurred, because after fifteen years, there are so many climbing and shooting varietals that programmers have begun to mix and match them in hopes of generating hit mutant hybrids ("I've got it, boss. A game where you climb *up* rope ladders while solving phase state logic puzzles and shooting space demons. Kids'll love it!"). Game lineage isn't like biological evolution, where an extinct line stays extinct. In game design, someone can come along two billion years later and say, gee, those trichordates actually had something going for them. I think I'll use them in a game. Between this Frankenstein crossbreeding and the hardware convergence, videogame genres are getting all blurry around the edges.

That said, genres do seem to hold together in the middle, weathering revolutions in chip speed and licensing. It's like the proverbial fourteen novels that have been endlessly rewritten throughout history. The costumes change, but the basic matrices remain. There are certain things that people want to see on a video screen. There are certain strategies that are inherently satisfying. There are certain ways of organizing obstacles that are hard to improve upon. Platform games, the Mario games for instance, clump together tightly as a genre. It's hard to crossbreed them without weakening the game play. Hybrids are generally scattered, sickly, and weak. And as a practical consideration, the game industry holds on to its list of genres because categories are expedient for marketing folk. Vendors, bean counters, and press agents love labels, and so the following distinctions will probably make it through the next videogame era (and maybe even into the next decade):

Action: The largest phylum in videogamedom, comprising most of the home console universe and virtually all arcade games; these games are also known as "twitch" games and "thumb candy."

Cartridge action games include the scrolling platform games of Mario and Sonic, which involve lots of jumping. These games, the Big Mac of the home videogame market (billions sold), put the player on an obstacle course where the emphasis is on movement. There may be some shooting, but it's mostly getting past things (e.g., *Pitfall, Donkey Kong, Prince of Persia,* and *Frogger*). A lot of these have now gone 3D.

Arcade games tend to fall into structural subcategories like horizontal scrolling games (run from left to right shooting, jumping, collecting treasure/bonus points), maze chase games, platform climbing games (jumping over gaps and over obstacles), shooters ("You are the last ship/marine left in a universe overrun by invading Enemy Alien Demon Beasts. Blow them all to hell"), and fighting games. Of course these combine among themselves to produce, like, horizontally scrolling games with maze interludes, but they all fall well within the purview of the action genre. There's also a category that could be called the "raining shit" games, like *Missile Command*, where things are just falling and you have to catch them or deal with them in some fashion. There's also the *Breakout* genre — the slider elimination game or bouncing ball game, which spawned *Space Invaders* and *Centipede*.

One of the reasons action games are such a popular category is that they provide a springboard for any kind of character, back story, or matinee flavor of the month. Traditionally, action games have been a catchall category for Hollywood licenses, hatching a slew of games based on movies that are mostly special effects anyway. These include some of the worst cartridges and arcade cabinets ever produced, as well as games that surpass the original Schwarzenegger/Stallone/Van Damme vehicles: *Batman Returns* (a good Super NES and Sega game), *Bram Stoker's Dracula* (a bad SNES and Sega game), *Home Alone* and *Home Alone 2* (awful), *Hunt for Red October* (worse), *Rambo 3*, *The Last Action Hero*, *Hook*, *Robocop*, the *Rocketeer* (ugh), *Wayne's World* (bogus), and most of the Spielberg oeuvre. Disney has spun *Fantasia*, *Aladdin*, *Beauty and the Beast*, and the *Jungle Book* into cartridges and no doubt has a pixellated *Hunchback of Notre Dame* waiting in the wings. TV studies have given us videogame versions of *American Gladiators*, *Family Feud*, *Jeopardy!*, and *The Jetsons*. In the world of Hollywood videogame licenses, cherished celebrities and animatronic characters become puppets in our hands. For a quarter, you can be Ah-nold in a cathode universe of exploding opponents. You can play your favorite $100 million special effects extravaganza (*Predator*, *Terminator 2*, *Alien 3*, which, let's face it, are big-screen videogames anyway). You can even watch your favorite Hollywood monsters fight each other, now that producers are playing Don King with digital beasties. *Alien vs. Predator*. *Robocop vs. Terminator*.

Following Hollywood's lead, the action game genre has also become a canvas for product placement: *Cool Spot*, a 1993 Virgin game for Sega and Super NES, stars the eponymous

7-Up spokesdot as an action hero rescuing his fellow dots from the Wild Wicked Wily Will, the feared Spot hunter. It's a shockingly good game. The sequel, *Spot Goes to Hollywood*, is a pastiche of silver screen action scenes — a mine cart chase, a Western shoot-out, a swashbuckling pirate scene, at Keystone Kops level, also starring Spot. Why just ogle six-packs on the shelf when you can play the product in a videogame. You can *be* the packaging.

Adventure: Whatever platform they're on, adventure games are about accumulating an inventory of items that are then used to solve puzzles. In Nintendo's *Legend of Zelda,* for instance, the hero Link must pick up useful objects before moving on to the next level. Zork, the most famous computer text adventure, works on a similar premise, stripped of the treasure-gathering and combat. CD-ROMs have produced a subgenre of adventure games, the first-person, character-driven narratives, which cast you into a tangle of dialogue and branching story lines punctuated by logic puzzles à la *Seventh Guest* and a spate of other interactive murder mysteries. And of course, *Myst.*

Fighting: By far the most popular arcade genre of the nineties, fighting games are basically comic books that move, pitting steroid-enhanced combatants against each other in hyperkinetic two-player death matches. Drawing from Hong Kong film choreography and martial arts, fighting games like *Tekken, Battle Arena Toshinden,* and *Virtua Fighter* feature airbrushed 3D polygon gladiators, complex signature attacks, and swooping Scorcesian camera angles, all of which require massive computer processing power and graphic flair. For this reason, fighting games have become state-of-the-art show cars of the videogame industry, as well as targets of right-wing politicians who deplore their increasingly graphic violence.

Puzzle: Unlike adventure games, where puzzles are obstacles to be overcome en route to the ultimate goal (find out whodunnit, rescue the princess, et cetera), in puzzle games, logic exercises are an end in themselves, usually in the form of colorful, two-dimensional, grown-up building blocks that stack in deceptively simple ways. The most ubiquitous puzzle game is the Macintosh system software version of the classic plastic novelty toy where you shuffle around mosaic squares one at a time to reassemble a picture, in this case the Apple logo. The most famous puzzle game is *Tetris*, in which geometric shapes fall from the top of the screen into stacking sedimentary layers.

Role-playing: Role-playing games, traditionally played on computers, superficially resemble adventure games — lots of monsters, treasure, and sword-and-sorcery backdrops. But compared to adventure games, RPGs have less abstract, repetitive action and repeat play. Instead, role-playing games unfold as long, drawn-out epic narratives involving a band of distinct characters that travel, fight, and plunder as a team. RPGs have their roots in 1970s tabletop role-playing games published by the TSR corporation and played in the dark with twenty-sided dice and pewter dragon figurines by brainy, ill-socialized teenaged boys (and the scary adults they later became). Ultimately, RPGs are about statistics, probability, and mapping — the number of experience points you have and how many spells that lets you throw, the amount of damage a particular hobgoblin can take and your chance of running into it in some dark corner of an uncharted maze. Personal computers simplified the requisite record keeping and took RPGs out of the closet by adding graphics, so that the player could look like a videogame jock rather than a hopeless *Dungeons & Dragons* geek.

In the RPG genre, epitomized by *Wizardry* and the *Ultima* series, you're given a complex set of rules and instructions and a detailed back story as follows: The King has been kidnapped (role-playing games are distinguished by their public service sensibility — they're the only videogames where you rescue male authority figures), and the Kingdom is on the brink of total anarchy. Monsters/demons/thugs/orcs/lobbyists have taken over, and chaos rules. You are a dwarf/wizard/mestizo warrior/butcher/baker/candlestick maker on a mission to defeat the foreign usurper, restore the monarchy, and save the day. In order to do this, you must accumulate experience points and earn chivalric merit badges that allow you to kill more effectively. You must also grab some magical number of relics (nine sacred scrolls, seven cryptic runes, five captive wizards, four stolen crystals, and a partridge in a pear tree). It's basically a digital version of the same old millennial crusade routine — unmitigated violence and pillage justified by the mystical quest rhetoric. Like, in *Final Fantasy Mystic Quest* for Super Nintendo, you're supposed to be "Freeing the Crystals of the Earth from the Forces of Evil," which sounds suspiciously like "Liberating Oil Reserves from the Running Dogs of Capitalism." Not surprisingly, these games incorporate an obsessive attention to the details of one's personal arsenal, be it a collection of longbows and halberds or an especially deadly repertoire of spells and prayers.

Simulations: Although arguably all videogames are simulations of something, players and programmers have a fairly specific idea of what "simulation game" is supposed to mean. What distinguishes simulation games is simulation for its own sake, rather than as a means to some end — say, blowing up space aliens. Most simulation games are first-person, pseudo-VR vehicle sims — planes, tanks, helicopters, nuclear submarines, manned space missions. Odds are, if it's received billions of dollars in military funding, you can buy a shrink-wrapped sim about it at Software Etc. The other big sim category is world-building games, a subgenre pioneered by Wil Wright with *SimCity*, *SimEarth*, and *SimAnt*. These sims are about constructing systems and watching them evolve — they're essentially digital terrariums for grown-ups.

Sports: Technically a combination of action and simulation, sports games are recognizably distinct enough to be classed as a separate category. From a design perspective, sports games may be totally unrelated to one another, but we all intuitively group them under the same rubric, regardless of whether the game is a first-person, point-of-view alpine ski slalom or a football game where you're looking at a map of the whole field, watching the game from a spectator's point of view. The category extends not only to major league sports bar spectacles but also to lesser-watched contests like bowling, soccer, snowboarding, pro wrestling, and bass fishing (*Super Black Bass* for SNES is a simulated twenty-four-hour bass-fishing contest featuring all the pulse-pounding excitement of a marathon casting and reeling session). This is only fair in a society that recognizes synchronized swimming as an Olympic sport.

Like every other aspect of professional athletics, sports videogames are dominated by celebrity athletes. There are dozens of NBA, NFL, and NHL games endorsed by the usual suspects — John Madden has made yet another career out of endorsing games by Electronic Arts — and tennis titles starring Pete Sampras, Andre Agassi, and the pre–drug scandal Jennifer Capriati, to say nothing of the PGA titles (in addition to separate Jack Nicklaus and Arnold Palmer titles, Sega has a golf Dream Team game studded with luminaries like Fuzzy Zoeller, Fred Couples, and Tommy Armour — sort of a middle-aged answer to *NBA Jam*).

Strategy. All videogames require some kind of strategy, but in strategy games per se, the game play and possibly even the goals of the game are abstract. In a sense, abstraction is the goal, just like in a card game or a board game. Actually, the most easily recognizable feature of a computer strategy game is that you have something on the computer screen that looks like a game board, although a lot of them are more complicated than would be feasible in a physical board game. Naturally, the strategy category includes straightforward adaptations of board games like backgammon or *Risk*. By now, most classic analog board games have been ported to the personal computer without much improvement, other than better scorekeeping, a constantly available opponent, and the gratuitous, gory animation sequences in *Battle Chess*.

Strategy games often have multiplayer versions — in fact, they are more likely to be multiplayer games than any other category. Other kingdoms are jostling against your band of hunter-gatherers even as they discover iron and evolve into rural agrarians. In *Civilization* and similar games like *Populous*, you're not just some SimMayor accountable to grouchy urbanites. You are an actual, card-carrying deity who has to throw his weight around with strategic earthquakes and plagues while viewing the whole playing field from an omniscient Judeo-Christian Sky God perspective. Invariably, these so-called God games take on a militaristic tone. They bear a striking resemblance to the other big subcategory of strategy games, namely war games, where instead of playing God, you get to play a Confederate general.

Ultimately, a true strategy game is about the consolidation of power. Unite third-century China. Ally or invade neighboring kingdoms. Marry your daughter off to a foreign despot to improve diplomatic relations. Fortify and defend castles in medieval France. Become the Holy Roman Emperor. Charge! Or play the CEO of a railroad/airline/microchip corporation for twenty years and build it into the most powerful antitrust juggernaut in history. Buy lots of ads, hire lobbyists, and force your competitors to knuckle under. Hire and fire. Downsize and watch your stock price soar.

Chapter 3
The Madonna/
Whore Complex of
ConsumerElectronics

While _Spacewar_ and its ilk hatched and bred as intestinal parasites of mainframe computers, the raw nucleotides of video paddle hockey were massing on a television screen in New Hampshire. In 1966 Ralph Baer, an engineer at Sanders Associates, was working on computer systems for the military. To lighten up the grind of Cold War circuit design, he hooked a computer to a TV set, built a symbol generator, and got two dots to chase each other across the screen. This peanut butter and jelly sandwich of computer logic and raster graphics was a gimcrack next to military mainframes, but it was kind of intriguing. So Baer assigned two engineers, Bill Harrison and Bill Rusch, to the blip project. It didn't pan out as a national security asset, but after a year it was shaping up as a nice game of video badminton.

Four years after Baer's original raster scan experiment, Sanders licensed the patents to Magnavox. Thus was born the world's first home videogame console, the Magnavox Odyssey, which connected to a TV antenna terminal. None of the Odyssey's games had color or sound, and players had to hang plastic overlays on the television screen, because the machine's twelve variations on tennis, ping-pong, and hockey were all really the same game played on different grids. Between the overlays and the antenna, the Odyssey demanded a good deal of fidgeting. But that didn't stop Americans from buying 100,000 of the things by Christmas of 1972. Two years later, Atari sold 150,000 of its Home Pong machines through Sears. By 1975, thirty companies were manufacturing clone TV game consoles, and amateur electronics mavens were building their own video paddleball machines from Radio Shack circuits and recipes in *Popular Electronics*.

Incipient video tennis fever built to malarial intensity in 1976, when General Instruments dropped a semiconductor bombshell: the AY38500 integrated circuit, which contained the guts of a home videogame system and six paddle hockey flavors on a single chip. This piece of silicon, which cost manufacturers five bucks, could be turned, with minimal effort, into a tennis/soccer/squash TV game console that sold for sixty dollars at Toys "R" Us. Suddenly, everyone and their dog was in the videogame business. By the end of the year, there were seventy companies churning out variations of *Pong* and clamoring for more circuits from General Instruments.

General Instruments ran out. Pumping out microprocessors at full capacity, it had shipped over a million McVideogame chips by the summer of '76. All the integrated circuits it could make had already been accounted for. Companies that had ordered early — Magnavox, Atari, and Coleco — got their allocations. All the other manufacturers just went bonkers, scrapping like rabid wolverines for the dwindling supply of semiconductors and further aggravating the chip shortage. Many of the parvenus hoping to cash in at Christmas never got the chance. There weren't enough parts to go around. Which meant that down the pipeline, little kids (and their parents) didn't get the SuperPong machine that Santa had promised. Would-be videogamers felt snubbed and lost interest. Retailers, fuming that the videogame companies had deprived them of those holiday greenbacks, mooned the industry when it came time to reorder. And as a result of the chip shortage and the tilt-a-whirl of supply and demand, the floor fell out of the videogame market, prompting an apocalyptic shakedown of would-be TV game manufacturers. Fly-by-night clone factories simply evaporated. Established players like Fairchild, National Semiconductor, and RCA hobbled around for a little while longer before their game divisions slumped over and died. Only Atari, the sole wounded survivor, persisted through the bloodbath, backed by Warner, which had bought the fledgling company when it looked like a great big cash cow. Suckers.

Just as home systems sunk into the quicksand of consumer disfavor, a new hardware platform provided videogames with a fresh dish of agar. Cheap handheld and tabletop models did a lot of the same things as home console videogames (sound effects, music, flashing lights, etc.). But they cloaked their technology in the guise of edutainment. Whereas *Pong* never pretended to be anything but frivolous electronic fun, these new plastic light machines — Merlin, Simon, Speak & Spell, Quiz Wiz — were ostensibly edifying as well as colorful and sweet. Digital memory games were the Flintstones vitamins of consumer electronics. Of course, their number was dwarfed by the profusion of portable sports games.* But they had a nice halo effect on handheld electronics in general.

Socially, portable electronic games and TV game consoles were totally different beasts. Unlike console units, handhelds were small and came in a rainbow of colorful plastic casing. They ran on batteries. They lived in a toy bin or the backseat of a station wagon or on the floor of a kid's room, not in the sacred "home entertainment center" that housed expensive stereo components and the almighty television. In short, the new electronic games weren't threatening. They were just a smarter breed of toy. But despite their contextual overhaul, these machines were made by the same people who'd just abandoned the TV game business — Mattel, Parker Brothers, Coleco — and were based on the same technology. In fact, they ran off the

---

* In 1980, there were forty-one handheld sports games, including eleven football, nine baseball, five basketball, and ten soccer/hockey games, one boxing and three bowling games, and one tennis and one handheld billiards game ("Electronic Games: Space-Age Leisure Activity," *Popular Electronics*, December 1980, 68).

same Intel and Motorola microchips as the ill-fated paddle hockey consoles. And game software, whether it ran on a TV or something that looked like a jumbo-sized calculator, was burned into the same kind of immutable read-only memory (ROM).

For a while, it looked like handhelds might be the future of electronic gaming. Portable machines like Milton Bradley's Microvision could conceivably have gotten smarter and faster and developed better displays and evolved into what we now recognize as videogames. But in the end, handhelds lost, for two reasons. First of all, by shifting from built-in software to cartridges, the videogame console developed a digestive tract. Whereas first-generation machines had essentially lived off stored novelty reserves, hitting the hall closet once players tired of preprogrammed blip games, second-generation machines like the Atari VCS could ingest new nuggets of software and jettison the husks of played-out cartridges when players were ready for something new.* Cartridges did to the videogame industry what the Pill did to sexual politics in the 1960s. Suddenly, software and hardware were separate enterprises. And once the games themselves were separate from the machines on which they were played, consoles were no longer big, expensive disposable razors. They were big, expensive razors with replaceable blades. This gave them an enormous advantage over self-contained toys like Super Simon.

The other reason console games won was that oversized calculators, however appealing, were no match for the television. America adores its television screens, and home videogames gave us a way to broaden our relationship with them. Atari rode the cathode ray tube to ubiquity, just like the

---

* The Atari VCS wasn't the first programmable home videogame system — Fairchild Camera and Instrument released one, the Channel F Video Entertainment System, in August of 1976. The Channel F, which sold for $150, played $20 "video-carts," the first of which added Tic-Tac-Toe, Shooting Gallery, and a game called Space Quadra Doodle to the machine's built-in repertoire of tennis and hockey. But Fairchild's budding Gillette strategy was nipped by the industry crash, leaving Atari to grab the baton. A year later, the Atari VCS flew off the shelves for $200, bundled with paddle and joystick controllers and a pack-in *Combat* cartridge.

VCR would a few years later. Home videogames even gave people the ability to manipulate action on the screen, which made them, essentially, the first form of interactive television. Stacked up against the allure of television and the tide of replaceable cartridges, prefab electronic toys were hard-pressed to compete.

By the end of 1978, videogames had bounced from the TV to the toy chest and back. They had successfully distinguished themselves as Not Toys, rising above the low-end, disposable world of handheld electronics. Now they had to define themselves against a new species of digital equipment: the personal computer. Just as TV games and electronic toys had overlapped, cartridge consoles and early PCs technically had a lot in common. In fact, the Apple II was built by former Atari engineers Steve Wozniak and Steve Jobs. The VCS in Atari's model name stood for Video Computer System, and there was no technological reason why late 1970s videogame machines could not have produced a usable PC.

And for a few years, computers were what videogames desperately tried to be, starting with the Bally Professional Arcade, which debuted in 1977 with lumpen aspirations to programming capability. After much fanfare and a series of delays, Bally's add-on keyboard and BASIC cartridge allowed Professional Arcade owners to write and store their own games on cassette tape — a small consolation when Bally decided to get out of the videogame business in 1979 and stopped releasing its own games. The 1978 Odyssey2 was sort of a mock computer — it had no actual programming functions but came with a forty-nine-character membrane keyboard, which was mostly used to play educational cartridges like Math-a-Matic. A year later, Magnavox released the *Computer Intro* cartridge and a spiral-bound manual explaining how to program your very own games in Assembly. (Squeezing out homemade Odyssey2 games in machine language on a membrane keyboard. Fun for the whole family!) Needless to say, *Computer Intro* was not a raging hit.

Meanwhile, Atari had formed a computer division and introduced the 16K Atari 400 computer, which was pretty useless, the 48K Atari 800, and a slew of Atari peripherals — disk drives, a dot matrix printer, word processing and accounting software — as well as a new assortment of games that did not work on the old VCS console. Atari didn't sell that many of these would-be computers. It did, however, sell 400,000 game-only VCS machines at Christmas. Realizing that computer features were gravy atop the beefsteak of video entertainment, Atari's computer division tried a different approach in 1983 with My First Computer, an expansion module that popped into the VCS cartridge slot and rested on top of the game console. Meanwhile, two third-party copycats, the Entex Piggyback 2000 Color Computer and Spectravideo's CompuMate, also humped the VCS trying to act like computers.

By the end of 1983, every manufacturer that had produced first-generation paddle hockey consoles and handheld electronic games was selling a pared-down home computer that also played videogame cartridges. Coleco entered the fray with Adam, a six-hundred-dollar system with all the trappings of a home computer (keyboard, cassette drive, letter quality printer, a word processor, etc.) plus *Super Buck Rogers Planet of Zoom*. Mattel's Aquarius project was similarly schizophrenic, encasing Microsoft BASIC in a white plastic box with bright blue buttons. Milton Bradley tried to hedge its toy line with a keyboard for the old Vectrex mini-arcade. Even the old Bally Arcade was relaunched as Astravision's Astrocade, a three-hundred-dollar superdeluxe game machine that ran off the same processor as Radio Shack's TRS-80 home computer but also came with pistol grip controllers and played *Galactic Invasion*.

To make matters even more confusing, computer companies like Tandy, Texas Instruments, and Commodore were slashing the prices of their low-end PCs to compete with the new, souped-up videogame machines. A dozen years before "convergence" became the buzzword of would-be multimedia computer cable, Internet set-top box manufacturers, videogames, and computers were foaming together in the same yeasty vat of electronics, entertainment, and shotgun marketing.

But just as game companies leaped out of the starting gate, the whole horse race was cut dramatically short by the second great crash of the videogame industry, which had nothing to do with consoles' computer pretensions and everything to do with an overabundance of awful videogames. Seven years after the crash of '76, a tide of ticky-tack clones washed 1983 Christmas videogame sales into the garbage disposal. Instead of hardware manufacturers, it was third-party cartridge producers that dealt the death of a thousand cuts, but the result was the same: a flood of less-than-thrilling games triggering a vicious cycle of discounting and loss. The more games merchants relegated to the discount bin, the more game companies slashed their prices just to compete.

When even the best games failed to rise above the dross, industry leaders blazed a scorched earth retreat, losing more money in 1983 than they'd made in all the boom years combined. Atari wanly gave the order to bury thousands of overstocked cartridges in a New Mexico landfill, capping a $539 million loss. Reeling, Warner responded in typical blue chip fashion and put Atari's R&D department into deep freeze. Mattel strangled the ill-fated Aquarius project by dropping its electronics division. Magnavox 86'd the Odyssey2, and Coleco euthanized Adam.

All these companies were right about the revolution in home computing. But seeing their industry shrink from a $3 billion anaconda in 1982 to a $100 million garter snake in 1985, American videogame manufacturers were not destined to ride that particular wave. Five years later, Nintendo staged a similar play to sell game machines as demi-PCs, banking on the buzz of computer networking. "By 1991," a spokesman told *Newsweek*, "Nintendo machines in the United States will be equipped with modems for communicating over telephone lines, allowing consumers to order stocks and shop directly from home. We want this to be an appliance that's in every home, school, and hotel room in the country."* The idea was to make the Nintendo ma-

* Michael Rogers, "Nintendo and Beyond," *Newsweek*, June 18, 1990, 62.

chine into a Dr. Seussian sneed — the fungible, all-purpose, omnipresent product that no one can live without.

But again, the cartridge-playing home computer was stillborn. It wasn't a matter of technological constraints. Americans just weren't ready to trade mutual funds with a joypad. Videogame machines, if they were to succeed, would have to return to the familiar appeal of television, their on-again, off-again spouse. It was a marriage held together, for better or worse, by America's Madonna/whore complex about the computer and the television. Televisions are creatures that exist solely for fun, bought and sold on the basis of their looks and their ability to entertain. If they're smart, fine, but their first duty is to amuse us.

Computers, on the other hand, are serious machines for serious purposes, and we are loath to view them as playthings,* especially when CD-ROM games are notorious for causing drastic malfunctions in system software — the risk of irretrievably soiling your Turbotax return with the binary offal of *Rebel Assault* simply isn't worth it. As work machines, computers sit on a kind of Calvinist pedestal. They are symbols for responsibility, and we like them to look responsible — heavy and stolidly understated, in some neutral corporate color like putty or charcoal gray. Flashy bodies would only tarnish their virtuous image and undermine our willingness to pay ten times more for them than for the most advanced videogame machines.

Guided by this double standard, we don't want to be reminded that videogame machines *are* computers. They are highly sophisticated computers with a narrowly defined task, namely, playing cartridges and optical discs for entertainment. But underneath the hood, they bear an uncomfortable resem-

---

* Repeating the results of a Hewlett Packard study of 4,000 consumers, most of whom rejected the idea of a computer as an entertainment platform, a 1995 market research report by DFC Intelligence found that even avid videogame players hated to play games on their computers. "A common attitude was a variation of the statement 'I work all day on a computer, the last thing I want to do is come home and sit in front of a computer playing a game.' Yet these same people had no qualms with sitting in front of the television to play a video game."

blance to the machines that reign over our desktops. A Sega Genesis runs off the same Motorola chip that drove the original Mac. The Sega Saturn is a 32-bit computer. So is a 486 PC. Nintendo's Ultra 64 processor, manufactured by Silicon Graphics, has the same bit width as Intel's Pentium and runs at over 100 MHz.

But never mind that. Fun is fun, and work is work — and we are sociologically incapable of paying our telephone bills on a Sony Playstation. And it's much harder to upgrade ingrained habits than to build a faster or more versatile set of microchips. Which is why, fifteen years after videogame machines tried to become computers the first time, "convergence" is still a myth. Ultimately, it's a design issue. Creating demand for all-purpose TV/computer hybrids is like changing the face of residential architecture. It's like getting suburbanites to give up dining rooms. The use of dining rooms has been on the wane in America for fifty years. But new houses are still constructed with dining rooms. Those dining rooms are then converted to home offices. But very few people buying (or building) houses say skip the dining room, let's use that space in another part of the building. It's a cultural fixture. So is the way we divide our time between computers and TV according to the rhythms of work and play. Technology may blur to the point where the guts of a game machine are nearly indistinguishable from the guts of a home computer. We may well buy the same chips twice. But one set will look like a computer and live on a desk, and another will look like a TV accessory and live in, well, the living room. When the dining room dies, that's where the multimedia sneed will go.

Chapter 4
A la Recherche du Arcades Perdu

It's ironic that the skills that young people use in high-tech computerized jobs should have been honed in video arcades because video arcades in the 1980s were intensely unprofessional places filled with smelly teenage boys — places like Playland on Forty-seventh Street in Manhattan. Lodged in the warren of glitz and grime that is Times Square, Playland is a place where orange and blue linoleum tiles checker the floor twenty feet wide and a hundred feet deep into a lightless recess of pinup posters and wood veneer paneling. The posters (all for sale) mostly portray glossy-lipped softcore sex kittens straddling chairs or motorcycles. But the lunch hour hodgepodge of teenagers in baggy pants and midtown businessmen seems oblivious to the airbrushed cheesecake vixens looming overhead. They're too busy playing *Marvel Superheroes* and *Ultimate Mortal Kombat*.

Off to the side, a forlorn *Pac-Man* machine sits, looking woefully small and dinky next to the seven-foot cabinets that surround it. Against the back wall, a couple of pinball machines blink their incandescent lightbulbs in a fruitless bid for quarters. At twenty-five cents, the old machines are a bargain, especially when you stop to consider that their price has remained constant for fifteen years. In fact, adjusting for inflation, a game of *Pac-Man* or *Frogger* will run you about twelve cents in 1981 dollars. All the new games cost fifty cents. Deluxe games like *Time Crisis* are a dollar. Nonetheless, the pumped-up martial arts games and networked Nascar races are clobbering the pinball machines and the *Pac-Man*s, just as Disney-style family entertainment centers are replacing seedy game rooms like Playland — just as Disney, for that matter, is reconfiguring Times Square itself. The dimly lit arcade of vidkid remembrance is going the way of the drive-in.

Videogame arcades have had a good twenty-year run — long enough to be taken for granted. But they aren't the first kind of coin-op play zone to flourish and then go extinct. Coin-op game rooms have existed in America, in various forms, for over a hundred years. Before videogames, there were pinball parlors, which provided a place for teenagers and deadbeats to hang out for considerable stretches of time without officially loitering. Pinball itself, like videogames, was relatively innocent. But it smelled like it might be dangerous. It was chaotic and vaguely aggressive, and there were girlies on some of the cabinets. Pinball was how James Dean or Marlon Brando might squander time while contemplating riskier pursuits. And it attracted people who at least dressed like juvenile delinquents. But more importantly, the pinball parlor was a place where sheltered suburban teens might actually come into contact with working-class kids, high school dropouts, down-and-out adults, cigarettes, and other corrupting influences, which made the place a breeding ground for parental paranoia, if not for crime. Although pinball machines themselves were hard to blame, in the public mind their milieu posed a threat to America's moral fiber.

Something about coin-operated amusements seems to inspire this kind of schizophrenic popular conception. Before pinball parlors, game rooms of the thirties and forties created the same stir in resorts and amusement parks. Before that, 1920s coin-op machines acquired notoriety as a frequent fixture in speakeasies. Prior to that, critics of turn-of-the-century penny arcades and nickelodeons argued that cheap, coin-operated thrills like the dreaded kinetoscope would foster a sensational-istic carnival mentality and drive the arousable masses to riot and iniquity. Of course, it was the masses and not the machines that concerned them. But the machines were a convenient touchstone for class tension because they cropped up just as cities were accumulating a critical mass of blue collar workers. Suddenly, there were droves of machinists and shop girls, all of whom had money to spend on low-cost entertainment. And coin-op machines gave them a way to spend their leisure dol-lars, nickel by nickel. So if you wanted to point to a source of working-class dissipation, nickel-in-the-slot amusement ma-chines were a nice, mute, nontaxpaying, nonvoting scapegoat with dubious ties to the underworld.

In the early 1890s, the big coin-op craze was phonograph machines, which gobbled people's pocket change while they stood around in lobbies, saloons, train stations, and fairgrounds. The high-tech cabinets of their time, coin-op phonograph ma-chines played cylinder recordings of speeches and popular songs through a listening tube, which the patron would cradle to his or her ear after inserting a number of coins. In central business dis-tricts, banks of coin-op phonograph machines lined the walls of bustling penny arcades, providing the midday crowd with a quick mental vacation:

[Companies] found that by grouping several machines to-gether in a downtown "parlor," with full-time attendants to service the machines and make change, they could attract large numbers of customers from the streams of pedestrians who passed by day and night. . . . To bolster their receipts, the parlor owners surrounded their graphophones and phonographs with other "automatic" amusement novelties, machines that dispensed gum, candy, fruit, and miracle me-dicinals such as "Roy's Positive Remedy Curing Headache and Neuralgia in 15 Minutes — 10¢ Per Package," and X-Ray machines and fluoroscopes that displayed the bones in your hands and were all the rage until experimenters, including one of Edison's assistants, discovered that repeated exposure caused flesh to ulcerate, hair to fall out, and eventual death.[*]

Coin-in-the-slot phonograph arcades boomed nationally in the early nineties (the 1890s, that is), before being superseded by the mid-nineties kinetoscope craze — a flotilla of picture peephole machines featuring films of flexing strongmen, highland dancers, cockfights, trapeze artists, contortionists, and trained bears.[†]

Ultimately, as with early video arcades, the proprietors of coin-op phonograph and kinetoscope parlors realized that their core customers were young males eager to play with the latest cutting-edge toys for five or ten minutes en route to work. After all, technological marvels like the phonograph and the kinetoscope were far too expensive for home use. And even when the phonograph became an affordable piece of consumer gear, the audio arcades always had the flashiest and most advanced equipment, plus all the latest cylinders before they hit the stores, plus a meeting ground where guys could discuss the nuances of different phonograph models and compare the size and variety of their home cylinder collections. In some cases, the phonograph parlors even provided a place to buy, sell, and trade on the underground market for homemade pornographic audio cylinders (a much seedier prospect than the twentieth-century video arcade, which at least offers a standard set of products. Parents may hate *Mortal Kombat,* but they know there aren't any mutant home-brew versions floating around that increase the prurient appeal of Acclaim's version).

Despite their popularity, the phonograph parlors inexorably gave way to the next turn-of-the-century coin-op wundertechnology, the mutoscope, which, unlike the earlier kinetoscope, featured a mechanical crank allowing the customer to speed up, slow down, reverse, or stop the action. Much was made of this feature, curiously foreshadowing the tone of

---

[*] David Nasaw, *Going Out: The Rise and Fall of Public Amusements* (New York: Basic Books, 1993), 126–27.
[†] Ibid., 132.

CD-ROM box labels a hundred years later ("You're in control. *You* turn the crank"). Back then, coin-op film machines were touted as emblems of the machine age, just as coin-op videogames would represent the bleeding edge of the digital era. Scores of amusement sites used "automatic" as a magic buzzword to attract novelty-crazed thrill seekers, exactly the same way the word "virtual" is used today. Everything was "automatic." Regardless of the images and sounds they projected (what we in the information age call "content"), the mutoscope was supposed to be entertaining by definition, simply because it was "automatic."

By the late nineties, phonographs and kinetoscope parlors were obsolete. And the mutoscope arcade was on the wane, slowly edging over the shady/respectable divide to begin its second life as a peep show (pornography being the perennial novelty). But in the wake of their outdated machines, turn-of-the-century coin-op arcades left behind a new kind of gathering ground that revolved around high-end technology that anyone could casually consume for a nickel, a dime, or, a hundred years later, a quarter. "The arcades," writes David Nasaw, "were casual institutions that required (and indeed sold) no advance tickets, had no assigned seats, and, as importantly, required no cultural capital of their audience. All viewers, regardless of social background or educational level, had equal access to the 'meaning' of the images viewed through the peephole or on the larger screen. One didn't even have to speak English to understand the story."[*] A hundred years after the phonograph machine, *Pole Position* cut the same swath across ethnic and class lines. The 1980s video arcade was one of the few truly diverse hangouts in teendom. It catered equally to preppies and high school dropouts, geeks and jocks, Chicano kids and rednecks-in-training. And, videogames being a great leveler, the arcade was more or less a meritocracy. It didn't matter what you drove to the arcade. If you sucked at *Asteroids*, you just sucked.

[*] Ibid., 158.

But unlike phonograph machines or coin-op kinetoscopes, videogames didn't have to attract traffic from the street. They were sheltered from the vagaries of climate and real estate by a bovine symbiotic host: the American mall. Although the first enclosed two-level mall, Southdale Center, in Edina, Minnesota, opened in 1956, the real wildfire of mall construction raged in the late sixties and seventies. By 1974 there were 13,174 shopping centers in Canada and the United States. By 1982, there were 20,304, including over a thousand megamalls of 400,000 square feet or more.* Fortuitously, these were concentrated in California, also the Tigris and Euphrates of the American videogame industry. In the cradle of military contractors and West Coast consumerism, the microchips that made videogames possible advanced in tandem with the mushrooming malls. As the malls landed, like retail mother ships, they carried coin-op game rooms into every metropolis, small city, large town, and suburban hamlet in North America.

In the first flush of 1960s malldom, there were no videogames per se. But there were some embryonic coin-op game machines that looked like TVs and worked by projecting film images off a series of mirrors. By the late 1960s these so-called "electromechanical projection games" were edging into retail stores along the eastern seaboard. The moment was ripe for someone to marry this new type of coin-op television game experience to the burgeoning phenomenon of shopping malls.

That individual was Tico Bonomo, an erstwhile candy manufacturer in upstate New York. Having just sold his stake in a successful confectionery, Bonomo Turkish Taffy, Tico was looking for a new startup venture when he spied a few of these electromechanical projection games and, with a growing sense of excitement, realized that a whole storeful of them in a shopping mall might be a good way to make money. So he opened the Time Out Family Amusement Center in the Northway Mall in Colonie, New York, in 1970. Amazingly, people seemed to

---

* International Council of Shopping Centers, National Research Bureau statistics.

like electromechanical projection games even more than they liked Bonomo's Turkish Taffy. So the following year, Tico opened a few more game rooms. And then came *Pong,* which sent pocket change flying out of mall patrons' bell-bottom pockets into the coffers of the newly minted Bonomo coin-op empire. By 1975, there were a dozen Time Outs. By 1978, there were twenty, just in time for *Space Invaders,* a second flood of quarters, and another round of expansion. As videogames replaced the electromechanical game cabinets and pinball machines, Time Out rode the twin waves of mall construction and videogames through the seventies. New malls hatched more arcades, spurring manufacturers to create flashier machines. And as the machines got better, their audience ballooned, drawn by a string of hit games like *Asteroids, Battlezone, Defender,* and *Pac-Man.*

At the center of this circular feeding frenzy was the arcade customer. And, much to local merchants' chagrin, that audience consisted almost entirely of fifteen-year-old boys, who were lured to glowing videogames in darkened rooms like mosquitoes to a bug zapper. "In the beginning," says George Mc-Auliffe, general manager of Time Out through a series of ownerships and president of the Family Entertainment Center trade association, "the philosophy was paint the stores black, and keep 'em dark, so that the TV screens stand out, and that was the atmosphere that customers wanted. But by 1979, we were trying to appeal to a wider age group. We wanted to open more stores, and shopping mall developers didn't want teenage hangouts. So we started to brighten them up, use more yellows and brighter colors. We were fighting this image that went all the way back to the twenties, associated with coin-operated games, that they were smoke-filled hangouts where nefarious characters did bad things. We had to brighten it up for the mall developer so that we could expand into more locations."

Thus began the arcade sanitation crusade, which meant, first off, that sometime around 1981, video arcades shifted their lighting scheme from black to a shade I like to call "clockwork orange," which was the color of pizza grease, only much more intense. It made everyone look like a poster boy for jaundice. But apparently, this bizarre tangerine hue achieved its goal, which was to pacify mall developers and convince Mom that the arcade was a safe place to dump little Johnny while she went shopping. "It was definitely a conscious decision to appeal to more women," McAuliffe flatly admits. "Before two-income families and career women, that was the shopper in the mall. That's where the money was. Those were the primary shoppers, making decisions about where they were going to allow their children. And if you had a place that appealed to them, they were more likely to bring that child to the mall and to feel comfortable leaving them there. And then Mom could go off and do the shopping, and meet up with the child and then maybe go to a food court." Basically, it was in everyone's interest to make the video arcade look like a viable form of free, unsupervised day care.

By the end of 1981, the arcade had become a fixture of urban and suburban life and the after-school hangout of choice for millions of teenagers. And arcade machines, doubly entrenched in the video arcade and the mall, were sucking down 20 billion quarters and 75,000 man-years annually. For the arithmetically challenged, that is: Five. Billion. Dollars. Which, added to the billion-dollar home videogame market, meant that joystick entertainment was raking in more than the U.S. movie industry and Nevada gambling combined.*

Inevitably, a fleet of speculators blew in to milk the craze. Many of them thought it would be a smart idea to open video arcades across the street from schools so that kids could run over at lunchtime. And after enough kids had been caught cutting class to spend their lunch money playing videogames, the backlash began. As with pinball, there was a shortage of credible arguments as to what, exactly, made videogames such a bad influence. But in the public perception, arcades smacked of

* *Time*, January 18, 1982.

moral turpitude.* Targeting videogame rooms as havens for delinquency, town fathers in communities like Snellville, Georgia, outlawed the games entirely, bringing their local ordinances into sync with the Philippines, where, half a world away, Ferdinand Marcos had banned coin-op videogames and given arcade owners two weeks to smash them.

Not only were video arcades becoming public enemy number one, but by the beginning of 1982, game manufacturers were getting sloppy, rushing machines into production with no technological innovation or improvements in game play or even marginally better graphics. By the end of the year, arcades were saturated with unexciting copycat machines, and the bubble burst. With the quality of games in a tailspin, high school videogamers got bored. And since every 7-Eleven had at least a couple arcade cabinets, you could cross the street to play videogames instead of cruising all the way over to the mall. As an escalating number of lukewarm games sparred for a jaded audience, the videogame industry began a painful freefall. And after a twelve-year sail, arcades followed suit. By 1983, thousands of game rooms had closed, leaving the survivors to stagnate in the lukewarm foot traffic of their malls, waiting for the new, shiny machines that would bring back the glory days.

Years went by. Layers of grime built up on the arcades' seldom-swept linoleum floors. Chewing gum collected on the roofs of old *Dig Dug* machines. But the new batch of miracle

---

* In an academic study ("Video Arcades, Youth, and Trouble," *Youth and Society* 16, no. 1, September 1984, 47–65), Desmond Ellis found these perceptions to be largely baseless: "For every hour [kids] spent in a video arcade, they spent ten watching television, five hours reading, and two playing a team sport." Contrary to claims that arcades were breeding hooligans, Ellis found that arcade attendance was positively related to academic performance and that the link between arcades and stealing/vandalism/assault was negligible. "Video arcades per se were not, as those authorities allege, a major cause of deviant behavior. Instead, video arcade involvement tends to increase the likelihood of deviant behavior only when such involvement is itself associated with weak parental control." That is, the small group of kids who were in arcades after 10 P.M. accounted for half of the deviant acts, which had more to do with the fact that their parents were letting them run wild than with their chosen late-night stomping ground.

games never arrived, and the teenagers only got cockier. As arcades across the country withered on the vine, larger chains bought up the rubble of a once-thriving industry at fire sale prices. On the West Coast, Sega put its American arcade operation on the block and went back to Japan to lick its wounds. The thirteen-store franchise was eventually absorbed by Time Out.

It was in this secondhand arcade chain that McAuliffe, Time Out's general manager, saw the salvation of coin-op entertainment. And it wasn't a new, shiny machine at all. "They had a couple of stores in which they were running Skee-Balls," he says, referring to the bowling-cum-ball-toss machines lingering in Sega's defunct franchise. "Prior to that, we never thought of it. Skee-Ball was always something you did at the Jersey shore or in an amusement park — more of a tourist venue. We were getting ready to take all these Skee-Balls out when we realized that they make money, and they're very steady, as opposed to a videogame, which you buy, and the sales curve starts out high and then trickles down. Skee-Balls were just a nice steady investment. Not only that, but women liked them. It was something they could understand. It was a skill game. Parents were intimidated by the technology in the seventies. This was something they could do with smaller children. And an operator can buy a Skee-Ball and it remains popular for ten years. They buy a video machine, and in six months it's not popular anymore. Teenagers are harder to impress. The real growth area is in the little kid stuff."

With the realization that preschoolers were more profitable than adolescents, the toddling of video arcades began. In came the Skee-Balls. In came the crane machines, driving coin-op entertainment out of the dazed-and-confused teenage bunker onto the putting green of romper room profitability. Crane games, grasping small plush merchandise in steel hooks, allowed Time Out to claw its way back into mainstream relevance. "What really drove the late-eighties arcade success," says McAuliffe, "was four-to-six-inch-high plush animals. People just loved it. In 1987, we had seventy stores. Between then and 1990, we had one [crane game] in damn near every store, and so did the rest of the industry, and they started to appear in supermarkets and other places. One of the things that kept it going was that you had this box, and the box stayed the same, but the merchandise changed all the time. You could do seasonal things with it to boost sales. So the people who got tired of little alligators, they could get hearts on Valentine's Day and rabbits on Easter and little flags on the Fourth of July."

Not only could you stuff this plush seasonal merchandise into claw machines, but it also fueled the other pillar of kiddie coin-op: redemption games. McAuliffe describes redemption games with a mixture of reverence and gosh-golly enthusiasm, brightening at the mere mention of them. "Redemptions are the ones that tickets come out of. It's the little kiddie games. That's the biggest part of our arcade. The whole industry has moved more towards redemption as a way to grow their business."

He invokes this term over and over. Redemption. Redemption. It's like he's trying to make good for all those years of playing REO Speedwagon over the Time Out sound system for legions of hormonal teenage boys. As if somehow, if only he could send enough tickets reeling out of Skee-Ball machines, arcades could return to the entrepreneurial Eden of Tico Bonomo. Install redemption games, and small plush merchandise shall set ye free.

Awash in pink bunnies and nylon froggy puppets, the arcade quickly lost its cachet for dissipated adolescents. The Skee-Ball machine was no place for any self-respecting teenager to strike a pose — it's kind of hard to be dangerous and cool when your five-year-old sister is lobbing Nerf balls twenty steps away. And after the high school heavy-metal crowd dispersed, arcades were safe for oncoming swarms of kindergartners screaming for the chance to win action figures and bouncy balls.

But what about the arcade from high school? What about nonsanitized places like Playland? McAuliffe turns grave. There's no turning back, he explains gently, pointing me forward to the shining future of kiddie coin-op. "The typical arcade that's in your mind-set will probably cease to exist in the next five years, because the ones that are successful now are what the industry classifies as family entertainment centers. They're incorporating pizza birthday parties. They may have bumper cars. They may have miniature golf. The traditional arcade needs to be married with these other elements, or it just doesn't make sense anymore." Video killed the radio star, the old song goes. Well, Skee-Ball killed the video arcade.

But surely the cavelike game room of high school remembrance has survived the onslaught of claw machines and Skee-Ball.

No. At Memorial City, my dilapidated hometown mall, the teenage stoners in Poison T-shirts and Mexican urban cowboys in acid-washed jeans have given way to a herd of baby boomers en famille lined up outside the multiplex. The video arcade of yesteryear has vanished, long since replaced by a 46,000-square-foot family entertainment center called Exhilarama, conveniently located next to the food court.

Exhilarama is remarkable for its complete lack of corners. It is one cavernous, all-encompassing formal garden of centrifugal rides, carousels, crawl cages, choo-choo trains, bumper cars, and virtual reality motion simulators. The videogames are arranged at precise four-foot intervals in a circle, their raster monitors completely washed out by Exhilarama's flood of fluorescent light. The whole place smells like bubble gum, a scent no doubt concocted and piped in especially to mollify the miniskirted former-mall-rat moms lingering around the Jackpot redemption console and fussing with their nails, oblivious to their howling preschool kids; or the blond-ponytail-sensible-shoes moms lined up next to Exhilarama's bank of seven Skee-Ball machines. Watching a four-year-old girl in pink overalls take aim at the *Striker* mini–bowling alley — she's intent, too, quite the little pro — it is clear that Skee-Ball is the perfect diversion for these coddled baby boomer larvae. Swathed in the security of their parents' mutual funds and sport utility vehicles, these kids are growing up with the limited cognitive palette and glacial motor skills of scaled-down bowling simulators, rather than, say, maneuvering for their lives against a ballistic arcade space monster screaming "Run, Coward! Run! Run!" In a crisis, no way is a Skee-Ball kid going to stack up against an arcade scrapper weaned on *Sinistar*.

And what does the Skee-Ball generation get for these so-called redemption tickets, anyway? Barney dolls from Taiwan, or some ersatz toy from the Exhilarama Prize Center: Frisbees, Slinkys, koosh balls, key chains, plush ducks, plastic back scratchers, and Barbie cameras, all hideously overvalued. Arcade games in their heyday were, at least, a straightforward transaction: you paid your quarter, you got to chase bits of light around for a few minutes, and it got your blood pumping. And then it was over. And if you did it repetitively, it was because the experience was thrilling enough to bear repetition. Redemption games, on the other hand, operate on the premise that this ostensibly pleasurable activity is merely a means to some greater material goal — in other words, Skee-Ball is a proxy for work. In the arcade, fun was something you paid for. In the family entertainment centers' redemption scheme, fun is your job, or rather, an unpaid internship that you take at your own expense so that you can *earn* all those fabulous plush prizes.

Basically, the redemption arcade is a giant, overpriced toy store housed in a high-tech, neo-Victorian circus, complete with putt-putt courses, downsized indoor Ferris wheels, and merry-go-rounds manufactured by Chance Rides, Inc., of Wichita, Kansas, which has supplied over a hundred North American malls with quarter-million-dollar carousels. Indoor theme parks, argue the industry bigwigs, are the future of coin-op entertainment.

In order to create this banana republic of family fun, the small, dingy arcade had to die. Its execution warrant was spelled out in the pages of *Shopping Center World*, in an article detailing the benefits of the "mini-anchor configuration." In this article, industry experts stressed the need to take arcade games out of the corners and back rooms, arguing that "out-of-the-way locations for games and other amusements often become prime teenager hangouts, and discourage visits from families — a prime customer target group. . . . People are looking for controlled environments where they can feel safe. The safer they feel, the longer they will stay."*

In the brave new world of family entertainment centers, videogames remain, but they have been hijacked from the shadow and skank of the arcade, which was everything Exhilarama is not. Arcades demanded alertness. They were dark. There was a whiff of challenge and danger and sweat in the air. You could be pissed off in an arcade — dissatisfaction was an acceptable frame of mind.

At Exhilarama, squeaky-clean fun is strictly enforced. Despite its funhouse references to the penny arcades and nickelodeons of a hundred years ago, this place does not cater to the type of people that dropped their change into phonograph machines and kinetoscopes. The patrons of family amusement centers are not latter-day machinists and shop girls. They are, according to a 1991 study by the International Association of Amusement Parks and Attractions, affluent professionals with college degrees, Visa cards, and kids. Hence, the family entertainment center is stridently wholesome. The family entertainment center is relentlessly bright. The family entertainment center is under panoptic surveillance.

Whereas the arcade proprietor of ten years ago kept an eye on the place but generally left well enough alone, the family entertainment center employs a crack security force equipped with stylish *Mission Impossible* ear mikes. Private security guards, in constant contact with local police and mall sentries, patrol the amusement ground, closing in on any rogue activity detected by crowd spotters and video cameras. The management could easily be more discreet. But this would be counterproductive, since this flamboyant attention to safety is a major selling point. All those video cameras and the phalanx of security guards aren't necessary to enforce safety. They're there to enforce the perception of safety. It's the same reason armed

---

* Jane Adler, "Amusement Tenants Come Out to Play," *Shopping Center World,* August 1994, 51–55.

guards stand outside banks in countries under military re-
gimes — to ensure all passersby that the situation is firmly and
irrevocably under control.

High above the fray at Exhilarama, middle-aged supervi-
sors eye customers suspiciously from their sky box observation
deck. Anyone obviously not Having Fun is suspect. On the
wall, a giant slogan in yellow all-capital letters reads: MORE
THAN JUST CAKE AND COFFEE IN THE CONFER-
ENCE ROOM. HAVE AN OFFICE PARTY HERE. Jenny
Holzer–type slogans are painted across the soaring teal and
purple walls of the entire facility, from the bumper car arena to
the Snack Zone. Amid the sensory overload, these mottoes
barely register. They're almost subliminal. But they say things
that are so insidious, you just have to laugh:

"HOW'S THE WEATHER? WHO CARES."

"THIS LITTLE PIGGY WENT EXHILARAMA."

"IT'S A JUNGLE OUT THERE. STAY HERE."

Stay here. Stay here until you run out of money. Stay here
until your children become teenagers and start causing trouble.
Then go home, go to work, and come back for your office party.
This is the kind of all-enclosing entertainment cocoon where
coin-op videogames now live. They are no longer part of a drop-
in, five-minute, human-scale environment. They are part of a
theme park deliberately designed to keep people from leaving.
They have been taken hostage by ailing fin de siècle malls,
which now face competition from catalogs, home shopping, factory outlets, and superstores like Wal-Mart, Home Depot, Garden Depot, Office Depot, Circuit City, Bed Bath & Beyond,
Petland, and Barnes & Noble. From 1980 to 1993, America's
mall time halved, while its entertainment budget (for things like
consumer electronics, restaurants, and theme parks, preferably
combined) doubled. And seeing the carpet slide underfoot,
malls have desperately tried to reinvent themselves by digging
arcades out of the shadows and bloating them with high-tech
cinema, amusement park rides, and virtual reality. Whereas a
typical Time Out was two thousand square feet and had forty
arcade games, the supermall theme park is 50,000 square feet

and has 150 arcade games, plus a miniature golf course. At the end of the day, the family entertainment center is just another kind of superstore grafted onto a shopping mall, throwing the video arcade into the same economic ditch as the independent bookseller (anabolic retail makes strange bedfellows).

Now that gigantic Fisher-Price toygrounds have subsumed the old arcades, the sharp-edged camaraderie of Playland has lost its physical catch basin. But it hasn't evaporated. It has simply slipped out of the face-to-face world and into pockets of cyberspace, suffusing online game dens with the same anonymous, white-knuckled competition once found in the old arcades. It's the other side of the looking glass. The physical arcade was also a kind of virtual social space. People assembled and spoke to each other, but it was the same kind of glancing interaction that takes place in train stations and airports, where everyone is en route. In the arcades, everyone was en route from the physical world to cyberspace. Every videogame cabinet was a gate from one world to the other; the interface, a system of buttons and joysticks and coin slots instead of latches and handles and locks. And the arcade was a kind of borderland where you made all those transitions — from spectator to player, from a person standing around the cabinet to a character on the screen, from the ricochet of signals in your brain to discrete physical responses with fingers and wrists, from level to level, from game in progress to game over and back (spending five bucks in the process of jumping back and forth twenty times). The arcade was where you jumped from the holding pen of physical teenagers into a disembodied game world.

Dialing into networked *Doom* rooms and online game sites, you're going the other way — navigating virtual space to get back through to real people. You're playing videogames from the inside out against people whose real names and circumstances you may never know. In this sense, online game space is even hazier and more dubious than the old arcades. You may not be able to smell your opponents. But you know their login names. You know when they're online. And you know they're lurking around the next *Hexen* corridor waiting to blow you to a bloody pulp. Somewhere on the other side of the virtual arcade is a real person who, in a friendly, schoolyard way, has it in for you.

This — and not the family entertainment center — is the true heir of the videogame arcade, the pinball parlor, the kinetoscope hall, and the phonograph saloon. A place like Exhilarama reeks of social mandate. Its technological centerpiece, the Skee-Ball, has been around for three generations. A networked *Doom* deathmatch, on the other hand, pushes the envelope of telecommunications, and Internet game servers spark all kinds of anxiety, because, you know, all sorts of unsavory people may be lurking online. And when any kid with a Sony Playstation can crash in with an X-Band modem — when it's not just white middle-upper-class suburban teens with $2,000 computers — then things will *really* get interesting. Because if you suck at twenty-first-century pinball, it doesn't matter what kind of machine gets you to the virtual arcade.

Chapter 5
The Classics

Along a narrow corridor on Astoria, Queens, video arcade machines are lined up against the wall, and kids are pumping tokens into them. Bleeps and explosions and the din of digital combat ricochet between coin-op consoles. But these machines don't luminesce in the half-light of a suburban game room. This isn't the mall. This is a museum in broad daylight. And this long corridor of arcade cabinets is an exhibit, ostensibly a historical survey of videogames at the American Museum of the Moving Image (AMMI). The exhibit is designed to illustrate how America's best-loved digital entertainment has evolved over the last twenty-five years. It is arranged in chronological order with scholarly blurbs mounted on the walls next to the hulking artifacts they describe. But the barriers that typically label museum objects as significant — the velvet ropes, the vitrines, the Plexiglas barricades — are conspicuously absent. And so the whole space is unsettlingly poised between a museum gallery (and the restrained, churchy behavior that implies) and a playground, where you're supposed to run around, make noise, and jump on things. Yes, you get to play with all the old machines, and they're aligned almost the same way they were when you were a teenager. But not quite, because the consoles are much farther apart than an arcade operator would plant them. They are privileged with space, like statues or really expensive clothing, and thus become Design Objects.

And this is when you realize, for the first time, that these cabinets, apart from containing your favorite videogames, are really just goddamn beautiful. Just the dimensions of a video arcade console give you the feeling that, yeah, this is the way it's supposed to be. Playing a 1980s videogame on an arcade machine is like viewing a 1930s Hollywood extravaganza on the silver screen rather than watching it at home on a VCR. It's a public rather than a private experience. And the proportions are completely different. Unlike the front cover of a cartridge, the sides of an arcade machine are big enough to hold life-sized illustrations of the grotesque monsters you're supposed to be fighting in the game itself. The *Centipede* cabinet, for example, is emblazoned with a six-foot, scabrous, red-eyed, yellow-bellied arthropod, venom dripping from its fangs. This adds a certain frisson to the game play. It's like seeing classic cars on display. Those huge fins didn't add anything to the motor's performance. But you can imagine (or remember) that flamboyant fins holistically enhance the driving experience.

In fact, the first machine in AMMI's exhibit, *Computer Space*, looks remarkably like a 1957 DeSoto. You can't look at its tumescent ovoid screen, grooved sides, and swollen base and not recall the dash and flanks of a large finned automobile, the Future Car that never was. This intergalactic-looking trunk of sparkling green fiberglass was the first coin-operated videogame in the world. Nolan Bushnell, who later founded Atari, built *Computer Space* in 1971.

As a videogame, *Computer Space* was a variation on the *Spacewar* concept — two spaceships battling gravitational inertia and each other. It had lots of rules and controls and was fairly complicated to play — too complicated for the bar patrons who were supposed to play it. They thought it looked cool — as a design object, it was gorgeous. But *Computer Space* was not simple and stupid enough to make it as mass entertainment. That came the following year with Bushnell's next arcade machine, *Pong*. *Pong* was the antithesis of *Computer Space*. The gameplay was minimalism itself: one dotted line and two glowing slashes on either side of the screen. Unlike its anthropomorphic predecessor, *Pong* was boxy and unadorned, its faux wood grain cabinet foreshadowing Bushnell's impending licensing deal with Sears. Two stainless steel knobs superseded the old system of multifarious thrusters and buttons. Whereas *Computer Space* was a marvelous dinosaur, *Pong* was the relatively unimpressive ratlike mammal scurrying beneath its feet that eventually conquered the world.

I wander down the AMMI arcade replaying the games that came out when I was twelve and thirteen. And it's like hearing a junior high school hit on the radio. You look up from a game of *Galaxian* half expecting to find yourself back in the mall as a teenager, surrounded by skanky metalhead kids in their Van Halen T-shirts and black rubber bracelets. That was videogame nation. That was the arcade mall, Foreigner-listening environment. And it's strange, because a dozen other people in the room are obviously also thinking this way. You can see it on their faces. They're thinking, God, I was a teenager in the mall obsessing about this cheerleader who would never go out with me, playing this videogame. There are a couple of mid-thirties baseball cap guys showing off for their kids. One of them is playing *Dig Dug* with his seven-year-old son — and beating him, probably something he couldn't do at home on the Super Nintendo. "Hah hah, still got it!" he hoots. "This is what Daddy used to play on lunch break."

It was a time bomb, really. You couldn't have that many American kids doing the same thing at the same time and not generate an immense aftershock of nostalgia fifteen years later. The shift from wildly popular to wildly retro was a radioactive decay process that started early in the Reagan administration and has now achieved critical mass. It is now impossible to mention Atari-era videogames at a cocktail party and not trigger a domino line of stories about the glory days of *Asteroids*.

"Remember *Joust?*" asks an investment banker at a Greenwich Village soirée. "That was my game. I was the champ. That was the best game."

"No," says his office-mate. "*Space Invaders*. It was great, because you could keep going a long time. But it just kept getting faster and faster. And you knew at some point it would overwhelm you, but you didn't know when. But you also knew you could take a lot of guys down with you before you finally died."

I take half a step back from this guy, careful not to make any sudden moves, and say, "Actually, I think *Missile Command*'s a better bet, if you want to get totally fatalistic. I mean, you've got six cities to defend against incoming nuclear missiles, and at first you can cover all of them. But eventually, the only way to really survive is to pick one city and cover that and let the rest go totally to hell. Like, fuck Washington, D.C., fuck New York, fuck Atlanta, I'm taking care of Madison, Wisconsin. It liberated you from all kinds of social responsibility." Now it's his turn to be nervous.

The most intense thing about *Missile Command*, though, was this weird crazy moment near the end, when the ICBMs were raining down and you knew you were just about to lose it, that was totally euphoric. Because you knew that you were going to die, that you were within seconds of everything going black. You're gonna die in three seconds. You're gonna die at this instant. You're dying. You're dead. And then you get to watch all the pretty explosions. And after the fireworks display, you get to press the restart button, and you're alive again, until the next collision with your own mortality. You're not just playing with colored light. You're playing with the concept of death. For a little kid, this is endlessly fascinating. One day, my little brother and I were playing the Atari version of *Missile Command*, and it got to that last desperate grasp for survival. He was maybe six or seven, and he let out this little scream, "YOWIE MOOEY!!!" It was sort of like "Kawabunga!" The same kind of exhilaration, laced with fear, before the final killer bombs exploded.

I looked at him. "What was that?"

"I dunno. Just a word." From then on, "yowie mooey" was

code language for the last point at which you can manage a given situation before it totally falls apart — that moment when you're just barely maintaining. Workloads. Deadlines. Relationships. My brother and I will be talking on the phone, and someone will say, totally deadpan, "Yowie mooey, man." And no further explanation is necessary. Lots of sibling code words spring out of videogames like *Missile Command*. Or *Sinistar*. *Sinistar* was an arcade game we discovered on a family vacation, in the basement game room of a restaurant in Durango. In the game, you fight off various intergalactic attackers, but all the while, a huge space station is being constructed in the shape of a death mask. And when the face of this villain is finally complete, he comes after you, shouting "RUN, COWARD! RUN! RUN! RUN!" in this incredibly loud, incredibly deep, resonant voice emanating from a mouth about twenty times the size of your little spaceship. It was the scariest thing we'd ever seen. That game inspired real terror. My brother and I used the phrase "Run, coward! Run! Run!" for years afterward.

This, I think, cuts to the heart of videogame retromania. Sure, other pop artifacts are evocative of childhood in the 1970s and 1980s. But none of those *Charlie's Angels* lunch boxes and iron-on shirts and TV sitcoms ran you down and tried to kill you. They just don't tap into the same kind of emotional intensity. Videogames weren't just iconic bits of plastic. They were more like music. They were a mental state.

And not surprisingly, people who've just purchased their first suits, cuff links, and tasseled loafers are more than ready to return to that state when they get home from work and realize that they are putative adults, aggressively targeted by the likes of Dewar's. No wonder they start casting about for the old Colecovision.

A burgeoning vintage videogame collectors' market is riding this impulse, driven by the inevitable recycling of pop culture, the growth of the Internet, and guys like Dave Stein, who is a human Frosted Mini-Wheat: corporate lawyer by day, rabid vintage videogame collector on evenings and weekends. After a hard day of legal wrangling, Dave goes home to a Manhattan high-rise apartment packed with forgotten hardware systems — Intellivisions, Odysseys, Colecovision, the twenty-year-old Fairchild Channel F, a Bally Astrocade and Emerson Arcadia, as well as the venerable Atari series. Shelves of cartridges line the walls and lie in boxes gleaned from liquidators up and down the eastern seaboard. Dave buys them by the dozen and trades them over the Internet and on occasional forays to videogame collectors' conferences in the Midwest, New Jersey, and the Bay Area.

"As many as my wife will let me keep in the house," he says, walking through a living room dominated by stacks of Atari VCS cartridges.

"Hey," says Dave. "Check this out. This is an old Vectrex. This is the most valuable system I own."

The Vectrex was a miniature arcade machine about two feet tall with vector graphics, like the original *Asteroids* arcade game. Milton Bradley manufactured it in 1982, shortly before the videogame industry crashed. Every fifth-grader coveted one of these machines, which were priced well over most parental toy-purchase thresholds.

Dave powers up the machine, which flickers to life playing the introduction to a proto–*Donkey Kong* climbing ladders game called *Spike*. Pencil-thin white letters glow against the blackness of a nine-inch monitor. "Our lovely and innocent heroine, Molly, has been kidnapped by the evil Spud! Only Spike can save her from this fate worse than death!"

"Help!" squeals Molly, an incandescent stick figure with a bow on her head.

"Oh no, Molly," squawks Spike, the stick figure hero with a star-shaped face, sounding uncomfortably like a post-op tracheotomy patient.

"Eek! Help!"

"Molly."

"Spike!"

As Dave jiggles the scaled-down controls, Spike scales a series of platforms, dodging spring-shaped enemies with rabbit-ear antennae to rescue the fair Molly. It's inexplicably evocative of a silent movie. "Darnit," growls Spike as he finally expires. Dave unplugs the machine. "These are impossible to find in mint condition. Last offer on the Internet was a thousand dollars."

Most of the games that litter Dave's apartment do not fetch Vectrex prices on the budding videogame collector's market, or even their original retail prices, for that matter, because most of them aren't all that rare. It's hard to charge a premium for something that's lying at the back of every childhood toy shelf in suburbia. Old *Pac-Man* carts for the VCS may have immense sentimental value, but there are hundreds of thousands of them out there. This will be a flea market item, sold adjacent to Emerson Lake and Palmer 8-tracks, for the next fifty years at least. There are, however, a few games that have become valuable cult items because they were never released or were pulled from the market in the wake of legal controversy. The holy grail, says Dave, is cartridges that saw very limited release as promotional items. Among these is a game called *Coke Wins*, the Coca-Cola corporation's cover of *Space Invaders*. It plays just like the Atari version, except that instead of aliens, the letters P-E-P-S-I advance inexorably across the screen, firing bullets. And every so often, where the *Space Invaders* UFO would fly across the screen, the Pepsi logo floats across the screen firing photon torpedoes.

"Our best guess," says Dave, "is that this program made it through all the design stages and then somebody in the legal department saw it and said, 'Are you crazy? We can't do this.' Someone decided it wouldn't fly, but nonetheless, there are at least half a dozen that have gotten out."

"Another one of the jewels is a game called *Chase the Chuckwagon* that was a Ralston Purina promotion. You remember the dog chasing the chuck wagon? Well, you had to send in a certain number of proofs of purchase from dog food and money, and you got this game, which is a horrible game, but since it's so rare, it's worth well over a hundred, a hundred and fifty dollars. Johnson and Johnson did a promotion called *Tooth Protectors*, where, with a certain number of toothpastes and some money, you could get a copy of the cartridge directly from them."

And then there are the games that verge on urban myth — games that everyone seems to have heard about but no one has actually played or even seen. All of these games seem to have been the subject of intense controversy, epitomized by the *Custer's Revenge* fracas of 1983 (a full decade before *Mortal Kombat* became the subject of congressional scrutiny). The story I'd heard — from people who claimed to have friends who knew people who'd seen the game once — was that *Custer's Revenge* was an Atari game in which an Indian maiden, tied to a pole, was ravished by an army officer, sparking protests by Native American organizations and NOW. But the story seemed too cheesy to be true, and its perennial status as Net lore only compromised its credibility. A significant minority of videogame aficionados believe it to be a hoax.

"Oh, it exists all right," says Dave. "I have a copy here somewhere." Dave roots around the videogame graveyard that was once a home office, digs up a small leatherette slipcase containing the notorious cartridge, and plugs *Custer's Revenge* into the Atari VCS. The intro screen flashes up, displaying a grossly rendered, buck naked cavalry officer sporting a hat, boots, gloves, and a pixellated erection pointed at a bit-mapped Indian maiden who is tied to a pole. Arrows fly toward him from the other side of the screen.

The game play is not subtle.

According to the instruction booklet, "The object of the game is to use your joystick control to advance Custer across the TV screen and 'score' as many times as you can with the beautiful maiden, all the time trying to avoid the arrows, and in game numbers 3 and 4, the prickly cactus as well. When Custer successfully reaches the maiden, repeatedly depress the 'fire' button. *Do not hold it down.* You receive one point for each time you 'score.' So press it over and over and over again as rapidly as you can. Watch how the maiden smiles and kicks up her heels and Custer 'flips his lid.' As Custer 'scores' a fanfare *Charge* is played. You do not have to wait for the tune to finish to 'score' again. Just keep pressing the button over and over again. P.S. If the kids catch you and should ask, tell them Custer and the maiden are just dancing."

Puerile? Sure. Vile? Yes. But it's impossible to picture anyone (a) actually getting off on this, (b) fantasizing about sex, thinking, "Yeah, it'll be just like *Custer's Revenge,*" or (c) trying to reenact the game scenario to spice up his marriage ("OK, honey, I'll be Custer. You be the Indian Maiden. Like Atari"). And besides, *Custer's Revenge* fails abysmally as a videogame. Dave agrees. "These games are absolutely horrible-playing games. The only interest anyone has in collecting them is not even a prurient interest, because looking at the graphics, one could not have a prurient interest in these games. It's just because they were so controversial and so hard to find."

"You mean there are *more?*"

As it turns out, American Multiple Industries, the publisher of *Custer's Revenge,* released two sequels, despite the protests and Atari's efforts to halt production. One was a *Breakout* rip-off called *Bachelor Party.* The other, *Beat 'Em and Eat 'Em,* was an X-rated variation of *Kaboom* involving various orifices and bodily fluids.

The Internet, not surprisingly, has created a buzzing collector's market for novelty carts like *Beat 'Em and Eat 'Em* and a virtual community for guys like Dave. "The Internet has really exploded the hobby," he says, "because it's given people across the country an ability to compare what's rare and what's not rare. Some games got dumped in California that never made it to New York, stuff that was incredibly rare because it was only released in Europe has now become much more accessible because people from Europe are on the Internet, and we've got a way to trade with them, to contact them and know that we have similar interests. And we didn't have that three years ago."

When you think about it, a videogame trading scene on the Internet makes sense. After all, the Net was built by a bunch of computer programmers and is dominated by a generation whose introduction to digital interactive media was early home video consoles. Now that these little Coleco jockeys have grown into college students and info-professionals, it's only natural that they would use the Net to buy, sell, and trade the video-game cartridges they coveted as children and relive the glory days (i.e., the early eighties). The way that grumpy retirees sit around the pool talking about how there was *real* songwriting before rock and roll, twentysomethings sit around the Net talking about how we had *real* videogames back when the brat pack was flying high. Pop culture has accelerated to the point where memories of 1983 arcade cabinets are painted in shades of sepia. A mere mention of *Joust* is enough to provoke maudlin reverie in rec.games.video.arcade.

"Man oh man, those sweet memories," writes an otherwise perfectly cynical student at George Mason University. "I still pine for a good game of *Gauntlet*. Remember when they used to make good games? You could go into an arcade and play a plethora of different games. The vector graphics. *Star Wars. Spy Hunter. Q*Bert. Donkey Kong. Marble Madness. Dragon's Lair. Tempest. Joust.* Do you think ten years from now people will be saying, 'Man oh man, I miss *MK3*. The sloppy controls, the cheesy graphics, and the run button. They don't make games like they used to . . .' Where did it start going wrong??"

The nostalgia rapidly snowballs as his classmate agrees, "These newfangled fighting games can be fun, but they get really repetitive after a while. I remember the good old days, with those great old platform and shoot-'em-up games. Anyone remember *Rygar*? Or *Rastan? R-Type, Robocop, Ghosts 'n' Goblins, Tapper,* the various *Donkey Kong* permutations. . . . They don't make them like they used to."

If anything, the latest games are considered wildly decadent. Listening to the old school reminisce on the Net is like listening to elder statesmen in the declining phase of an empire hankering for the days of the young republic. Sure you guys can sit around the table and gorge yourself, then go to the vomitorium and throw up. We went and conquered Persia. We didn't have 3D-rendered polygons like you young folks, with all yer flashy graphics and 360-degree orchestral scores. We had primitive graphics and 4-bit sound effects, and we *liked* it. We loved it.

Because our games didn't *need* all that fancy eye candy. Because our games were *real* games.

"Anyway," says the forum's arch-purist, "I think that the primitive graphics in those games were actually a benefit, because they forced me to use my imagination to picture the scene in *Indiana Jones,* or *Yars' Revenge,* or any of them. Nowadays, there is no imagination required, the realism is so advanced. It's like reading a book — the book will always be better than the movie because although the movie is more realistic, with the book you can tailor each setting and event to your own personal tastes in your mind's eye. I am not, by the way, putting down the current systems, I just don't think that because games are primitive it means they are less fun. They are more fun in some cases."

The discussion peaks with a rhetorical flourish from a CD-ROM game programmer: "What is *Doom,* really, besides a first person rehash of *Robotron 2084* or *Space Invaders?*" he asks. "The graphics of Atari 2600 games may be ancient and laughable now; the game play concepts and theories are not."

Actually, there is considerable debate among videogame nostalgics as to what constitutes "classic." Like most forms of popular culture, it boils down to "what was popular when I was a kid." But underneath the thick, soggy layers of nostalgia, there is the legitimate argument that many of these game consoles and arcade machines were the first of their kind. One can justifiably argue that the Atari 2600 (1977) is a classic in the way the Nintendo Entertainment System (1985) can never be, because Atari's machine was the first cartridge console to gain mass acceptance. Atari, Intellivision, and Colecovision are all from a period when videogames were breaking into the mainstream and creating a culture of their own, during the first rise and before the first fall of the videogame industry. Comparing a *Pong* console to a Sega Master System is like comparing a '57 Chevy to, say, a '79 Mustang. One is from the period that created car culture. The other is simply a machine whose sentimental value will rise as its original owners wax nostalgic for their youth, the same way that Nintendo and Sega's 8-bit consoles will be regarded as classics by twenty-first-century yuppies who have abandoned, rediscovered, and recycled their old toys into retro reference points. And of course, that process is already beginning as third-generation machines like the NES languish in the hall closets of America. A brief period of obsolescence is the noble rot of popular culture.

Even "classic" videogame boosters on the Net are cynical enough to realize this. As a vidkid at Loyola puts its, "The fact is that the kids who 'grew up' on the NES (and never even saw a 2600) are still too young to feel nostalgia for their childhood — they're still kids (or teenagers). Trust me, 10 years from now NES systems will be just as collectible as 2600's are now. Do you know why? All those generation X'ers will be feeling nostalgic for the system of their youth and they will pay outrageous prices for obsolete junk. Smart money is investing in NES staples now! These X'ers (or whatever they're called) will come back and say, all these modern games suck, they have no depth, they're all just this or that kind of game. Man, those games when i was a kid were the best!"

Or, in the words of Steve Ryner, custodian of the Classic Arcade Game World Wide Web home page, "Any full-size, arcade-dwelling, quarter-sucking video game I played in Junior High is a classic." Given the web population's proclivity for amateur tribute (mostly to themselves) it comes as no surprise that they've seeded the web with a carefully tended garden patch of retro vid shrines like the Q*Bert Home Page, the Pac-Man Page, and a monument to Colecovision, all inscribed with elegies for a kinder, gentler era, illustrated with screen shots of cute characters in action and illuminated in the old arcade cabinet typefaces (videogame packaging typography is a fetish unto itself).

In some cases, retro devotees have actually re-created home-brewed versions of the original games — *SuperPong* for Windows '95, say, or *Indenture,* Craig Pell's rendition of *Adventure* for DOS, which was received with hosannas by Atari saps everywhere ("I was quickly overcome with a mixture of tears from sentimental rememberings, awe from the near-perfect 'copy' I was playing, and a rather 'high' feeling that naturally comes when a few million long-forgotten and inert synapses suddenly begin firing again!").

It didn't take long for the videogame companies themselves to cash in on this wave of classic cartridge nostalgia by releasing commercial revivals of their own. In 1995 alone, three software companies, including the mighty Microsoft, issued retro compilations on CD-ROM, exactly the way Rhino Records converts vinyl apocrypha into encyclopedic CD revivals. In a sense, Activision's *Action Pack*, an assemblage of fifteen vintage Atari games remastered for PC and Macintosh, was a companion disc to Rhino's *New Wave Hits of the Eighties*. It almost begged you to throw the audio disc into shuffle mode as you turned on the computer and just wallow in nostalgic synesthesia. Devo. Split Enz. Flock of Seagulls. *Pitfall. Kaboom. Chopper Command.*

Scarier still is the idea that people who grew up on *Defender* have actually reproduced, raising the prospect of a second-generation joystick battle between parent and child. But yes, says Activision's CEO, Bobby Kotick. "In our focus group testing, parents told us they liked the idea of the *Action Pack* because they will be able to play games with their kids on equal footing." Like, sure, kiddo, you can kick my ass in *Battle Arena Toshinden,* but let's see how ya do with *Centipede.* Yeah, look who's got the high score *now.* Back when I was a kid, *all* the games were this good.

But of course they weren't. We conveniently forget this, much as classic rock radio listeners forget that music really *wasn't* like that in the sixties. Classic rock stations do not play what radio stations played twenty-five years ago, because most of that music was awful. Thousands and thousands of songs came out every year, and most of them faded deservedly into oblivion after two months. But the great and semi-great stuff persists, and programmers duly port it to the next platform, casting a very skewed picture of what music was like in 1966.

Similarly, the hundreds of egregious videogames that came out (and actually caused the industry to crash in 1983) are buffed out of memory by a tide of greatest-hits anthologies.

If the Activision *Action Pack* was a digitally remastered greatest hits CD, *Microsoft Arcade* for Windows and *Microsoft Return of Arcade* for Windows '95 were a tribute album of slavish covers. According to the company's oily press release, "These games bring back nostalgic memories of spending long afternoons in game halls and pizza parlors with pockets full of quarters. For a few minutes each day, players of Microsoft *Return of Arcade* can use their home or office PCs to relive the days of their youth." Upon closer inspection, however, Microsoft's approach to translating these games is less like transporting a castle stone by stone than making a plaster cast of the entire structure and reproducing it in polyurethane foam. Rather than base the translations on the original programs, Microsoft filmed the games being played and then wrote code that approximated the footage. Microsoft later bragged about how closely the reverse engineering mimicked the original arcade experience. But it's odd, considering Microsoft's access to the original code from *Asteroids, Centipede, Battlezone, Missile Command,* and *Tempest,* that they would choose to construct nearly perfect simulacra of actual arcade games. Microsoft never used the original game code itself. They merely simulated it. The end result was a set of experiences that's almost indistinguishable from the originals. But not quite. Because in their effort to render perfect representations of the original arcade classics, the Microsoft programmers missed one subtle but important element, buried deep in the original code — the watermark of authenticity.

The bugs. They left out the bugs.

Players who'd spent time with the games could sniff out the ruse at once and turned up their noses in disgust. After all, releasing a classic arcade game without the bugs was worse than colorizing a classic black-and-white movie. It was like remaking a classic black-and-white movie (starring Brad Pitt and Pamela Anderson). A lot of the meat of the old games was in the bugs that slipped into the binary soup, despite programmers' checks and double checks. In *Asteroids,* for instance, there was a bug that let you shoot the spaceship early if you lingered by the side of the screen. In *Space Invaders,* if you shot the saucer on the seventeenth shot you got 5,000 points. In *Defender,* if you got a million points, everything you hit would give you a free ship. To videogame lovers, these little glitches are like the familiar catch in the ignition of your car, or a trick in the back-door lock of your parents' house. Getting a version stripped of bugs is like losing your favorite plush animal as a kid and then having your mom buy you another one that is exactly the same but it's not the same because it lacks that patina of dust and car grunge and doesn't have a stain on the toe.

The Microsoft simulacra are mired in the same ontological DMZ. Visually, they're doppelgängers of the original games, and they behave a lot like them as well. But they lack the essence (and, some would argue, the ineffable magic) of the original code. Can they really be called the same games? It's almost a question of Platonic ideals — say, the Platonic ideal of *Space Invaders.* The fact is, you can take the code of *Space Invaders* and emulate it line for line on a computer. But what is *Space Invaders?* Is it the code? Is it the arcade cabinet? Was it the idea in a Namco engineer's mind when he made it? Where is the actual game? As we move to the thingless digital society, we have to confront issues like this, which seem to crop up with disturbing frequency as chunks of content are bent, beamed, and repurposed into one storage medium after another. With videogames, these questions are particularly messy, because these retro artifacts were digital from the get-go. It's not like there's a canister of celluloid locked in some vault to which you can point when the satellite transmissions and digital videodiscs blur together and say, there, that's the master. Videogames were always just copies of code.

If any game company has an implicit grasp of these issues, it is Williams Entertainment, the original manufacturers of *Defender* and *Robotron,* recently rereleased as *Williams Classics* for the PC and Sony Playstation. Taking an archival approach, Williams software engineers treated the source code with the digital equivalent of white gloves. Instead of bending it to fit the new machines, they constructed an emulator that hangs from the rafters of a PC or console operating system, convincing the central processor that it is actually an arcade machine that can interpret the original code. So the entire game runs verbatim, with every nuance exactly as it was. The exact code runs through the emulator, and you can see the setup screens for arcade employees. And most importantly, all the bugs are there. In a microworld, where there is no physical dimension, only information, that's all the authenticity you can hope for.

As trivial as it sounds — these are, after all, games — this process of translating old code for new hardware actually points to a huge can of worms that is just cracking open in other arenas. The truism among technology mavens is that hardware increasingly resides in software — all the crucial information, the real meat of a computer's usefulness, is shifting from the physical components to the strings of ones and zeroes that run through them. The Internet, for example, is more a set of agreed-upon software protocols than a set of wires and computer chips. You could use a telephone line or a cable or a wireless cellular pager or a satellite dish to check your e-mail. The hardware, increasingly, doesn't matter. It's the software that gets you where you need to go. Essentially, the chicken doesn't matter. It's the egg that counts: all the information on all the databases and computer networks in the world. But what happens when these (New! Improved! Better! Faster!) computers we've designed are too slick to run that rickety old code? Computer manufacturers have to keep releasing next generation hardware every eighteen months. But what happens when they're too sophisticated to run the software that makes the world go round. Big problem. It's as if cars suddenly got too good to run on gas. Given that it's simply too expensive to keep hiring armies of data processors to translate the old information into new, fungible forms, global data brokers will at some point have to do what Williams Entertainment did with *Robotron:* graft phantom limbs onto newly minted machines. In fact, that may be the test of the highly evolved new processor — is it smart enough to couple with a primitive predecessor?

With the arrival of Pentium and Power PC chips, the answer is, for the first time, yes. "Because PCs now run at hundreds of megahertz, they can basically simulate exactly the old hardware system and execute the original code," says Eugene Jarvis, a Williams game designer. "It plays as the original. The only thing you're missing is the controls, which I still think is a big part of it, especially with *Robotron*. I mean, you gotta have those two joysticks there to reach true nirvana, and you gotta have that machine to slam against the wall, and you need that glass there to break with your fist.

"It's funny, seeing that stuff on the PC," he says, "because I actually did some of the original games back in the early eighties."

"Wait a minute," I say. "You mean you —"

"I programmed *Defender.*"

"Omigod!" I squeal. "You. Wrote. *Defender.*"

I can't believe this. I've interviewed actors, rock singers, and various other figures of mass and cult celebrity. But I've never been starstruck. Until now. I can't believe I'm actually talking to the guy who wrote *Defender.*

"Yeah," he says. "*Defender. Defender 2,* which was renamed *Stargate. Blaster. Robotron.* And *Narc.* That was the game where you're out busting drug pushers in the Reagan era."

"That piece of themed propaganda for the War on Drugs?"

"Well," says Jarvis, "I always thought players were intrigued by the whole drug culture, and it seems like so rarely does a videogame make any kind of statement about anything — it's always a battle against some generic army, or the space aliens, or the little munchkins. You never see any kind of political statement or any kind of topicality. I thought players were intrigued by drugs. Originally I wanted to do a game where you were the drug dealer or something, but then I realized that might not go over so well. And so I figured, you know, it was like the whole Reagan thing, OK, be the narc. Up until that point, nobody would ever envision themselves as being the narc. It was the total antithesis of hip. But the pendulum was swinging. Say no or DIE. It put a little Schwarzenegger hard edge to the thing. And the game did really well."

The surprising thing about Jarvis is that, after all these years, he's still making games, unlike most of the programmers from the arcades' heyday. "I'm probably one of the only people left from my generation that is still doing videogames," he says. "They're all managers or died of a drug overdose or whatever. I'm one of the few people still doing game design on a daily basis. I just realized that that was what I enjoyed doing and I feel like, hey, this is my life's work."

"But still," he says with a sigh, "it's amazing, the transition in the last sixteen years. *Defender* was my first game, back in 1980, and it was just me and a couple other guys programming it. These days when we do a videogame, it's almost like a Hollywood team. We have a guy just writing musical scores for the game, four or five guys doing the artwork, a couple guys designing the cabinets, and three to four programmers. It's a huge, huge thing. It's a different era. The games are much more cinematic and a lot more visually oriented. Whereas back, if you look at *Defender*, technology didn't give you much to work with. You couldn't really razzle-dazzle people. You did your best to razzle-dazzle them with what graphics you had, but you had, like, sixteen colors and three blocky things. So a lot of the work just went into the play of the game.

"You had to figure out what your game was about. What is the essence of the experience I'm gonna give people? It's a hard thing, in the design, to say, what can I do? *Defender* was the first game that scrolled, and then with *Robotron*, I just stuck the guy on one screen. It was kind of about confinement. You are stuck on this screen. There's two hundred robots trying to mutilate you, and there's no place to hide, and you'd better kill them or they're gonna kill you, coming from all sides. It was an incredible sweaty palms experience. It's just the confinement. You are stuck in that room. You can't run down the hallway. You can't *go* anywhere else. You're just totally focused. A lot of times, the games are about the limitations. Not only what you can do but what you *can't* do. Confining your world and focusing someone in that reality is important. You spent months and months and months just playing the game and percentaging it and seeing how you could create maximum frustration in the player. If a player smashes a game, that's actually the best thing you want. You want a strong reaction. If a player does not care enough about a game to kick in the coin door or break the glass, then you know it's not a good game.

"One reason the nostalgia is so strong is that players were just so involved. You're there replaying those games and going, oh God, if I'd only gone left I would've been all right. How could I have blown that? You're totally living that experience. Just the emotion, the survival nature of the videogame — you're tapping into the most powerful human instinct. Survival. Fight or flight. That is so hugely intense that in some ways it becomes too intense. People really lived the games. They dreamed the games. I know a guy who quit his engineering job at Boeing to play *Defender* full-time — there was actually a circuit of tournaments, players would go around and play *Defender* at tournaments and make money — he actually earned his living for about a year traveling around the country playing *Defender*. And to watch him play that game was like watching a virtuoso violinist or watching Marsalis on trumpet. It was just unbelievable the way he had the chemistry — all these angry, nasty aliens trying to waste him, and he'd just calmly waltz through and blow the shreds out of 'em. It was amazing. It was almost like he'd taken over the game and made it his own. He was doing things I never envisioned, never thought of, tactics I never dreamed of."

When Jarvis watches young game designers, guys in their twenties, playing his games around the office, it's like Les Paul watching Jimi Hendrix. They've been doing this stuff since they were toddlers, and it's as natural to them as breathing. "There's this guy at work who plays *Robotron* at level ten difficulty. Just to watch the tactics," he says, "and how he circles the field and avoids the enemy, there's this whole gestalt at work.

It's a miracle how the human mind processes this stuff and says, OK, I'm gonna move to the right. *And it's right.* It's just a huge parallel process going on, and all the synapses, the neurons just going *kachong.*"

Meanwhile, Jarvis's own kids have moved on to the next generation of videogames, even as *Defender* has attained classic status and its original champs are sliding into adulthood and the outer envelope of middle age. "I was twenty-five when I did *Defender,*" he muses. "Now I've got a house, three kids. They're probably more into today's games than they are into the old games. Like, my twelve-year-old son, he's into a lot of *Doom* and stuff. My thirteen-year-old daughter plays a lot of *SimCity.*"

There is a generation gap, he says, even with videogames. "In some ways," he says, "I feel kind of lonely because I'm into instant gratification. I want games that any idiot can just step up to that game and do it. I'm not into *Street Fighter, Mortal Kombat* games, which are all based on secret hidden combinations — down down left up right hard kick left, and like you flip the guy over three times and smash his head in with a pickax. It's like an elaborate game of rock, paper, scissors. That's what it's all about. It's like, there's three hundred types of rocks, papers, and scissors, and there's a certain timing element to it as well, but it's essentially the same thing. It has that same kind of randomness, with the illusion of strategy and control."

Games like *Streetfighter* and *Mortal Kombat* are generations away from the games Jarvis designed as a twenty-five-year-old. They've catapulted from total abstraction to full frontal gore and realism. But in a sense, the new crop of fighting games completes an evolutionary cycle in game play. At the dawn of the videogame era, with *Spacewar* or *Pong* or *Tank,* you played against another human being, mano a mano, or rather blip a blip. And then in the late seventies, with the advent of *Space Invaders,* the machine became your opponent. And it was really cool just to beat the machine, because you were tired of your buddy kicking your ass all the time. And everybody just wanted to clock themselves against the machine. And then in the mid-eighties, with games like *Narc* and *Double Dragon* and *Gauntlet,* you found games with a cooperative play mode, where it was you and your friend against the machine, and you could work together as a little gang and beat up all the drones in the machine and rescue the princess. And now, with the modern crop of fighting games, *Killer Instinct* and *Tekken* and *Virtua Fighter,* it's back to kicking each other's asses again.

Which brings us back to the American Museum of the Moving Image, a gallery where you can trace this evolution down a corridor of machines that is and is not a videogame arcade. As the exhibit's curator explains it, "Artifacts in museums are usually things that you don't touch and play with. They are things that you just look at and contemplate. That's subverted in this exhibit, where you are actually abusing this thing that is supposed to be an artifact. In a sense, those games aren't really the artifacts. The real artifact is the entire line of a particular game in all its forms, and the arcade machine is just this vessel through which you see that. We don't painstakingly restore these things, because they aren't artifacts in the traditional sense. If the *Space Invaders* breaks down, we'll just get another one. That doesn't work with a Rembrandt. The arcade kind of transcends that distinction between two kinds of museum objects: the objects that are collected — the painting, the sculpture, the artifact — and the interpretive objects — things that aren't in themselves the valuable object but help you to interpret whatever the object is."

In this way, the arcade exhibit that comes with game tokens is consistent with the museum's other holdings — the old movie cameras, the antique televisions, the zoetropes and cinematographs — because all the projectors and the sprockets, the celluloid and the silicon are means to the end, which is the experience of watching *Some Like It Hot* or playing *Donkey Kong.* The hardware gathers dust or breaks and is repaired. The reels and semiconductors are swapped for copies in better condition. And everything ends up on optical disc at the end of the day. But ultimately, it is not the machines themselves that are important. It is those patterns of light they create. It is the choreographed splashes of color and the quirks of response that tattooed videogames into our minds as children and that trigger the rusty synapses of nostalgic adults. It is hitting the space saucer on the seventeenth shot that makes you a teenager again (for a few euphoric seconds). It's not something you can touch, taste, smell, hear, or see, but it is the code, finally, that counts.

Chapter 6
Why *Doom*
Rules

On December 10, 1993, the University of Wisconsin computer system fell to its knees as thousands of college students from around the world stormed its file transfer (ftp) site. As the network strained against the sheer weight of Internet traffic, waves of undergraduates continued to charge the system. They were all after one thing: *Doom.*

Bits and pieces of Id Software's apocalyptic videogame had been floating around the Net for months — screen shots, a demo, a faint buzz that had quickly built into a deafening roar. College kids had been playing an early test version in networked multiplayer deathmatches from computer science buildings across the country. Up to four people could play from remote locations, using a high-speed T1 line or on a college localnet. It was the most brutally frightening game anyone had ever seen. Players would just sit there, squirming in their seats with an expression of unadulterated terror, until four in the morning.

And now Id was putting a free shareware version on the Internet, starting with the Wisconsin ftp site. By this time, *Doom* was already a cult phenomenon. It had inspired such grassroots hysteria on the Net that Jay Wilbur, Id's PR point man, couldn't get past the throngs of Doomheads to upload the file they were all waiting for. A mob scene brewed an international Internet chat channel, #Doom, as over a thousand people sat on their haunches bitching about the delay. It was as though a thousand people in line for Nine Inch Nails tickets had formed a human wall, blocking out the one guy who could open the ticket booth.

At midnight, Wilbur called the Wisconsin system operator, who told him to type in all the necessary data and be ready to press enter at the sysop's signal. "Go!" yelled the admin, simultaneously increasing the system load limit by another fifty people. Wilbur hit enter. But by the time he arrived a few seconds later, the load had already topped out. Eventually, the sysop had to kick people off the server so that Wilbur could upload the program. When everything was in place, the sysop opened the file transfer floodgates, whereupon thousands of Doomheads stampeded into the University of Wisconsin ftp site like rabid ferrets and crashed the university's computers campus-wide. The network was propped back up, only to be toppled again. All told, 15 million shareware copies of *Doom* — the first two episodes of the game — were downloaded around the world. Once the shareware audience had mainlined the initial stages of game play, 150,000 full versions of *Doom* were sold directly through Id, qualifying the game as an instant best-seller.

Doom was a watershed event on par with the Atari 2600, because it changed the way videogames circulate and reproduce. Atari's machine housed videogame code — the impalpable string of ones and zeroes, the game itself — in a plastic cartridge. Videogames already had essence. Atari gave them a very successful kind of body: rugged, mobile, and interchangeable. The Atari 2600 cartridge gave videogames a way to proliferate in any home with a TV. Similarly, *Doom* gave videogames a way to proliferate in cyberspace. *Doom* is poised like some sort of liverwort between water and land. It alternates between physical and virtual generations, shifting into shrink-wrapped form just long enough to make money. Down the line, you can see a point where videogames will be sold in electronic form and

jettison their bodies entirely. *Doom* points the way. *Doom* is a ful-
crum.

Of course, it didn't succeed just because it was online. It
also had to be riveting. No problem in that department —
within a year, *Doom* was hailed as the 3D Game of All Time by
every videogame publication, was released on every next generation home videogame platform, and had made cameo appearances on *ER, The Single Guy,* and *Friends.*

The inevitable Hollywood development deal came as no
surprise to anyone familiar with *Doom*'s premise: You are a
combat-hardened marine stationed on a moon base near Mars.
"With no action for fifty million miles," the back story goes,
"your day consisted of suckin' dust and watchin' restricted
flicks in the rec room." When suddenly, the lull of monotonous,
grunt-ridden boredom is shattered by the inevitable Urgent
Distress Message from terrified scientists conducting interdi-
mensional transport research on a nearby moon. Their computer systems have gone completely berserk, their experiments
have gone horribly awry, and now they are groveling for imme-
diate military support because, "something friggin' evil is coming out of the Gateways!"

Demons from hell, naturally.

Leave it to the fuckin' eggheads to tinker around with their
little subatomic colliders and bring on the Apocalypse, then run
away, tails between their scrawny little legs, whining for help
from the armed forces. But that's OK. You'll defend them. You'll
save the day. Because you're a big, strong, beer-guzzling, porn-
watchin', gun-totin' soldier. Never fear. Space Marines are on
the way.

So you get to this moon where all the shit's flying. Your
squad buddies are immediately killed (the scientists, of course,
died long before you got there). Now you are the sole survivor,
stranded with only a pistol, rapidly blasting your way through
an avalanche of evil incarnate in a frenzied quest for bigger and
bigger guns. As you progress, the pistol gives way to a shotgun,
a chain gun, rocket launcher, plasma rifle, and the euphemisti-
cally abbreviated BFG 9000. Blast away, but try to avoid ex-

ploding barrels of fuel and toxic waste and collapsing ceilings. There's also a whole range of surveillance toys and protective gear — infrared goggles, radiation suits, Kevlar vests, titanium-derived combat armor, and of course, ammunition. As hyperbolic as this scenario is, it's amazing how closely it cleaves to the real-world arsenal of riot control and combat troopers.

But sometimes, particularly when you're single-handedly fighting off an army of demons, you need more than firepower. And the twenty-first-century military understands this, which is why the battlefield is also littered with drugs they've engineered to enhance your combat performance — stimpacks (quick injections of booster enzymes) and berzerk packs (which add a jigger of adrenaline to the stimpack's intravenous cocktail, sending you into a superhuman rage of enhanced fight-or-flight muscular prowess). *Doom* definitely does not cleave to the Just Say No school of videogame pharmaceuticals. No abstract power-ups, health revival icons, and tokens of invincibility. Screw that. You get hypodermics.

Once you have all your guns, toys, and drugs, *Doom* is basically a hopped-up first-person 3D shoot-'em-up. It's a pretty straightforward descendant of Atari's *Battlezone*. But a decade of technology has made all the difference in graphic realism. And a decade of serial killers, celebrity murder trials, and special effects action movies have made all the difference in the standard of stylized graphic violence. *Doom*'s machismo makes *Pulp Fiction* look like *Waiting to Exhale*. The game has a major attitude — which is summed up nicely in the magazine ad for *Doom 2*: "Bloodthirsty DEMONS from Hell. GUT-SPLATTERED Hallways. A Big-Ass, Nasty GUN in your hand. Life is GOOD."

It's all so deliciously clear-cut. There are no annoying ambiguities in *Doom*, no behavioral gray zones or questions about the appropriate way to interact. If it approaches you: destroy, stand back, and enjoy the spectacle of supernatural protoplasm blasted to shreds by heavy artillery. It's open season on anything that moves — your deceased squad members, now zombies in need of deep lead therapy, as well as the supernatural plethora of imps, demons, flying flaming skulls, cacodemons, and truck-sized Barons of Hell (the occult equivalent of *Jurassic Park*'s Tyrannosaurus rex).

The *Doom* universe gives you fire and brimstone by way of cyberpunk — everything that flies at you seems to combine medieval demonology with advanced robotics: Revenants (skeletal robodemons with combat armor), Arachnotrons (cybernetic spiders engineered in the Hell Department of Robotics), and Cyberdemons (missile-launching leviathans with goat legs). Religion doesn't provide depictions of evil this vivid anymore. Unitarianism, folk mass, and the Anglican church's nouvelle Muzak vision of hell have watered down fear-laced entertainment and violent spiritual epics in church. And we miss those honest to God, pitchfork-carrying, cloven-hoofed, Lake-of-Fire, shit-kicking devils. We love that stuff. *Doom* fills that niche.

Even the word "doom" is resonant. The concept of doom. Especially when you factor in all the scary technology lurking around the late twentieth century and the threat of rogue dictatorships blowing up Seattle with surplus Soviet nukes. In *Doom*, you get to resolve that sense of moral decay, political instability, and technophobia. You get to be global supercop, *Blade Runner*, and Oral Roberts, all rolled into one.

You get to visit a place where there is no way to humanize the enemy because the enemy is, by definition, Evil. Not just bad. Not misunderstood. Not the victim of childhood abuse, ethnic discrimination, faulty antidepressants, or low self-esteem. Not a belligerent race of aliens on *Star Trek* with whom you have some responsibility to negotiate and understand. It's the devil, OK? It's printed, right there in the instruction booklet: "They have no pity, no mercy, take no quarter, and crave none. They're the perfect enemy."

Yum.

We all crave the perfect enemy. Political leaders employ squads of propagandists to create these monsters — the Evil Empire, Manuel Noriega, al-Qaddafi, Saddam Hussein — so that we can fly over and stomp on them. The makers of *Doom* understand how deeply satisfying this concept can be. In fact, before Id Software released *Doom,* they sold a quarter of a million copies of *Wolfenstein 3D,* which pits you against the entire Nazi war machine on your way to face down der führer himself. Substitute floating skulls that belch lightning for SS soldiers, and you have *Doom.* In both games, you get to play out that cherished underdog scenario: Everything was Good, but then Evil swept in, crawled over the whole goddamned place like swarming army ants, and you are the Orkin man. You, and only you, are the hero. No teamwork, no delegation, no profit sharing. Just the Lone Ranger, transplanted to Mars. We in America like this.*

But beyond the basic tribal shoot-'em-up premise and the social itches it seems to scratch, there is something more important that sets *Doom* apart from the hundreds of first-person 3D shooters on the market. And that crucial element is: *fear.* Other games have great graphics, but none have triggered the same degree of deep, primal terror. As one IBM engineer said in a Usenet discussion, "Many 1st person games have come and gone on the old hard drive, but *Doom* remains top dog. Remember the first time you played *Doom2* and you heard the "meow" of the Revenant? MY GOD!! I was actually scared!!! *Witchaven* didn't do anything for me. . . . No I take that back, it made me appreciate *Doom* even more."

For hundreds of thousands of people, *Doom* has invoked the kind of horror that you only experience as a small child when the lights go out and the monsters in the closet and under the bed come to life. Ultimately, you know you're safe — you can always race for the door. You can always turn off the computer. But for a moment, you're exquisitely frightened. It's the kind of fear that turns us on and makes us feel alive and sends us on skydiving expeditions and roller-coaster rides. *Doom* gave you a way to get that same thrill from your very own dorm room.

---

* In role-playing games, the "hero" is a party of four to six people of various abilities — a warrior (strong but dumb), cleric, magician, et cetera. The essence of these games is teamwork and delegation. Each character pulls for the team, and rewards contribute to the greater glory of the group. These games are strictly a niche item in the United States. They are wildly popular in Japan.

It also galvanized a cult of Doomers on the Net who sat around commiserating about how goddamned scary this game is, and how this makes it superior to any other game, anywhere, ever. When a slew of *Doom* imitators hit the market, these emotional fish stories fell under the rubric of the Good Old Days. "I've never been so knee wobbling terrified," wrote one nostalgic Doomer, "as the first time the Cybermutant from *Spear of Destiny* came running after me, you know the one with the machine gun in his chest and four ax-wielding arms, and he ran faster than anything else in the game. And I'll admit how crazy I am: To this day, especially in a deathmatch, when I'm looking out a window, I'll sit up as high as I can in my chair and peer down at the bottom of my monitor so I can see as much of the ground as possible:)."

"*Doom* came along," replied a Net.entity logging on as Cyberdmn, "and i was foolish enough to play it with headphones in a dark room.......and there were many times i would shut off the computer, saying "I ain't playin this any more!" It scared the piss outta me. This, i think, is why it is STILL the rage that it is...DOOM, DOOM II, nothin better." A virtual chorus chimed in agreement, adding dozens of testimonials to the body of *Doom* lore. And then an Italian summed it up in seven words, posting from a server in Bologna: "*Doom*," he wrote, "takes you into its own world."

This was doubly true, because Id not only created a compelling fictional world for *Doom* players but gave them a stake in it by releasing the actual source code of the game itself, allowing Doomers with a modicum of programming skill to add to the game, essentially picking up where the game's authors left off. They could create custom soundscapes, tweak the game's configurations, or even create new levels, entire episodes of the game. Releasing the source code gave players all the keys to the castle — teleport commands, the ability to acquire an instant arsenal, walk-through walls, etc. But after all the shortcuts and secrets were laid bare, the challenge then became to compose better variations on the *Doom* theme than anyone else. The *Doom* source code itself became a kind of world. And the online *Doom* constituency trancended the mere sharing of cheat codes to become a virtual kustom kar kulture — a community based on shared, self-made chunks of the *Doom* universe called .wad files. Players became a part of *Doom*'s world not just because they played the game but also because they constructed bits of it. They competed not just as players but also as creators.

Of course, this source code homesteading was all a part of Id Software's marketing plan: create a universe, hook people on it, then expand. *Doom II: Hell on Earth* was released ten months after the original *Doom*. It featured some new weapons and hazards (charming moats of toxic waste) but used the same 3D engine. It sold 1.2 million copies. Two months later, volume three of the *Doom* saga, *Heretic*, was released as shareware (the first episode for free, a full version available for sale from Id). And on October 30, 1995, just in time for Halloween, the final descendant of the *Doom* dynasty, *Hexen: Beyond Heretic*, landed on store shelves everywhere. It was an idea whose time had come: release a free, stripped-down version through shareware channels, the Internet, and online services. Follow with a spruced-up, registered retail version of the software. It worked well with Id's previous double whammy, *Wolfenstein 3D*, and it succeeded beyond anyone's expectations with *Doom*.

A small startup company called Netscape took note and followed suit.

Chapter 7
Virtual
Construction Workers

Having grown up wandering through game worlds from Atari *Adventure* to *Castle Wolfenstein*, a generation of vidkids can appreciate the care and craftsmanship that goes into a high-quality virtual environment: artful dimensions, good doorway design, well-placed obstacles, easy-to reach ammunition. Two decades of cartridge games breed a deep familiarity with the conventions of vector graphs, tile maps, and 3D, rendered polygons. And even if videogames haven't prepared us to be fighter pilots, as Ronald Reagan liked to think they would, they have prepared us for high-paying jobs in the booming virtual construction industry. The manufacturing economy may be sputtering, but there are plenty of assembly jobs in the videogame industry: computer-aided drafting, 3D model making, texture mapping, object design, puzzle building, landscaping, backgrounding, and polygon animation. At this point, game worlds have become so immense and complicated that their construction requires crews of postcollegiate code carpenters and graphic design masons working sixteen-hour days for months or years, either as company employees or independent contractors. It's like building a skyscraper, or a cathedral, or some kind of fabulous gargantuan sea vessel.

"I do the carpeting for the *Titanic*," drawls Billy Davenport, a twenty-six-year-old graphic designer from Tullahoma, Tennessee. Billy drives a pickup truck, sports a red Co-Op Feeds gimme cap, and happens to bear a striking resemblance to Bo Duke from the *Dukes of Hazard*. Fifty years ago, he'd have taken a job that involved wood planes, sandpaper, circular saws, and lots of varnish. But in the age of interactive interiors, he does digital wainscoting and furniture finishing for CyberFlix, a CD-ROM developer in Knoxville. CyberFlix has produced a string of award-winning CD-ROM games — a space opera, a postapocalyptic shoot-'em-up, a Western, a horror title — *Lunicus*, *Jump Raven*, *Dust*, and *Skullcracker*, respectively. The company is staffed by a squad of fresh-faced lads, and its principals have been written up in all the usual magazines for the sort of garage triumph that has long since become cliché. Their current project is *Titanic*, a mystery adventure set aboard the notorious Edwarian luxury liner that, for the purposes of this game, has been painstakingly reconstructed as a perfect scale replica of the original. The doors swing the same way. The taps work. Every deck, cabin, corridor, and engine compartment corresponds to its actual counterpart rotting on the bottom of the North Atlantic. This process involves two construction crews. The 3D crew builds the skeleton and strutwork on high-end workstations from the original plans and blueprints. At this stage, the ship is architecturally complete, a schematic phantom floating in virtual dry dock.* Then the 2D guys come in and put the skin on it.

Essentially, what guys like Billy do is gild two-dimensional

---

* In an eerie twist of fate, Paul Haskins, one of the 3D artists who spent two years digitally rebuilding the *Titanic* in cyberspace, is the direct descendant of an Irish shipyard worker employed by Harland and Wolff, the Belfast shipbuilder that assembled and launched the original *Titanic*. Reconstructing the behemoth vessel in cyberspace added a haunting sense of karmic return to the normal stress of the workday. The ship, he explains, was as long as three football fields and had nine decks. "Re-creating that digitally in 3D, we were working with data files of immense proportions and a huge amount of complexity. Naturally, it hit a chord with me — I'm working with mathematical calculations to re-create the kinds of things my grandfather helped craft out of iron and steel."

surfaces onto this transparent 3D structure. They shrink-wrap the frame with textures and interior details. Imagine walking through a house where every wall, ceiling, and floor was trompe l'oeil, where every texture, from the furniture upholstery to the play of light on the silverware, was painted on. This is how a CD-ROM environment is built. In this case, the visual shrink-wrap comprises the original fixtures and surfaces and provisions of the HMS *Titanic*. So for the past year, Billy has been coating the walls with authentic *Titanic* paint colors, hanging wallpaper duplicated from period photographs, putting in the domed skylights, laying seventeenth-century Arabian-style mosaics in the Turkish bath, and fashioning plaster moldings in the lounges and galleries.

Billy takes a craftsman's pride in his 2D design work. "We have a room where you start out in the game, and I've outfitted the desk with postcards that you can actually flip over and read, and magazines like *Brave New World* magazine, and I've designed the covers for 'em, so you can pick those up and look at 'em. There's a lot of detail in there that we don't even expect people to actually look at. It's like, if you were just tryin' to half-ass it and get through it, you might make a lamp, but you might not make the electric cord that goes *behind* the desk. We're tryin' to get all the detail in there. There's a lot of games that you look at today, and a lot of people don't take the time and energy to go in and really work with their maps to make 'em look real, so they end up coming out lookin' plastic or fake."

This is the sort of thing you don't think about in the real world, where, if you get closer to an object, you see it in more detail. In a game world, this isn't necessarily true. If there are cans in a cupboard, a graphic designer has to come up with the wood grain and vintage food labels so that the 3D guys can map them onto the planes and cylinders in some corner pantry of the *Titanic*. Every level of resolution is deliberate, to say nothing of all the dirt that must be strategically strewn and the corners that have to be ground down. Because in the end, what conveys reality is signs of deterioration. And all that scuffing and staining and denting requires endless hours of meticulous work. It's historical restoration in reverse. But it tends to attract the same kind of radical perfectionist. On the *Titanic* project, Billy's pride and joy is a scrapbook on the mantel in the opening scene. "I made it so that when you click on the scrapbook, it opens up, and then all the pages are just full of imagery, you know, ephemera, things like that. So I go out and I find all the stuff to go in the scrapbook and put it in there. That's the fun job. I could spend a day or I could spend a month on that book."

As players, we have come to expect a certain level of realism and depth in videogames, and that level continues to rise. So now game companies have to employ people to crumple up the scenery. And this kind of work is incredibly labor-intensive. It is not a glamour job. That's the Silicon Valley fantasy of what it's like to work on videogames — this vision of a thirtysomething millionaire cruising down the Pacific Coast Highway with a cell phone in one hand and a fistful of stock options in his pocket. The reality is that most of the people who assemble videogames are just out of school. And they're not chin-scratching liberal arts majors from Ivy League universities hugging the track of an old boy network. They're fresh out of some technical institute. They're trade school graduates. And they're pulling double shifts six days a week. "I worked thirty-six hours in two days last week," Billy says with shrug. "But they try to make it as accommodating as possible. We've got showers, you know. And they stock the refrigerators with Cokes. Everybody gives you Cokes. They want you gettin' wired so you stay there all the time. And they got some couches. So I mean, you can stay here forever."

Indeed, CyberFlix HQ does possess that twenty-four-hour Kinko's Copies atmosphere — full of equipment and overworked twentysomethings, simultaneously frenetic and oddly mellow. Because, as hard as everyone's working, there's no whistle at the end of the day. Because, well, there is no end of the day. In fact, there is no daylight to speak of, because the vertical blinds have been drawn to shut out the sun, leaving the downtown loft in complete darkness, save for the glow of computer monitors and a few lava lamps. CyberFlixers like it this way. They have showers. They have caffeinated beverages. They have Blow Pops, Pop-Tarts, and Atomic Fireballs and a Ping Pong area. They can go for days. And at this point, they have lost all circadian perspective, because the beta deadline for *Titanic* is a week away. Along every wall, white boards outline the grid of work still to be done. Blueprints of the *Titanic* hang outside the testing room, where half a dozen twentysomething programmers are rooting out the bugs in the latest draft of the game. From outside, you can hear them heckling the hell out of it.

"Knock-out gas? Who came up with *that* term. It's like some old *Batman* show or something."

"Just click the top one, stupid."

"I dunno how much longer I can play this game."

"Well you've been at it about six hours."

"You shoulda seen the redneck we had in here yesterday to test. He was like, 'Damn, do you mean to tell me you can't kill shit in this game?' He was just like, outraged."

It has been a very long day. It's been a long week. It's been a long month. But at six o'clock on a Friday, everyone is still here, fully engaged in the most labor-intensive facet of the game: puppet scripting. In the course of *Titanic*'s espionage mystery drama, you have to converse with dozens of photorealistic characters aboard the ship. Each one of these characters has dialogue, and all of it has to be dubbed from recorded voice-overs onto the mouth movements of animated talking heads. Or rather, the mouth movements have to be manipulated to lip-synch the audio. This involves reducing words and phrases to their phonetic building blocks, which go into one end of a proprietary authoring tool and come out the other side matched with appropriate lip shapes. So, for instance, "I've no use for that" becomes "iv no os for that." This is not difficult — it requires roughly the same amount of technical expertise as macramé. But translating five hundred pages of screenplay into phonics is like one of those absurdly tedious home crafts projects, knitting a car cover, say, or latch-hooking a wall-to-wall carpet. It is a nontrivial task. At this point, every spare computer in the office has been put to use as a scripting machine, and everyone, from the creative director to the receptionist, is frantically stitching together video and dialogue. The entire staff of CyberFlix has abandoned their official job descriptions to become digital assembly-line workers.

In this regard, working at a videogame company is pretty much the opposite of working at a Fortune 500 corporation, where it's important to arrive at a certain time and dress a certain way, to look as if you're working hard while cultivating a network of contacts by spending a lot of time on the phone. At CyberFlix, dress code is nonexistent. Schedules are brutal, but entirely flexible. And the concept of face time does not exist. Getting the work done is all that counts — sheer, unadulterated output.

On every bulletin board in the building, someone has scrawled a running countdown in capital letters: 6 DAYS LEFT.

"They're keeping us pumped up on amphetamines and cheap pornography," cracks a 3D model maker, the infamous Alex Tschetter, resplendent in his mohawk, earrings, and multiple tattoos. "Whatever it takes to keep us here, whatever we want. The best part about this time is that you can come in looking like a wreck, reeking of booze, whatever, and they're never gonna fire you for it, because they need you." Alex is a burly former construction worker from the flatlands of Florida who happens to be a gifted computer animator. He also has a lengthy criminal record. No one bothers him.

Alex does not respond well to Authority. He was, in fact, kicked out of computer design trade school for accosting an instructor before the director of the 3D design program interceded on his behalf, took him under her wing, and introduced him to the wonderful world of high-end workstations. Given sufficiently powerful equipment and enough personal space, Alex hauls like a sled dog. He comes in at an unspecified hour, usually before noon, and stays for marathon sessions, bolting together 3D models on his souped-up SGI workstation. He functions in his own personal time zone. But he's allowed, because his work is jaw-droppingly good, and he cranks it out at a prodigious rate, and because his personal demeanor engenders a healthy respect — the kind of respect you would accord a large, friendly pit bull.

"Luckily enough," he says, "they've been thoughtful not to force any kind of real schedule on us. Just get in when you can and do your shit. So I just go to work doing whatever I have to do, build sets and do props, little things here and there where it needs to fit in, do movies, and help. While I've got big jobs off running on the SGI, I just jump around and do little different things, 2D work or whatever. As long as it takes is as long as you've got to spend, and if you're here friggin' eighteen hours a day, so be it. And it's kind of very strange for me," he says, "because up until I came here to do this, I was always working construction, my whole life, and I felt sorry for the poor bastards trapped in air-conditioned prisons all day, and I thought it was so much fun to be roaming around on the job site, getting sun and running around and hollering and screaming. And that's all well and good, but you ain't never gonna make shit. You're gonna die poor or you're gonna die pissing away your social security check in some stinking little bar, and that's no good. So I just decided to take the step and at least do this for a few years to say that I could do it, and make some money out of it. If something went horribly wrong here tomorrow and I got kicked out or fired or I had to leave, I would just throw some things in the truck, get out, and go someplace else and do it. Because this industry is just replicating itself at such a disgusting rate and everybody's got something to do. And sure, not everything is quality, but it doesn't matter. It's like, you got money? All right, pay me, I'll do it. Give it up. And then you just do it and move on again."

Digital construction workers are the most technologically sophisticated migrant labor force the world has ever seen. Demand for their skills is at an all-time high, and they go where the work is. And the jobs are everywhere, because demand for computer-enhanced entertainment is skyrocketing. Game jobs are plummy because they're artistically demanding. But they are dwarfed by the more mundane (yet lucrative) opportunities to create flying 3D logos for local television stations, animated cumulus clouds for national weather shows, snazzy zooming statistics in industrial videos, and adorable computer-generated mascots.

And, Silicon Valley notwithstanding, the crackerjack video-game jobs are increasingly happening in out-of-the-way places. Hit games have a way of germinating in left field, in places like Spokane, Washington (*Myst*), and Mesquite, Texas (*Doom*), and Knoxville, Tennessee, home of CyberFlix. Making a game isn't like making a movie, which requires lots of site-specific infrastructure and schmoozing. Games aren't tied to the Bay Area the way that movies are tied to L.A. The tools are mobile and so are the people who use them. So the work can happen anywhere. Increasingly, it doesn't matter where you are. It only matters where your imperial corporate partners are. In the CyberFlix lobby, there are three clocks, marked Tokyo, Orlando, and Knoxville. This is the underlying irony of "indie success" in the game industry. Once the code is finished, the spunky individualist phase comes to an abrupt halt and the media empire machinations begin.* Most "garage multimedia" outfits harboring any talent are affiliated with some multinational behemoth — a movie studio, a telecommunications company, or a global distribution octopus like Bertelsmann.

In the big picture, "rogue" game producers are less like indie record labels and more like punk rock bands. In their own self defined environment, they create a particular kind of thrilling experience, which ends up as a string of ones and zeroes on an optical disc distributed by some media giant. In this case, CyberFlix signed a three-disc deal with Paramount after their

* A chart of media empire investments in the interactive entertainment industry looks like a billion-dollar game of *Twister*. Having lost hundreds of millions of dollars opening (then closing) multimedia divisions, the Jolly Green Giants of Hollywood have decided it's a better idea to buy pieces of independent companies that actually know what they're doing. In addition to the Tinseltown contingent, hardware manufacturers like Matsushita, Philips, Sony, Toshiba, phone companies like GTE and AT&T, cable companies like TCI, television networks, and finger-in-every-pie conglomerates like Disney and Dreamworks have twisted themselves into a tangled web of mutual investments with the likes of Sega and Microsoft, Silicon Graphics and IBM, strategic software tool developers, indie game producers, and of course, each other.

first disc's initial glimmer of success. Now they're distributed in North America by GTE (which, like every other telecom concern, is lurching into the entertainment arena). In Europe and Southeast Asia, CyberFlix games are distributed by BMG. In Japan, by a titanic toy company, Bandai. Of course, there are strings. CyberFlix's project roster also includes production work for GTE and a *Mighty Morphin' Power Rangers* title for Bandai. But it's a small price to pay for global distribution and a home base in Smoky Mountain trout-fishing country.

And in their own slightly deranged way, the 3D modelers, animators, and programmers of CyberFlix belong here in Knoxville, where the three largest employers are the University of Tennessee, the TVA, and Oak Ridge National Labs. The regional economy is already based on high-tech make-work programs for gearheads and construction crews. And as it turns out, most of Knoxville's young codesmiths are the spawn of Atomic Age engineers. These are kids whose dads built missiles and dams. CyberFlix's president is the son of a Martin Marietta physicist. Half the people on the payroll are related to architects of the Cold War or the Tennessee hydroelectric power grid. And now that those jobs are gone, children of the Smoky Mountain military-industrial complex have nothing better to do than play in punk rock bands, become snowboard thrashers, and start new media companies. And somehow, it's fitting that they should make their living on machines whose technological great-grandparents number-crunched nuclear impact, and that they should use these machines to build videogames set in outer space, the postapocalypse, and aboard a massive, sinking steel ship — and that they should do it here, in the cradle of the atomic bomb.

Chapter 8
Ditties of the Apocalypse

So I'm on the phone with this twentysomething multimedia publicist, and he's telling me about his weekend. "Man," he says, "were we ever a scene outta *Friends*. Bunch of my friends and I were playing this drinking game where we imitated, then guessed, all the audio effects from the old Atari 2600 games."

"Omigod. That's sick. You know you're acting page one out of the demographic playbook here."

"I know," he says.

"So, like, could you do a few?"

"The sound effects?"

"Yeah."

"OK," he says. "Here's the sound effect *Pitfall* makes when you die." He warbles the plaintive descending arpeggio that signals Game Over for Pitfall Harry. "Here's the sound of dragons in *Adventure* crashing into the walls. Brrrsch! Brrrsch!"

We reminisce at length about the early bells and whistles of Atari 2600 games. The sound of Mario jumping over a barrel in *Donkey Kong*. The wakka wakka dot-eating noise of *Pac-Man*. The random yet strangely melodic calliope jungle of *Breakout*. The ear-popping squeak of Frogger leaping into home base. The rumble of ICBMs exploding in midair over the silos of *Mis-*

sile Command. Having heard these sound effects several hundred thousand times, we have them indelibly burned into the crannies of our minds, and even a fleeting, drunken imitation is enough to spark Proustian reverie.

When most of the people now impersonating young professionals started playing videogames, sound effects were just explosions and other action-oriented sonic cues. But then, sometime in the mid-eighties, someone decided that games also needed a musical score. Thus began the diamond-drilling of digital buzz-clips into our collective skull. These sonic nuggets lodged like burrs, in part because, like advertising or carnival ride music, they were minimal and repeated ad infinitum. This wasn't some kind of Skinnerian plot. It was simply a matter of draconian technical constraints.

"The hardware was pretty primitive — you couldn't do that much," says Rob Hubbard, one of the grizzled old-timers of videogame sound design. Now a music point man for Electronic Arts, Hubbard started composing game music in 1983, when he was still living in Newcastle, England, and scraping together a living as a studio musician. As professional insurance, he bought a computer, taught himself assembly language, and started creating videogames for the Commodore 64. Then he started getting paid for it. "At that point," he says, "I thought, well, this'll just be a little fad which will last about a year, and then I'll have to get a new gig, so why not milk it."

Back then, videogame music was purely a matter of computer programming. In the small coterie of veteran videogame musicians, the apocryphal story of Rob Hubbard involves him sitting in an English pub scribbling ones and zeroes on a cocktail napkin. That was videogame music. "You were given a tiny, tiny little bit of memory," says Hubbard. "And you had to create pieces of music that were recognizable and sound effects that were believable on four voices of an FM synthesizer chip, one of the hardest chips in the world to program. That's all they had to work with, so it was really a lot of ingenuity and not so much about music and sound as it was about programming and doing the best you could do with the tools you were given in order to make an acceptable sound. In those days, we used to do like four minutes on the title screen — ten or twelve minutes total. I used to do them overnight. And it was all 100 percent assembly language. Those machines were just little baby machines, you know. You really had to work very hard to make them sound like anything at all, to make something that didn't sound really awful.

"In those days," he says, "you only had three-voice polyphony or four-voice polyphony, and you had to do everything with that." What this means, basically, is that only four sounds could happen at any given time. And if two of those sounds were game-play-related — bullets, say, or explosions — that left two sonic slots for music. A high hat and a kick drum. Or, if you chose not to use those, a bass and a piano. But only two voices at a time, to include a bass line, some kind of percussion, and a melody. It was like mixing an album on a four-track, except each track could only hold one note at a time. No chords.

"Trying to get all that to happen was a bit of a feat," says Hubbard, with typical British understatement. "You had to do a lot of voice peeling and shuffling. Now, the Sony Playstation has twenty-four voices and Saturn's got thirty-two. On PCs people have MIDI and digital sound effects, and you don't have to worry about having enough voices. But back then, you had to be extremely creative with the way you thought about things. In those days, I used to write really outlandish stuff, and people used to dig it. Just outrageous harmonics and stuff, a lot of weird bitonal stuff and parallels at the bottom. Outlandish stuff. I would never, ever, ever think of doing stuff like that these days. I wouldn't try to do anything outlandish now. But back then, a lot of people thought it was cool."

At some point, Hubbard's assembly-language rendition of *Pet Sounds* earned him a kind of odd fame among early computer game enthusiasts. "People used to recognize me in shops," he says, his northern inflection kicking up a notch. "At one point, I dared not venture into the computer shop! It's not like that now, of course, but I had people turning up on my doorstep in England wanting to see what I was up to. People would call from

Japan at, like, three o'clock in the morning saying they'd got this game with music that I did and wondered how I was doing. It was great, but I got a bit uncomfortable about it after a while."

Hubbard emigrated to the United States in 1988 and started working for Electronic Arts. Now he works on 32-bit machines and CD-ROMs for Windows '95. He doesn't actually write music anymore. His job is more a matter of resolving production snags and managing deadlines than composing bass lines. But then, the days of one-man videogame projects are long over. Budgets have exploded, and job descriptions have narrowed. It's a highly compressed parallel of what happened to science. Three hundred years ago, a Renaissance man could get a grip on pretty much every kind of science out there. Now you could spend your life collecting doctorates and still not know more than a tiny fraction of a scientific subspecialty. Fifteen years ago, Hubbard recalls, "it was possible for people like me to do a full game, to do all the graphics, write all the code, write the sounds. A lot of people did that in the old days. That has changed to where now people have to specialize. A lot of the people who write music for CD-ROMs don't know anything about code. They don't know anything about design. We've gone from people creating all this stuff in their back bedrooms to now having chains of twenty to fifty people involved with a project. You now see a lot of people from the music industry wanting to do this stuff. It's going to end up very similar to what it is in Hollywood."

Needless to say, the big-name, seven-figure composers will not be scoring videogames in assembly language. They'll want to confect the music and let the programmers worry about how it translates into bits and bytes.* They are also unlikely to limit themselves to the memory constraints of a cartridge —

---

* Of course, this implies a certain loss of precision — moving away from code is like switching from a stick shift to automatic. But what videogame sound jockeys lose in technical maneuverability, they make up for in ease of use. They can sit at a keyboard and loop sound samples instead of line editing programs in some arcane computer language.

try telling John Williams (of George Lucas film fame), "Yeah, and could you keep it down to 8 megs, Mr. Williams." I don't think so.

This is why the transition from cartridge to disc is so important for sound design. Except for Nintendo, every game company on earth has switched to CDs, not as a concession to artists but because CDs are much cheaper to manufacture. But the upshot is a massive expansion of legroom for musicians. Whereas a fully loaded cartridge contains maybe thirty-two megabytes of memory, a CD can hold over 600 megabytes. That's enough space for a composer, and not just master miniaturists like Rob Hubbard, to score a soundtrack. With the transition to CD, the firm lines between games and the rest of the entertainment world start to break down.* Now we're starting to see synthetic sixty-piece orchestras unfurl cinematic scores in the sonic background of an action adventure videogame.

We are also starting to see videogame divas. Case in point: George Alistair Sanger, aka the Fat Man. The Fat Man's promotional bio begins with arresting statistics, like the fact that he's sold more music than Madonna or Garth Brooks. Of course, Sanger's musical stylings came packaged with 20 million copies of best-selling games like *Wing Commander* and *Seventh Guest,* but that's much of a muchness. The press kit also includes a comic book starring the Fat Man and his posse of cowboy composers battling computer bugs and working under deadline for Client Bill. And then a reminder, printed on cow-pattern stationery: "FOR AN INTERESTING FEATURE ARTICLE GIVE US A HOLLER." It's pure Barnum: the singing cowboy persona, the drawl, the gold nugget suit. Everything about Sanger's country-and-western drag is leveraged on Hollywood glitz.

But then, this is the entertainment industry. As Hollywood

---

* Albums on audio compact disc have been a common fixture for ten years. Digital video discs (DVDs) — movies stored on high-density, standard-size CDs — are already in the Sony pipeline. Putting videogame code on optical disc brings the audio and video quality into sync with these other media. Whether CD-ROMs are as much fun as albums or movies is another ball of wax. But the production values are superb.

pours money into multimedia, image becomes more and more important to would-be interactive players — musicians, artists, producers. Being digital has nothing to do with it. The Fat Man seems to have figured this out while everyone else was still huddling around their workstations.

"Information isn't the valuable commodity," the Fat Man declares, echoing less flamboyantly dressed media futurists. "The valuable commodity is information sorting. And actually, style is the most sophisticated form of information sorting." This from a man who cites Ravi Shankar, the Beatles, Disney, and Andy Warhol as his primary influences. "It's taking shape now," he says. "There are a couple people who are starting to realize that this is show business. I like to think that someday, it'll be like bass players in the seventies. Someone'll see someone walkin' down the street dressed like Bootsie Collins, and they'll say, oh, he must be a bass player. And they'll see someone walking down the street in a Nudie suit and go, oh, computer game musician."

This scenario is not as far-fetched as it seems. Spencer Nilson, now head of the Sega Music Group, started out as a struggling rock musician, switched to videogames, and saw his fan base mushroom. "After a year at Sega," he says, still in a mild state of disbelief, "I went to a couple of these trade shows. And all these kids were flocking to me, because they knew who I was, and they knew all my music. And I thought, *man,* I'd been struggling out there putting out solo records and selling 40,000, 50,000 units here and there. And here, I've got hundreds of thousands of kids who know my music better than people I've known for years. Kids were sending me cassettes and asking if I would make copies of the music, because they couldn't do it off their machine and they wanted to take it on their summer vacation and play it at the beach. And that's when it hit me that there was a whole other industry here."

So Nilson did what any other honorable employee of a multinational entertainment corporation would do. He seized the marketing moment. If kids were yelping for videogame music, they'd probably be willing to buy it at Tower Records. And

Tower Records deals with record companies. So Nilson started a record company. At Sega. A Sega-owned record label, with its own A&R reps, its own roster of bands, its own recording complex, and its own executive producer, namely, Nilson.

"We've spun off and created an 11,000-square-foot recording record facility with publishing companies and a new label distributed by Polygram," says Nilson, easing comfortably into the proprietary tones of a music industry bigwig. "The umbrella for the facility is the Sega Music Group. The name of the label is Twitch Records, and it's right in the heart of multimedia gulch in San Francisco. We're just down the street from *Wired*, and Team Machina, which is a high-tech toy developer here."

The irony of the situation is that Sega can ensconce Twitch Records in the type of luxe environs that major labels can no longer afford. Indie label presidents from Seattle to Chapel Hill can only fantasize about the equipment Nilson has expensed to Sonic the Hedgehog. "The facility alone is world-class," he says, "and we're already doing record projects here that are unrelated to Sega, just because of the facility itself. I mean, I have 11,000 square feet with six full-time people. I've got everything from a huge A suite, which is a world-class digital mixing suite, to studio D, which is a small mastering lab and CD burning room. We've got twenty-five-foot skylights — it's an incredible space. The studios are so big and so airy and comfortable. But that was by design. That was the whole idea, that throughout the eighties, when things started being generated off of samplers and drum machines, the studios started cutting their rooms in half and in quarters. And it's very difficult to find large ambient recording spaces anymore. And now bands want to record that way. They all want to be in the room at the same time. They don't care so much if you hear the drummer through the guitar mike. The unplugged thing has caught on. And it's great, too, because then you really hear the song. You can't hide the song in that kind of production. It has to be a good song."

Once Twitch has these pop rocks on the mixing board, Nilson's job, as he describes it in smooth media empire–speak, is to "create other media, other entertainment forms from the original game experience, and use that experience to break new bands that then spin off debut albums from the success of the game — very similar to the film model."

In other words, this is basically a multimedia stealth operation, using a CD-based game machine as a Trojan horse for music "content." The idea is that if a hot Sega game sells a couple of million copies, that's a couple of million teasers for some band that also has an album out on Twitch Records. And every time kids play that game, they hear a commercial for the album playing in the background of that riveting Final Kombat Slalom Racer Destruction scene. Their hearts are pumping. Their adrenaline's kicking in. And then later, when they're cruising through the local music megamart, they hear *that song* and their vital statistics soar into Pavlovian overdrive. Ka-ching! This glorious consumer moment is made possible by the wonders of Corporate Synergy.

"So," says Nilson, "we've really positioned ourselves to be part of the entertainment industry, not necessarily just the game industry. Because it's very hard to differentiate the two. I mean, you have these games that are games in the middle but are feature films on the front, back, and sides. With the level of production and the video technology and compression on these platforms, the delivery system is quite impressive. And the Sega Saturn is a set-top monstrous box. It's designed to be a network server, and it's designed to download digital information from satellites. It's not just a little game machine. It's really set up to be that one box that sits on top. And you feed your cable into it. And you feed your modem and everything else into this one box that happens to reside on your television and the sound happens to pump out through your speakers. As opposed to being in the office watching a little postage stamp video display on your computer that has terrible speakers. I mean, that's really the thing that separates the Sega game experience from anything on a Mac or a PC or a Nintendo, for that matter, which is still cartridge-based. And that is going to be one of the downfalls of that whole design. There is no getting around the fact that they take longer to make, they're more expensive to make, and people aren't as comfortable with them as they are with the CD." And besides, you can't pop a Nintendo cartridge into your car stereo on the way to the mall to buy the latest Twitch Records release.

So who are these bands, anyway? Who are these great unknowns waiting to launch their careers off a videogame score? Where does Sega find these people? How does this work?

"Well," he says, "there's a kid out of New York, Staten Island, and I heard a demo of his at his record company. And he was perfect for a project I was working on. And I called him up. To make a long story short, in two weeks he did twenty-seven pieces of music. And we're not talking cartridge music. We're talking fully produced sixteen-track digital tracks that he produced in his bedroom in a Staten Island apartment. It was over an album's worth of music. Fifty-five minutes. His name is Ron Thal, and he's been featured in *Guitar Player* magazine this past winter and he has a debut album out on Shrapnel Records. And they're comparing him to Frank Zappa. I mean, the guy is brilliant. And he was inspired by the fact that he was getting to do a videogame. The way we had to work things with his record company, with the contracts, he didn't get paid for six months. But it wasn't about the money. It wasn't about anything but the fact that he was going to immortalize himself in a videogame."

But the immortal stamp of a videogame musician is like the immortal stamp of Scotty Moore or one of Phil Spector's studio musicians. It's not exactly a ticket to prima donna rock stardom. It's the fin de siècle answer to Tin Pan Alley.

"It's very blue collar," says Nilson. "There are a lot of staff composers. And at Sega of Japan, they have two or three people per cube with headphones on, composing original music. At least a hundred people, on several floors. It's like working in a closet with a piano at the Brill Building in New York.

"The Japanese are *amazing* at what they can do with the chip," he says. "It's night and day sometimes, when you hear the same chip, the same amount of memory, everything's the same, and you hear what they can do with it, and you hear what we can squeeze out of it. I mean, they do all the music in programming text. They don't use a keyboard interface and then try to convert it to MIDI and say, 'Well, that's close enough, and at least it captured my performance,' which is the way I approach it, the way any person I know would. They don't try to treat it like an instrument. They don't treat it like anything but a chip. So they line edit everything. They go about it from a programming standpoint. What are the capabilities. What are the ranges. What are the depths. They chart out the music and then convert it into code and put it in that way, and it sounds amazing. I mean, Yuzo Kashiro did *Streets of Rage* and *Streets of Rage 2*, and that stuff is downright great house music, and it's coming off the Genesis. It's thumpin'. It's slammin'. And he's got no more than we do.

"They use a whole different type of code," he says, clearly awestruck. "It's *perfection*. It's perfection, regardless of what they had to work with. It's absolutely as good as it can be, technically. It's much more entrenched in their way of doing things and in their culture. Now, you may argue about the style of what they're doing or the authenticity or just the cheese factor. But that totally aside, what they've chosen to do, they've pulled off to the nth degree, with echo and delay and production techniques on something that has *no mixing capability* other than changing the pitch value. We're not talking about a process where you put it all on tape and then you tweak it and mix it and compress it and overdub, which is what games are now and what we've done always in film and records. That wasn't an option."

Basically, the Japanese have just kept rolling down the road that Rob Hubbard was on in 1983. But while Western videogame musicians abandoned programming code for musical instruments and individual performance, the Japanese kept writing ones and zeroes on bigger and more powerful machines. Today, Sega of Japan may be working with the same hardware as their counterparts in San Francisco, but they are approaching it from the opposite direction — from the bottom up, rather than from the top down. They aren't thinking in terms of how to deconstruct and compress music sufficiently to stuff it into the machine. They are calculating the exact number of vibrations per minute that will coalesce and coagulate into a Virtua Fighter leitmotif.

But ironically, the code virtuosos of Japan have achieved mainstream musical success that dwarfs their American counterparts. Eschewing Marshall Stax, embroidered cowboy suits, and gold lamé, they have beaten impresarios like George Alistair Sanger to the pop charts. Game music in Japan has come into its own. There are radio and television shows devoted to reviewing it. It's huge there.

Of course, so is karaoke, and it has yet to break the novelty threshold stateside. At any rate, Sega is throwing a lot of money at this. "This is not an offhand venture," insists Nilson. "We're really going about this with a serious business plan for ten years out and how this is going to develop into a major part of the industry." Twitch Records' first releases hit the shelves in the summer of '96. And who knows, today's Sega session band may be tomorrow's Skinny Puppy. The next Sonic theme song may be as annoyingly overplayed as the tune from the week's most popular post-adolescent melodrama.

At the very least, the postcollegiate beer bets of 2012 are riding on this one.

Chapter 9
Cartridge Wars

Forty minutes from downtown Seattle, Mount Si cuts the horizon like a sullen cigar store Indian in profile. Ice crevices slice down into pools of slush and gravel, water-gorged tufts of grass and conifers and gullies of cracked stone. At the base of a steep meadow, the vertical dimension halts abruptly, cut off by a concrete slab the size of five football fields. The monolith is perfectly horizontal. It diffuses light with the flat sheen of a computer rendering. This is Nintendo's North Bend Distribution Center — the way station of every Game Boy in North America. Filled to the rafters, North Bend would hold half a billion *Yoshi's Island* cartridges. It's sort of a monument to global computerized inventory control.

What happens here is the blood flow of an entertainment economy. A stream of cheaply assembled Product pumps in through the pulmonary artery of the Third World manufacturing sector. Sorted Product courses through this massive aortic warehouse, bound for the capillaries of retail, which exhale Product to consumers. Orders flow back to the warehouse through the venous channels of digital inventory databases and thence to the factories of Central America and China. The automated stream of packaged entertainment stays liquid, never getting the chance to sclerose in storage. Sell. Order. Sell. Order. Sell.

Every day, thirty truckloads of shrink-wrapped plastic and silicon arrive from factories in Asia and Mexico en route to 9,000 electronics boutiques, toy emporiums, department stores, and Wal-Marts north of the Rio Grande. At North Bend's inbound receiving bay, two barrel-chested, mustached loaders lift plastic-coated cartons from China onto an Adjustoveyor belt. As Mario and Luigi hoist box after box of red Game Boys from the People's Republic, a bar code scanner reads the containers into the factory, ticking off numbers on an LED display — how many boxes loaded, how many to go. One after the other, the boxes ride the conveyor belt overhead to an automated pallet stacker that labels each pallet with its own ID number. Then the robots take over.

Because cartridges have a tendency to mysteriously disappear from the warehouse floor, all software loading in North Bend is done by robots that wheel through a steeplechase of wire-guided scanners embedded in the floor. Each robot is named after a hit Nintendo game and zooms around making gooselike honking noises. The most troublesome and unpredictable robot is named after Mario's evil twin, Wario, because it jumped the track once and tried to go the wrong way. It had to be forcibly shut down. Each robot has a separate off switch, and the warehouse supervisor assures me that somewhere there is also a central switch that shuts down all the robots in the event of an Asimovian mutiny.

There is some residual human participation in this process, but only at the most picayune level. When a Babbages store in some suburban mall needs just one Virtual Boy, three *Wario Land* cartridges, and two green Game Boys — not whole boxes of things, just a grab bag of merchandise — the robots punt this piddling order to the Pick By Light system, which involves human beings doing their best impression of robot product sorters. The way this system works is that open boxes of consoles and cartridges sit in slots above an array of LED panels and lights. For each computer-indexed order, a series of red lights blinks on, and a Nintendo warehouse worker rolls a cardboard bin down a conveyor belt from light to light, reading numerals off each LED, taking the designated number of boxes out of the slot, and punching a button, at which point the lights turn green. When you get to the end of the line, the next order comes up, and you roll another cardboard bin the other way, at top speed, while the computer prints out an invoice. To gain a full grasp of the Pick By Light system, I insist on filling an order myself, maniacally tossing items into a cardboard bin bound for the Wal-Mart at 2135 Main Street in Snellville, Georgia (three Super Game Boys, one Super NES with *Yoshi's Island*, three Virtual Boys, two SNES with *Donkey Kong Country 2* and *Diddy's Kong Quest*, and four *Wario Land* cartridges — in under thirty seconds. Not too shabby). Essentially, it's just like *Kaboom* or *Burger Time* or any one of those videogames where parts must be dispatched as they're falling from the sky. The Pick By Light record, during Nintendo's holiday rush, is 5,700 orders filled in eight hours by six people. This process is 99.5 percent accurate.

The other 0.5 percent is taken care of at the next level, the Verification Station, where all the boxes are rescanned under data-enhanced, digitally encrypted video surveillance, then automatically wrapped in white polymerized cellophane that says "100% ACCURACY ENSURED BY ELECTRONIC VERIFICATION" in red letters. Wheels suddenly pop up from the conveyor belt, shooting the boxes toward their exit bays, where they are numbered, videotaped again, sealed inside bar-coded tractor-trailer door seals, and sent on their way. This is an operation worthy of Fort Knox. But then, a truckload of Nintendo merchandise is worth between half a million and two million dollars. Carriers have had trucks abducted.

From loading in to trucking out, the whole process is choreographed from North Bend's Central Control Room, a claustrophobic bank of refrigerator-sized computers that looks just like NASA Mission Control. Orders pour in over the network every two hours, in waves. The person who picks them up and orchestrates all the robots has the best job title in North

America: Wave Planner. Being behind the Wave Planner control console has to rank right up there with being behind the wheel of a large piece of construction equipment, or having your finger on the switch that triggers a test of the Emergency Broadcast System. It's an unsung form of despotism. The Wave Planner gets to twiddle the frequency and amplitude of who gets what, and has to make sure that everyone catches the current wave of Product at the optimal moment.

The process is almost balletic. On the day of a hit videogame release (after months of multimillion-dollar buildup), hordes of breathless kids launch a kind of Normandy invasion of America's toy marts. There are monstrous lines. There are waiting lists. Shortly thereafter, the supply of this blockbuster cartridge mysteriously evaporates, even from behemoth retailers like Toys "R" Us. Those without the foresight to shell out fifty bucks, sight unseen, in advance, are stranded without Product. A few weeks later, the second wave of Product arrives to appease them and tempt a third tide of more cautious cartridge collectors, who by this time have heard the game's glories described by the legions who seized the first wave of Product. Having already "beaten" the game, the diehards are already paddling toward the next crest of frenzied demand and limited supply, which has all been calibrated in advance by the marketing folks and the Wave Planner.

This alimentary tube of videogame distribution, epitomized by Nintendo, is designed to prevent the kind of catastrophe that destroyed the videogame industry in 1983, when a flood of execrable games drowned companies like Atari and Coleco in a sea of consumer contempt. Within the space of a year, the $3 billion industry shriveled to a fortieth of its previous size, and American manufacturers never recovered. Meanwhile, Nintendo introduced the Famicom in Japan. Unlike its American counterparts, Nintendo maintained iron-fisted control over the game supply with a lock-out chip that prevented outside companies from releasing software for the system — all in the name of quality control. With the Famicom's 1986 American debut as the Nintendo Entertainment System, Nintendo kept the draconian development process in place, along with a number of ham-fisted marketing tactics. When the antitrust smoke cleared, Nintendo had to take a less openly fascist approach to dealing with merchants and software developers. It also had to take credit for single-handedly reviving the videogame industry, setting the stage for the cartridge wars of the nineties.

The cartridge wars — Nintendo versus Sega, Mario versus Sonic — were essentially about whose blades justified the purchase of one $250 razor over another — the competitors' blades being mutually incompatible. Nintendo sold millions of NES consoles because they came packaged with *Super Mario Bros.* Sega released the Genesis in 1989, but only began to crawl out from Nintendo's shadow in 1991 with the introduction of *Sonic the Hedgehog.* Among the current crop of machines, it's a three-way scuffle between *Virtua Fighter 2, Battle Arena Toshinden,* and *Super Mario 64* for the Sega Saturn, Sony Playstation, and Nintendo 64, respectively. It's all about software. In this business, software drives hardware with jackboots and a riding crop.

In this regard, kids are far more sophisticated than their parents. Adults are easily snowed by abstract hardware statistics they don't understand ("Well, Grant, *I've* got a 166 megahertz Pentium with a 500 megabyte hard drive, 14 megs of RAM, and a quad speed CD-ROM drive"), and then use their new screamingly fast, top-of-the-line, twin cam turbo-driven machines to run the same database they've been using for years. But you'll never hear a kid asking some salesman, "Excuse me, is that Sony Playstation running off a 32-bit RISC chip? A VLSI CPU? How many megahertz?" A kid will evaluate the latest software firsthand, determine, in a very empirical way, what's cool and what sucks, and make a hardware decision on that basis. Kids have a ruthless set of criteria for separating great games from the dross, and they render judgment with no pretense of critical distance. Unlike their mush-mouthed elders, who will rationalize tickets to a lousy movie by playing up the cinematography or costume design or some cameo performance, kids will unequivocally trash a bad game, regardless of the marketing fanfare.

Because kids subject videogames to such intense scrutiny,

videogame companies devote a huge amount of energy to figuring out what kids want. Not only do they periodically corral prepubescents, adolescents, and twentysomethings into in-house focus groups, but they also assemble hundreds of *echt* videogamers into testing laboratories. The Sega Testing Lab, for instance, trawls the Bay Area youth base for eighteen- to twenty-eight-year-olds by posting flyers and taking out ads, much as a bone marrow transplant clinic or sleep deprivation study would solicit young, healthy males from the local college population.

Contrary to popular belief, not just any joystick jockey with an excess of spare time can become a tester. There is an arduous screening process. "Believe it or not," says Mark Latham, the testing lab's twenty-eight-year-old director, "you have to have a really good education. You have to be very good in English. We basically give testers when they come in English tests, basic math tests, a small battery of tests. It's like an SAT. Roughly, only about 20 percent make it. Because what they have to do is they have to write up these incredibly complicated situations. You know, I was doing A when B happened and then I went over to this section and then C happened, in this linear order type thing. And if they write it in a convoluted way or in their own vernacular, it isn't terribly valuable. And the number of people with that talent is pretty slim, who embody both the playing ability and the IQ to articulate and write it down." In other words, an evaluation that reads: "Like, I got to the eighth level, and it was way hard, and like, there was all this weird stuff going on at the top of the screen, but I totally got past it" is not going to cut it at the Sega Testing Lab. It's not enough just to master the game in forty-five minutes. Afterward, you have to produce a detailed debriefing document.

"There's a certain military aspect to it," says Latham. "We even use military vernacular. We have the test leads, which are kind of like little generals, and we have lieutenants. For a given project, you assign the test lead, and the producer depends on this person to be their number one contact in test, and they're the person who they communicate with daily about where the product's at. And then below the lead are two lieutenants, assistant leads. And the assistant leads mainly communicate with the large temp and perm base on all the bugs and pull it all together."

The "perm base" is the small sliver of Sega's testing lab payroll that works full-time with benefits and health insurance. The rest come from temp agencies, which is appropriate, given the audience for whom these games are being honed. Sega's core customers are between the ages of eighteen and twenty-eight. Thousands of them are temps. In fact, working at the Sega Testing Lab is sort of a temp dream job — a karmic eddy of videogames perfected by temps, for temps.

What this nomadic workforce does, on a day-to-day basis, is (a) spot programming bugs and (b) drive the subtle process known as "balancing the game." Balancing is the videogame equivalent of all the fine-tuning that boutique beer brewers talk about in radio commercials — the ratio of malt to hops, artisanal decisions about the bottling process, etc. In the videogame test process, this means increasing or decreasing the number of enemies, the amount of ammunition, and other factors that determine the pace and difficulty of a given game. This, again, is based on all kinds of market research about stress levels and frustration thresholds of adolescent videogamers, no doubt conducted by gray-flannel consulting firms for exorbitant amounts of money. The balance of a game is essentially arbitrary — it just depends whom you're trying to sell to. At Nintendo, I'm told that titles arriving from Japan are regularly made slower and easier for their American release. The theory is that Japanese children are more proficient at videogames and what they consider challenging fun would simply frustrate and quash American grade-schoolers.

Sega's testing lab director bristles at Nintendo's theory that American kids can't compete at the Japanese level of videogame virtuosity and must therefore be coddled. "I love this perception that they have to make it easier for Americans." He snorts. "As I've pointed out to both Japanese and the Europeans, the American consumer is the most demanding and educated consumer, and because of that, they demand a more balanced experience. It's not a lack of ability. It's because we're such great educated and insistent consumers, and their marketplace would be far better off if they had the same type of consumer. I mean, they're quite full of it. And the Japanese games that come to us are horribly balanced, in my opinion, and way too difficult. And the reason why is because in their marketplace, they judge products on how long it takes them to complete it and not the quality of the experience."

Of course, the American balancing process has its pitfalls, which bear an uncanny resemblance to the pitfalls of movie-making by committee. Too much testing, like too many focus group screenings, can irreparably curdle a videogame, as Latham readily admits. "There was a game — and I won't say the title, to protect the innocent — it was a kid's licensed game, and it got delayed for a while, so it was in test for a long time. And so the test people kept saying, this is too easy. This is too easy. And then they would make it a little harder, a little harder. Well because it was in test for so long, these guys became so perfect at playing this game, because they'd play it every day, and they kept saying make it harder, make it harder. This game, when we shipped it, made little kids cry. It was just abusive. At Christmas, small children were crying at the fireplace. It wrecked their self-esteem. This game actually broke the land speed record for moms returning in VW station wagons to Toys "R" Us because their kids were screaming. This is what happens to a producer if you listen too much to test, because test really represents the hardcore edge of our audience. And this is what the Japanese and the Europeans always sell to, is the hardcore edge. And as you know, in America you don't get anywhere by selling to the fringe. You sell to the masses."

Selling to the masses, in this case, entails the same kind of big-budget hype and blockbuster groupthink for which Hollywood studios are famous. The production cost of videogames, like summer special effects movies, continues to spiral upward. Gone are the days when one guy in a basement could pull together a videogame for five hundred dollars. Now the process entails battalions of coders and graphic designers and about $2 million, and it has to produce a megahit double platinum home run. Which, in turn, requires legions of publicists and promoters and an eight-figure advertising campaign.* The staggering cost of all this is, of course, used as a bullet point, for shock value in press releases, to drive home the point that this Product is indeed megabig, bigger than big, the videogame equivalent of *Terminator*, *Jurassic Park*, and *Independence Day* combined, and that, as the autumn days grow short, this Product will be everywhere, and kids will buy it.† They will buy it in Toys "R" Us. They will buy it at Tower Records. They will buy it at Circuit City, Best Buy, Babbages, Software Etc., Target, Blockbuster, and Kmart.

Not too long from now, they will also run it on play-per-view off a cable channel or jiggle joysticks for a buck an hour online. Before we get movies-on-demand, interactive television, or any other media empire fantasy distribution scheme, kids will be playing some *Sonic the Hedgehog* sequel off a satellite network. Kids know what they want, and they're not afraid to use new technology to get it. Need to learn a whole new machine to access a kick-ass videogame? No problem. Kids don't have Platform Issues. Whether *Battletoads* plays on a Sega Saturn,

---

* Acclaim's wildly successful *Mortal Kombat* "premiered" on September 13, 1993, when it was simultaneously released on four videogame platforms, boosted by a $10 million marketing campaign. The release, dubbed "Mortal Monday," was a raving success, and *Mortal Kombat* sold over 6 million copies, raking in $150 million for Acclaim. On September 9, 1994, Acclaim reprised *Kombat*'s success with "Mortal Friday," another $10 million kickoff, for *Mortal Kombat 2*, which earned $50 million its first week on the market.

† Nintendo is particularly enthusiastic about publicizing its own expenditures. Actually, they've taken this tactic into another dimension by emphasizing not the production costs of the games themselves but rather the amount of money being spent on advertising and promotion. At the 1996 Electronics Entertainment Expo, the videogame industry trade show, Nintendo's twenty-foot backlit billboard radiated: "Launch budget of over $50 million. . . . A breakthrough campaign of print and television, with over $20 million of media support. . . . Major brands like Kellogg's, Blockbuster, and Nickelodeon are lining up their fall promotions behind Nintendo 64." What's important is not that Nintendo spent a lot of money developing *Donkey Kong Country*, but that it will spend $16 million to put the game on the back of cereal boxes. It's hype squared.

Nintendo 64, Sony Playstation, or PC-CD-ROM, on a console or over a modem, is immaterial to a third-grader. Conversely, the hottest machine in the world is going to bomb if there's no good software for it. Trend gurus dress these conclusions up in lots of jargon, impressing fifty-year-old executives with what any seven-year-old understands: Hardware slips away. Channels change. Content rules. A couple years playing videogames makes you more or less the model Information Age customer. That's why the videogame industry is so far ahead of publishers and movie studios in the brave new world of "interactive entertainment." Videogames, unlike books or movies, are digital from start to finish and have been for twenty years. And they're the only medium whose entire audience can master any new piece of equipment in forty-five minutes. That should keep the robots of North Bend rolling well into the twenty-first century, until the ripples of Product break invisibly across our telephone lines.

Chapter 10

Video**game**
Porn

As endless ribbons of shiny, shrink-wrapped plastic cartridges cascade from the loading doors of Nintendo's Willie Wonkan thumb candy warehouse, children throng toy emporiums from Tokyo to Tacoma. They put themselves on Toys "R" Us waiting lists months in advance. They skip school to idle in endless lines, salivating in anticipation of this new, indispensable, Top of the Pops software product. They act just like little grown-ups waiting to buy *Windows '95*.

But unlike *Windows '95* owners, kids have to attain a certain level of proficiency with *Donkey Kong Country 2* before they can brag to their friends. They can't just stand around the water fountain at recess and casually bluff about how much easier and more productive this software has made their lives. ("Oh yeah, *Diddy's Kong Quest?* Got it on my system. Runs like a dream.") Generalities don't cut it. In the pecking order of schoolyard videogame one-upmanship, you have to demonstrate incredibly detailed and specific inside knowledge of the system du jour (imagine your social status suddenly contingent on the ability to outline *TurboTax* installation procedure for Power PC line by line at office volleyball tournaments, and you begin to grasp the crushing pressure involved here). It's not enough to be the first kid on your block to own the hottest videogame. You have to know to throw a crate against the first right wall in the Parrot Chute Panic level or risk dismissal as a hopeless, clueless poseur. Videogame strategy is the grade-school equivalent of the sports bar statistics that weave rapport between former jocks. It's not the hidden power-ups and fatality moves per se. It's the combination of arcane knowledge and hand-eye coordination that lets you join the gang.

This is when the typical second-grader discovers the information economy, where you pay a premium for short-lived, narrowcast expertise — in this case, $4.95 for a copy of *Next Generation, Electronic Gaming Monthly, Game Pro, Nintendo Power,* or *Flux.* Like the secret decoder rings of yore, videogame magazines give kids the keys to the castle of high-status trivia. If you open any of these garishly printed videogame glossies, you'll see pages and pages of codes, strings of letters separated by commas — indecipherable ribbons of alphanumeric gibberish to the uninitiated. Children memorize this stuff by rote and drill, not unlike musical scales. They may not be able to locate Idaho on a map, but they know every secret combination in *Virtua Fighter 2* by heart. Every month, manufacturers unleash a new pantheon of videogame heroes and villains, each with their own set of killer combination moves, to fuel a new, slick batch of plastic-encased videozines.

Not coincidentally, the price and variety of plastic-sealed videogame periodicals corresponds to the shrink-wrapped magazines on the other side of the newsstand, the ones that artfully pose topless nineteen-year-old covergirls. It's curiously symmetrical: *Nintendo Power, Game Pro, Flux. Playboy, Hustler, Juggs.* As one media scholar wryly observes, "These pictures constitute a kind of techno-porn: children spend hours ogling the fascinating places they might visit in a new game, eyeing the magazine's uncloaking of those secret sites to which they have so far failed to gain access."[*] Like the adult publishing industry, the videogame press prides itself on lavish foldout sections, runs

[*] Henry Jenkins, "X Logic: Repositioning Nintendo in Children's Lives," *Quarterly Review of Film and Video* 14, no. 4, 1993: 55–70.

Make pad Thai!

Ingredients:

- ☐ 8 ounces (227 g) dried flat rice noodles
- ☐ 2 tablespoons (27 g) brown sugar
- ☐ 2 tablespoons (30 ml) fresh lime juice
- ☐ 3 tablespoons (44 ml) soy sauce
- ☐ 2 teaspoons (10 ml) vegetable oil
- ☐ 3 green onions
- ☐ 1 garlic clove, minced
- ☐ 2 eggs, beaten

Optional toppings:

- ☐ dash of Sriracha or other hot sauce
- ☐ bean sprouts
- ☐ prepared chicken, shrimp, or tofu
- ☐ chopped peanuts
- ☐ chopped cilantro
- ☐ lime wedges

Serves 4

Cook with a grownup assistant. Be careful when working with knives and the stove.

If you can't find rice noodles, linguini can also work.

Step 1

Prepare the noodles according to the package instructions. Then drain them.

Step 2

Thinly slice the green onions. Put the green slices and the white slices in separate piles.

Step 3

In a small bowl, use a fork to whisk together brown sugar, lime juice, soy sauce, and (if you're using it) hot sauce.

Step 4

In a large nonstick skillet, heat the oil over medium-high heat. Add the pile of white onion slices and garlic. Keep stirring over the heat for about 30 seconds.

Sriracha hot sauce is named after the Thai city where it was invented, Si Racha!

Step 5

Add the eggs and cook, scraping the skillet with a spatula, for about another 30 seconds.

Then move the eggs to a plate.

Step 6

Put the drained noodles, green onions, and sauce in the skillet. Cook, tossing constantly, until the noodles are soft (about a minute).

Step 7

Divide the noodles between four serving bowls. Add some of the egg to each bowl.

Add as many of the optional toppings as you want. Serve with a wedge of lime to squeeze over the noodles.

Yum!

Pad Thai

The name pad Thai roughly translates to "Thai-style stir fry."

Pad Thai (say "pad tie") became Thailand's national dish soon after the country known as Siam changed its name to Thailand. Today, pad Thai is a favorite meal everywhere from fancy restaurants to street vendors to home kitchens — like yours!

hotline advertisements, and cultivates a throbbing channel of feedback from its readers.

The videogame fans panting hardest are invariably *Flux* readers. Of all the game rags, *Flux* is the most pungently redolent of adolescence and the essential grossness of teenage boys. Between videogame articles, comic book synopses, fantasy role-playing games, and death metal album reviews, *Flux* is an orgy of fourteen-year-old male power fantasies, awash in sweat, blood, and other bodily fluids. This magazine reeks of authenticity. A typical issue combines the *FX Fighter* Complete Move List, a strategy guide to *Battle Arena Toshinden* trading card games, and a profile of Glenn Danzig's peephole-into-the-apocalypse comic book company, as well as the usual Babe-ality page and *Flux*'s signature Don't Ever Do This section ("Never buy a carton of crickets at the pet store and leave it — opened of course — in someone's house. Their family will spend months of sleepless nights before they find them all. . . . Never get a bunch of friends to always carry screwdrivers and slowly dismantle your school. . . . Never leave cartons of milk in out-of-the way corners over a long holiday weekend"). And no copy of *Flux* is complete without a slew of letters from shocked PTA mothers and incensed high school feminists whose florid gusto rivals the Penthouse Forum letters. *Flux*'s editors gleefully print this invective, and *Flux* readers eat it up, lick the bowl, and beg for more. In the words of one afficionado, "This 'thing' which you call a magazine is vile, filthy, disgusting, and shows many ways for a person to get in deep trouble. In other words, I love it!"

Jonathan Rheingold, *Flux*'s associate publisher, is the editorial mastermind behind this tumescent pulp. Rheingold, who grew up in Brooklyn listening to Black Sabbath, Ozzy Osbourne, and Iron Maiden, is basically the *Flux* reader ten years later. After a seven-year stint at Harris Publications, proud publisher of *Guitar World*, Rheingold has spread his editorial wings and now publishes comic books and videogame titles. "I publish *Vampirella*," he says with a grunt, Brooklyn accent thick as cheese on a deep-dish pizza. "You know *Vampirella*? She's like, a female vampiress." When Rheingold got the idea to do

Flux in 1993, he wanted to tap into the videogame market, but with a twist. "The kids that were playing *Mortal Kombat* were also watching *X-Men* and listened to Pearl Jam and were into all this stuff," he says. "Comic books like *X-Men* and *Spiderman* are becoming videogames by Acclaim. There's been a tremendous amount of synergy. Obviously guys like Katzenberg, Spielberg, and Geffen have this vision as well — cross-pollinating all these different forms of entertainment." Obviously, a magazine that covered all of it would cater to this vision. The Katzenberg vision. The Spielberg vision. The Rheingold vision. The vision of a magazine for legions of preteen boys precipitously poised between Hot Wheels and actual dating.

"All the *Flux* reader wants to know," says Rhengold, "is, is a game cool? Or does it suck? And we say what sucks, and we say what's cool, with no holds barred. We have a review section in the back, where our mascot dog reviews the videogames. We have a TV dog, where the dog is humping the TV, like, yes yes, oh yes, more, yes. If you get a humping dog, that means the game rules. And then we have the licking dog, and the dog's like licking himself. And that's like, it's a satisfying experience, you'll get off on it. So if the game's real cool, but not awesome, they get a licking dog. Then we have the bone dog, who has a bone in his mouth and is wagging his tail, and he's like, yeah, knick-knack paddywack, who cares. And then there's the pissing dog. Like, if a game sucks, the dog's like, pissing on it. Some of my advertisers freak. They say, how could you do this. How could you have a dog humping a TV. I'm like, c'mon, you ever watch Beavis and Butthead? Those guys are like, setting shit on fire. This is what the kids want."

If *Flux* holds a mirror up to the sweaty-palmed adolescents of America, *Nintendo Power* caters to their little brothers. Run out of Nintendo's corporate headquarters in Redmond, Washington, *Nintendo Power* is *Flux*'s polar opposite. It is the *Pravda* of the videogame industry. It is also the largest videogame magazine in America. With a circulation of 750,000 and a mainline to the marketing department, *Nintendo Power* is essentially an exquisitely produced product brochure that kids can buy at the newsstand for four dollars. *Nintendo Power* doesn't take advertising, because *Nintendo Power* is advertising. In over a hundred pages of advertorial content, there is nary a negative review. It's sort of an editorial *Animal Farm* where all games are fun and exciting, but some games are more fun and exciting than others, especially if they are developed by Nintendo's in-house development team as opposed to an outside licensee. These games are always at the top of the magazine's Power Charts — lists of the top twenty Super NES games, the top ten Game Boy cartridges, the top team sports games, etc. — although there is no explanation of how these charts are calculated.

It is very easy to condemn *Nintendo Power* as a prattling mouthpiece of corporate marketing. But it's not quite that simple. Because the games developed by Nintendo's programmers and pet software companies generally are superb, given the massive amount of money, brainpower, and technical support they get from the mother ship. You won't see any pissing dog icons in *Nintendo Power*, but the games at the top of their Good/Better/Best ratings are usually the best. That doesn't make the magazine any less smarmy or cloying. But then, you don't have to wonder about the integrity of a glowing review followed by five pages of the manufacturer's ads. You don't have to worry about an incestuous relationship between advertising and editorial because there is no division at all. In a twisted way, it's reassuring. In the videogame press, advertising and articles are such a hazy, hyperbolic blur that it's comforting to know, for once, what kind of propaganda to expect. Paging through *Nintendo Power* is a profoundly unsettling experience, but not because of corporate bias.

It's the incessant, pine-scented chirpiness that sets your teeth on edge. The whole magazine chimes like a perky airline stewardess explaining what to do when cabin pressure drops and oxygen masks fall from the overhead compartments. The same sunny tone is used throughout, for promotional news blurbs as well as the answers to questions like "How do I do the Kombat Tomb Uppercut?" And somehow, this is more disconcerting than *Flux*'s World Wrestling Federationesque dirtbag overkill. It's like hearing a Disneyland attendant giving cheerful instructions on how to strangle a dog. For instance, instead of columnists, *Nintendo Power* has "Counselors." Whether this is a summer camp analogy or a reference to junior high school psychological evaluation is unclear, but all these counselors really want to help you. They want to help you help yourself. They want to help you find the locked door in World 3-2 of Yoshi's Island.

But sometimes, even the Counselors can't help you. Sometimes, you need TOP SECRET CLASSIFIED INFORMATION, which is published in a colorful four-page spread on page sixty-four of *Nintendo Power*. This TOP SECRET CLASSIFIED INFORMATION consists of puzzle solutions, special passwords, access codes to hidden bonus levels, immortality, invincibility, and unlimited ammunition (For Extra Lives, press Left, Up, Q, Select, Select) sent in by Secret Agents, who all have their own three-digit identification numbers. So you know that your Super Power Codes or *Street Fighter Mega Man* moves are coming from Agent #444 or #596. As it turns out, all these Secret Agents are actually *Nintendo Power* readers who respond to the magazine's solicitation for tips and codes ("If you've got an awesome tip or a killer code, send it in! Be sure to include your three-digit agent number, so we can give credit where it's due. What are you waiting for? Warm up those brain pans, stretch those thumbs and get moving!"). Why be a mere reader when you can be a Nintendo Secret Agent, with your own special ID number?

At *Nintendo Power* headquarters, all the correspondence of Nintendo Secret Agents is assembled into huge, framed collages that line the walls. Videogame letters to the editor seem to have spawned a new genre of envelope art — fantastically decorative Magic Marker line drawings of Earthworm Jim, Donkey Kong, the Animaniacs, and Mortal Kombatants clustered around the *Nintendo Power* postal address. This is the art of the Faithful, accompanied by the gushy prose of the successfully brainwashed. There are no violent fantasy scenarios or juvenile jokes, just the tender prose of well-behaved, rapturously appreciative kiddie consumers.

My guide around this marketing wonderland is Jenne Pierce, one of Nintendo's battalion of game tip hotline operators, or Counselors (the catch-all title for any Nintendo employee who comes into contact with the game-playing public). Jenne's fresh-scrubbed blondness is perfectly set off by her neatly pressed Nintendo Game Counselor uniform — black jeans and a denim work shirt, fastidiously accessorized. Without the little red Team Nintendo Mario logo embroidered on her shirt pocket, she could pass for a Gap employee or TGI Fridays waitress. As she leads me through the brightly lit beige Nintendo's offices, I notice that all the walkways have whimsical street names, clearly marked at the intersections of carpeted cubicles. At regular intervals, spherical gray plastic planters dangle office ivy tantalizingly overhead, tempting you to jump up and smash them for bonus points or extra lives.

"What's with the street signs?" I ask.

"Oh yeah," she says. "All our hallways are named after videogame characters. Mother Brain Lane, Koopa Troopa Trail, Torpedo Ted Turnpike. All our conference rooms too. It makes it a really fun place to work." As we amble down Diddy Kong Drive, Jenne describes her job as a Nintendo Game Play Counselor. Every hotline employee gets a Virtua Boy, a Super NES, a Game Boy, and access to the game library. Jenne smiles a sparkly Aquafresh smile. "They encourage us to practice."

After weeks of intensive training, she explains, journeyman Game Play Counselors can "cross-train" for a variety of new, exciting phone jobs at the Nintendo customer service center and eventually earn the rank of Superagent or Advanced Superagent. "That's what I do," says Jenne. "I'm an Advanced Superagent."

"Does it say that on your business card?"

"Um, well, no, but every year, I put 'Advanced Superagent' on my tax return, on that line where they ask you what your job is, and the IRS hasn't said anything about it yet."

"Wow."

"Yeah. I love working here!"

Honestly, I believe her. But something about this place says "model POW camp." It's totally spotless, and it's filled with jubilant motivational statistics. On a bulletin board outside the hotline phone bank, there's a running ticker. "Calls received today: 115,278. Letters received today: 2,133. Calls received to date: 48,579,515. Letters to date: 1,564,008." An LED sign hangs overhead with the number of calls on line, calls on hold, calls being answered in French and Spanish, and the number of customer service reps and Game Play Counselors on duty. At any given time, there are three hundred people working the phone lines, answering general how-do-you-plug-this-thing-in questions and giving out game tips. The customer service line used to be toll-free, but the traffic was overwhelming, even for Nintendo. "Before we started charging a toll," says Jenne, "we'd get one and a half million calls on a busy Saturday."

Tip line traffic was always manageable. The tip line is, and always was, ninety-five cents a minute and is disproportionately staffed by young, female operators like Jenne, some of whom have answered more than 100,000 calls as Game Play Counselors (a plaque lists them as members of the Hundred Grand Club). All Nintendo phone workers must be signed on to the telephone 90 percent of the time, leaving 5 percent of working hours for "wrap-up" paperwork on each call and not more than 5 percent "idle." Voice boxes attached to the telephones monitor call time automatically. It's a lot like a catalog order phone bank. Or a phone sex line. This is the flip side of telemarketing. This is the networked, one-to-one, customized trackable database the Third Wave marketing gurus keep talking about. This is where Nintendo introduces grade-school kids to the concept of software customer service. By the time kids are old enough to install their own home computer software, they'll have two decades of experience with tech support staff. They already know all about the software/hotline/magazine/direct mail connection, and that the people on the other side of the phone know all kinds of things about you, like how old you are, what system you're using, and how far you've gotten in *Super Mario World 2*. They know that companies publish magazines telling you that one brand of toys does in fact define an entire lifestyle, and they do all kinds of things to get you actively involved. *Nintendo Power* does what other corporate advertorial infomercials try to do, only much, much better. It makes *Windows Magazine* look like kid stuff.

Chapter 11
Mario über
Alles

Of course, *Nintendo Power* didn't invent videogame hype. They just perfected it. Before Mario, there was a yellow, limbless, ravenous disc licensed from Namco of Japan. Midway's photon-nibbling *Pac-Man* was the monster arcade hit of 1981, spawning a school of sequels and ripoffs: *Ms. Pac-Man, Baby Pac-Man*, the beanie-capped *Pac-Man Junior, Professor Pac-Man, Pac-Man Plus, Super Pac-Man, Mr. and Mrs. Pac-Man, Pac-Attack, Pac-Land*, and *Pac-Mania*. By 1982, *Pac-Man* had become the quintessential eighties arcade icon, Forrest Gumping its way onto the *New York Times* best-seller list,[*] *Billboard*'s Top Ten,[†] and the pages of *People* magazine.[‡] *Pac-Man* wasn't the first videogame block-

---

[*] *Mastering Pac-Man* and *How to Win at Pac-Man* were both best-sellers in 1982. But then, this was the novelty-crazed era when *The Simple Solution to Rubik's Cube* could sell a million copies.

[†] The title song from Jerry Bruckner and Gary Garcia's LP *Pac-Man Fever* hit number nine on *Billboard*'s Top Ten in March of '82, prompting a spin-off single, "Do the Donkey Kong."

[‡] *People*, the bellwether of American mass culture, actively fueled the *Pac-Man* craze by sponsoring a celebrity *Pac-Man* competition hosted by Harry Anderson, pitting sitcom fixtures like Scott Baio, Donna Dixon, and Jimmy Van Patten against the stars of hit shows like *Trapper John, Archie Bunker's Place, Greatest American Hero*, and *The Waltons*. It was a landmark gathering of people who would later turn up as eighties-edition Trivial Pursuit questions. ("Pac-Mania! Scott Baio of *Joanie Loves Chachi* and an Arcade of Celebs Match Wits with the Hot Video Game," *People*, May 31, 1982, 68–70).

buster — *Pong, Asteroids,* and *Space Invaders* had hit, and hit big — but there were no videogame characters per se. Pac-Man had a personality. Sure, it was the personality of a paramecium with only two behaviors — engorge or flee. But he had a certain prokaryotic flair. Women thought he was cute. But most importantly, he gave the player something to identify with. Pac-Man gave videogames a face. And a face, however featureless and crudely rendered, gave videogames entrée into the celebrity-obsessed mass media. *Asteroids* and *Pong* could make money. But Pac-Man could become a star, with the requisite merchandising bonanza. Within months, Pac-Man was on pillowcases, backpacks, lunch boxes, Hallmark cards, and gift wrap. He had his own Saturday morning television show and a Pac-Man Christmas special. As one Midway executive crowed to *Time* magazine, "I think we have the Mickey Mouse of the '80s."*

Of course, Pac-Man wasn't the Mickey Mouse of the eighties, because Mickey Mouse was the Mickey Mouse of the eighties. In economic terms, Pac-Man was a mere flea on Mickey's ear. But when Nintendo launched its own cute, round, colorful arcade hero, the modus operandi was clear: build the videogame character into a celebrity à la Disney, and license, license, license. Nintendo never wanted to be the one-time windfall beneficiary of a hit like *Pac-Man.* They want the whole Eisnerian enchilada. What they want is a comparable collection of billion-dollar superstars who work for free — no agents, no prima donna tantrums, drug habits, sex scandals, or aspirations to direct. Disney has taken thirty years to breed this flock of golden geese. Nintendo took less than a year to vault Mario into that league. In a climate of megadeals and media empires, Nintendo has one eye constantly trained on the Magic Kingdom. Donkey Kong see, Donkey Kong do.

"Well, Disney has a lot more experience at this," says Peter Main, Nintendo's vice president of marketing, "and that's why

* "Pac-Man Fever," *Time,* April 5, 1982, 48.

I unabashedly say we don't care where we borrow our smarts from. Disney's been through it. We try and learn everything we can from publications, conversations, licensing arrangements which we've been involved with them on in the past. We look to them for learning."

Main is one of those impossibly well groomed, silver-haired executive types that you see in commercials for life insurance and mutual funds. His brand of geniality calls to mind golf courses, cuff links, and genteel barbecues. His cuticles are perfect. He has just turned a roomful of truculent journalists into a herd of lambs plaintively bleating for *Super Mario 64* cartridges. And now he is explaining Nintendo's plans to groom its videogame characters into a stable of stars. It's like the old Hollywood studio system. Today, Mario and Donkey Kong. Tomorrow, Yoshi, Kirby, and half a dozen other digital starlets scrapping for a bit part in some 64-bit Mario vehicle. By degrees, Nintendo builds up the visibility of a minor character, and pretty soon, they've got another videogame icon.

"We just passed the billion-cartridge mark in the fall," says Main. "This is the total number of cartridges sold worldwide on our three platforms, which is an astounding number. Mario games, of which there were twenty, account for fully 120 million of those. And therein lies the whole story, I guess. How valuable is this? Why has it been so pervasive? Is it the game or is it the character, I think, is a chicken-and-egg type of question. It's both working together, and importantly, we are preserving the equity in that character between those games so as not to preempt the great expectations."

"It doesn't show on our balance sheet as our most important assets," he says, pausing for a perfect Mutual of Omaha moment. "And yet, at the end of the day, these characters are unquestionably our most important assets. When you can take a character like Mario — and forget about the seven-figure income that we still realize off of Mario year after year after year from people we allow to license it, to put his likeness on a T-shirt, on a lunch bucket, on all these things that happen around the world — if you take 120 million pieces of software and you multiply it by an average of, probably, over the history of this thing, say, thirty dollars, in order to have accomplished that with other people's characters, were we able to sell that many games, you would've had to pay somebody else roughly 15 percent of that amount to borrow the equity in their characters, and that starts to put the real live dollar value on what that thing is worth, and it's staggering. It's over a half a billion dollars in revenue that would've been paid to somebody else."

Nintendo's in-house characters are its crown jewels. And the company is fastidious, to the point of paranoia, about safeguarding their reputations. Every time Mario mugs for a sweatshirt or a soccer shoe, Nintendo chaperones the process. And every licensee is scrutinized as a potential Nick Leeson ready to drown Donkey Kong in a toilet bowl of tasteless merchandise. Main turns stern, puts on his I'm-sorry-ma'am-but-we've-arrested-your-son-for-shoplifting voice, and launches into an exhaustive litany of Mario do's and don'ts.

"We have our own guidelines and character books that say how he's gotta look," he says. "For example, we have guidelines on the very important area of personal appearances. And we do have these $25,000 outfits for Mario and Yoshi and Donkey Kong and long guidelines against what kind of events they can be at and can't be at. They can't be associated with alcoholic products or tobacco products. They can't be involved in any kind of sale. If they appeared at an opening of a new Wal-Mart store, they would never be allowed to say, "Get the great new Mario game over in aisle three at $54.95." They are there. There are poses they can strike. They cannot speak, they cannot touch. You go through all those kinds of things." Having some rent-a-Mario molest grade-school boys in the back aisle of Nobody Beats the Wiz would not do wonders for the Italian Plumber Equity Account. But barring that, well-managed videogame icons yield bumper crops of licensing cash.

Appropriately enough, the man who rakes and hoes Nintendo's merchandise hacienda is Al Kahn — the man who gave the world Cabbage Patch Kids. Burly and bespectacled, Kahn looks like he should be taking fertilizer subsidies for a canola crop in Iowa. For all intents and purposes, he is a corporate ramora, nibbling off of Nintendo's great white shark. People like him — whole companies — exist because characters like Mario and Donkey Kong are famous. Even in the cutthroat merchandising market of the nineties, Nintendo's roster of licensees is staggering. Apart from the usual clothing items — T-shirts, sweatshirts, shoes, bicycle helmets, and other kidwear — there is a line of Mario golf shirts and a license for neckwear and formalwear sets "to include vests, cummerbunds, and bow ties in 100 percent silk and 100 percent polyester." There is a set of fishing rods and reels emblazoned with Nintendo characters. There are comic books and *Donkey Kong Junior* novelizations, prismatic stickers, pogs, and temporary tattoos. There are musical ceramic mugs that chime when lifted, musical ceramic lamps that ring when lit, musical ceramic cookie jars that play when opened, and a musical ceramic coin bank that plays a tinkling videogame theme when a coin is dropped, in gleeful anticipation of the cartridge for which the coins are ostensibly saved. There is a Hong Kong licensee on Hoi Shing Road that's taken Nintendo's Game Boy idiom as an unrelenting theme, suffixing every nugget of plastic and silicon that rolls off the assembly line with the tag "Boy": Watch Boy. Radio Boy. Cassette Boy. Walkie-Talkie Boy. Calculator Boy. There is a Nintendo tabletop "claw" machine, no doubt filled with one or more of the above.

The whole panoply of licensed products reaches its apogee with consumables that are literally consumable: packaged snack foods. In most industrialized countries and a growing number of third world nations, you can actually ingest Donkey Kong and Mario in the form of 3D-pressed dextrose candy, frozen pudding pops, edible molded sugar cake decorations, soft drinks, and dehydrated fruit-based and granola-based portable snacks, not to be confused with the Brach candy company's global, exclusive license for "fruit snacks to include all shapes, forms, and textures including but not limited to items known as roll-ups, bite-size fruit snacks, fruit by the foot, filled fruit snacks, and string thing." And of course, there is the inevitable sweetened cereal license, a Ralston Purina product called the "Nintendo Cereal System," consisting of extruded wheat and sugar morsels shaped like popular Nintendo characters.

Basically, kids will consume Nintendo characters in any wearable, playable, or edible form. With that in mind, Kahn views everything that kids wear, play with, or eat as a potential Nintendo licensed product. He keeps a database of every product category that kids even sniff at, with a list of the relevant companies and what they're churning out.

And it's the little kids that count, because little kids are the ones that gobble up the merchandise. "If little kids like a character, they try to emulate that character by having things around them that assist in that emulation — the clothes, the cups, the lunch boxes and what have you." Kahn sighs at the enormous range of Nintendo products kids can buy to emulate their cartridge idols. "There's a whole litany of things kids will do if they fall for that character." For kids, videogame icons take on the totemic significance that a major-league baseball jacket or a celebrity golf club or, say, Michael Jordan's shoes hold for adults. The idea is that if you consume every Mario artifact you can get your hands on, if you can play the Super NES game in a Mario Brothers sweatshirt while scarfing down an individually wrappaged Mario Brothers snack, then through some mysterious process of celebrity transubstantiation, you can become Mario, or at least take on some of his abilities. It's kind of like Pinocchio in reverse — millions of real boys dreaming of someday turning into a digital marionette.

But once they get to be teenagers, it's all over. They've outgrown the relentless, slavish devotion to licensing that drives the parents of toddlers and preteens out of their minds when a particularly annoying character like, say, Barney, becomes a licensing behemoth. Grade-school kids are the bread and butter of the licensing industry, fortunately for Nintendo, whose audience is skewed younger than its competitors, e.g., Sega, whose teen consumers are already too cool for Sonic sleeping bags and night-lights. 3DO and Sony are similarly unlikely to license lol-

lipops, spiral notebooks, and pencil boxes to the twentysomething set. Atari has become a retro T-shirt in the rave scene, but
that's the extent of it. When it comes to selling videogame
celebrity souvenirs, high school students are a lost cause.

Apparently, so are girls, because they pay attention to their
toys for more than three weeks before moving on to the next
plastic action figure. "Girls are much more independent," says
Kahn. "They make up their own play patterns." And at this
point he's actually frowning, as if this is some kind of problem
to be solved. And then, suddenly, he brightens. "Boys, on the
other hand, need rigidly defined play patterns. If you run out of
story lines, another character comes in and captures their interest. Boys get caught up in one thing after another — when you
lose them it's because they get caught up in something else."

Appropriately enough, this scenario is the premise of Disney's 1996 blockbuster, *Toy Story*. In the film, a young boy gets
a new Buzz Lightyear astronaut doll for Christmas and tosses
aside his faithful cowboy puppet, Woody. The interesting thing
about *Toy Story* is that while the film was made into a beautifully
rendered Nintendo game (Nintendo, in this case, borrowing
from Disney's jumbo piggybank of character equity), there
aren't any videogame products in the movie. Which is odd,
since the average kid's toy chest includes either a Sega or Nintendo machine, or at least a Game Boy or Game Gear. In a
movie composed on Silicon Graphics computers — the same
company that manufactures the guts of a Nintendo 64
console — videogames are conspicuous by their absence. But in
a sense, videogames would have been redundant in *Toy Story*,
because the movie itself sprang from the same technological
tank as *Donkey Kong Country 2*. Woody and Buzz Lightyear were
born digital, flashed briefly onto the silver screen, then slid ef-
fortlessly into the silicon memory of a Nintendo cartridge.
Watching them cavort in a movie theater, under the auspices of
Disney, it was almost as if Mickey were tipping his hat to
Mario.

Chapter 12

Having a Wonderful Time . . . Wish I Were Here

West of House
You are standing in an open field west of a
white house, with a boarded front door.
There is a small mailbox here
— opening lines of *Zork*

Before videogames had characters, there was no need for them to have stories. The plot was pretty restricted: See target. Fire. We didn't care *why*. Who needs a back story for skeet?

But it couldn't last. Eventually, technology allowed game designers to animate squads of thumbnail-sized digital homunculi. And once you had people on a screen, even blocky little stick figures pushing the gestalt of human anatomy, they needed a reason to be there.

Presented with this narrative dilemma, game designers scratched their heads and settled on the same premise that silent film directors had used seventy years before: kidnapping. Dastardly villain kidnaps helpless blond heroine. If it worked for the *Perils of Pauline,* it would work for *Donkey Kong.* Kidnapping is a great story line if you have very limited technology, because it's self-explanatory. See damsel. Rescue her (by jumping over barrels, hitting henchmen with mallets, etc.). You don't need any plot twists or psychological perspective. Players don't care about King Koopa's motives for abducting Princess Toadstool. They just know that Mario and Luigi have to rescue her. That understood, they can get down to the real business of the game, which is jumping and malleting. The choreography of an arcade game *is* its plot. A coin-op contest has a narrative the way that NBA playoffs have a narrative, or the way that *Swan Lake* has a narrative, or the way that Disneyland's movie-themed barge rides have narratives. The drama is motion, set inside a well-designed volume of space. The story is kinesthetic.

For example, *Time Crisis*, a Namco arcade game, has no plotline to speak of. What it does have is a foot pedal that allows you to duck behind crates and around corners while gangster bullets whiz past your head in three-dimensional audio. It's a gut-wrenching Hollywood shoot-out in the dark. It triggers a groovy endocrine response. But have you ever heard someone describe a chase scene? It's like hearing someone describe a luge race. You have to be there. Arcade games may be increasingly cinematic, but it's the cinema of Hong Kong. In a kung fu flick, it's not important why two characters are poised on a particular roof ledge or who's supposed to be avenged. You just want to see them fly through the air. They could recite the Hong Kong phone book, and it would hardly detract from the martial arts movie experience. Likewise, it doesn't matter that there is no dialogue in a Stallone movie. No one cares what he says. They pay to see the pretty explosions. In fact, if the ever-shrinking script of a modern action movie shriveled to its logical extreme (a one-page memo outlining pyrotechnics and facial tics) it would be a pretty decent videogame. No flashbacks. No zippered story lines. Just explosions and fight scenes episodically arrayed like firecrackers on the Fourth of July.

This line of Roman candles essentially defines *Mortal Kom-*

bat: The Movie — the only successful cinematic adaptation of a videogame to date. The martial arts scenes, which begin within five minutes of the opening credits, continue unabated until the end of the movie, with just enough intervening narrative to move from one fight scene to the next and the faintest suggestion of psychological drama furnished by Christopher Lambert. Naturally, costumes are a proxy for character development. *Mortal Kombat* isn't a movie. It doesn't even try to be a movie. It is a ninety-minute arcade session projected onto a large white screen. And if you accept this and just let yourself wallow in the Velveeta, you get to watch a really great videogame played by an ace joystick jockey called the director, who knows all the secret strikes and combo moves and skillfully somersaults through progressively more difficult combat scenes to fight the Big Boss in the end.

This progress from level to level is what keeps the serial plot of a videogame from getting boring. There is no seventh-inning stretch. The action just keeps getting faster and more complicated until you either win or die. Every opponent is quicker, stronger, and more slippery than the last and demands more rapid and complex responses. Each stage pitches the game further up the slope of a long neurological crescendo. This kind of stepwise buildup isn't unique to videogames. You can see it in cultural tributaries like professional wrestling and martial arts comics. After each conquest, a bigger, meaner character appears, and the doughty hero faces a tougher battle.

In a comic book series, this can continue indefinitely in the timeworn cliff-hanger tradition. But on a game cartridge there is only a limited amount of storage space. So at some point the game has to end. And it has to end in a satisfying, climactic kind of way. Hence the Big Boss — the biggest, ugliest, fiercest opponent in any given game, whose demise results in an elaborate rumbling pyrotechnic display and victory screen. The Big Boss emerged as a videogame convention in the mid-eighties with Nintendo's scrolling platform adventures (e.g., *Super Mario Bros.* and the *Legend of Zelda*). Before Nintendo, in the Atari era, home games were based on arcade software, which repeated the same screens over and over. The field in *Asteroids* would become more dense and treacherous. The killer androids in *Robotron* would multiply. But there was no variation in scenery, just an increase in difficulty. This formula was intentionally designed to maximize the quarter-sucking potential of an arcade cabinet. An arcade game's raison d'être is to live in an arcade for as long as possible. The game is supposed to last. And the best way to make it last is not to give it an ending.

Cartridge games, on the other hand, are not built to last, because home console manufacturers do not make money when a kid keeps playing the same game. Cartridge game companies make their money the minute a kid walks out of Toys "R" Us with a new game cartridge, at which point the marginal profitability of that cartridge falls to zero. The only way the cartridge game company makes more money off that kid is if he buys another cartridge in a reasonable amount of time. Voilà, the digital narrative develops a finale. When the Nintendo Entertainment System and Sega Genesis replaced arcade games as the engine of the videogame industry in the mid-eighties, the structure of videogames shifted decisively from the open-ended spirals of the arcade heyday toward the current narrative chassis, which looks like a freight train. The object is not endless replay. The object is to explore the latest videogame universe until the sidewalk ends. Then you buy a new world.

At this point, the videogame becomes an exploratory expedition, with the same atmospheric flavor and narrative hang-ups as any other travel account (equipped the ship, sailed, hit lousy weather, shipwrecked, met the natives, traded or fought with them, plundered, starved, etc., and on and on). As MIT cultural scholar Henry Jenkins has observed, the rescue plot of a Nintendo game is merely a pretext for exploring and colonizing new territory.* Now that Columbus has become persona non grata in the politically correct multicultural worldview,

---

* "Nintendo and New World Travel Writing: A Dialogue Between Mary Fuller and Henry Jenkins," unpublished paper, 1996.

videogames can give millions of little kids the thrill of charting new continents, subduing the savages, and slurping up their treasure, without infecting millions of people with nasty Western diseases. None of the casualties in a videogame are human, and they don't even really die. They just disappear in an evanescent burst of sound effects and bonus points. As virtual conquistadors, we can re-create the Renaissance encounter with America, minus the postcolonial guilt. These virtual New Worlds are the final frontier on a planet that seems to shrink daily.

The final frontier used to be outer space. Previous generations dreamed of exploring other galaxies. Even people in their twenties and thirties can remember watching *Star Trek* reruns and thinking it would be cool to visit another planet. And then in 1986, every schoolkid in America was corralled into a darkened cafeteria or classroom, shushed, and made to watch the space shuttle explode on television. After that, no one wanted to be an astronaut anymore. We just went back to the arcades and shot space all to hell. No one was going to Mars, but there was a whole constellation of videogames to conquer. Virtual space became the last frontier to push against, and the only one that showed no signs of running out. No matter how many platforms, screens, and warp zones you put behind you, there was always a new, more richly rendered world to explore, just in time for Christmas. Sure, videogames were consumer entertainment. But then, so was the space program, which cost taxpayers far more on an annual basis than the national supply of Nintendo games. What was the conquest of space compared to these stunning treks through uncharted fantasy architecture? How could satellite footage of Venus possibly compete with the next screen of *Super Mario World?*

In the alien landscapes of Nintendo and Sega, Mario and Sonic assume the duties and the heroic status of astronauts. They bounce around foreign planetary surfaces and become our gleeful, gravity-defying eyes and ears and our moon buggies through game space. "Mario's journey may take him by raft across a river of red hot molten lava, may require him to jump from platform to platform across a suspended city, or may ask him to make his way through a subterranean cavern as its ceiling collapses around him," writes Jenkins. "The character is little more than a cursor which mediates the players' relationship to the story world. . . . Once immersed in playing, we don't really care whether we rescue Princess Toadstool or not; all that matters is staying alive long enough to move between levels, to see what spectacle awaits us on the next screen."*

As with all competing spectacles, videogames have to offer something even more breath-taking each time the player pops a cartridge into the slot. And so what we get is an ever more elaborate and exotic set of digital tableaux against which the same action repeats:

> Streetfighter II, one of the most popular Nintendo games in recent years, basically centers around a kickboxing tournament which could have been staged in any arena. The game, however, offers players a global array of possible spaces where the individual competitions can occur: a Brazilian dock, an Indian temple, a Chinese market, a Soviet factory, a Las Vegas showplace. All of these details constitute a form of visual excess ("eye candy" as computer enthusiasts call it), a conspicuous consumption of space. Such spectacular visions are difficult to program, unnecessary to the competition, yet seem central to the game's marketing success.†

In a sense, Nintendo does to flying and hopping what Merchant-Ivory does to drawn-out, tentative love stories among pale, repressed people. If you go to a Merchant-Ivory film, you know certain emotional cards will be played with a new set of hairdos and hats, corsets, stagecoaches, and panoramas. If you load a Mario game, you can expect the same kinesthetic con-

---

* Ibid., 11–12.
† Ibid.

ventions applied to a new set of castles, catwalks, and clouds. The geographic novelty runs up against an overwhelming sense of familiarity. It's like a Hard Rock Cafe or Planet Hollywood, where different magical celebrity objects line the walls from city to city but the menu stays the same. Only the eye candy changes. Videogames are the purest kind of entertainment architecture — architecture with no physical substance at all, just production values. These are the theme parks of the mind.

And because cartridges are so disposable, the themes can be completely arbitrary. Manufacturers just keep updating them, depending on the current political climate. During the space race, for instance, alien invaders in videogames were either amphibians or historical hybrids like, say, intergalactic Viking terrorist marauders. Now they're imperialists from a parallel, Asian-speaking dimension or marginalized Earth groups like Nazi skinhead motorcycle gangs. Instead of taking place in some asteroid belt, videogames of the nineties are set in a twenty-first-century one-world state, although they can't agree whether this is good or bad. In the current slew of dystopian CD-ROM adventures, either all the governments of the world have united to fight off the invading enemy, or else they've united to terrorize us all, and they *become* the enemy. One step beyond that, there are game scrims that paint the world in a state of total anarchy. This is the most popular videogame premise of the mid-1990s. It recurs with grim regularity on the shelves of Circuit City and Nobody Beats the Wiz: The world is a bombed-out industrial wasteland ruled by either a totalitarian one-world state or the law of the jungle, sometimes both. The economy is in ruins — all the manuals stress this. Forget lack of food and water, rampant disease, and environmental havoc. The economy is in ruins. The *Dow* is flatlining. This is the seventh seal.

So, OK, the world has gone to hell. Now the aliens invade, not to colonize or enslave us, but as corporate raiders scouting the junk heap planet Earth for scrap parts and recyclable containers. Your mission: Defend the garbage-ridden shambles you call home. Since it's a wreck anyway, you have carte blanche to blow up anything that falls into your path. That's the great freedom of the postapocalypse. If the world's on fire, you might as well grab a can of gasoline and have a little fun.

Millenarianism is a godsend to videogame producers, who can now repackage all the old driving, fighting, and shooting games as Mad Max gladiator contests. In these games, you are not only the hero but also a celebrity, usually a contestant in some globally televised blood sport involving humans and radiated mutants or robots. Namco's *Battle Cars*, for instance, takes place in a twenty-first-century world where "pollution is rampant and the earth's inhabitants become crude and uncivilized. Huge tracks are built to hold races for the entertainment of the public, to keep them amused and under some control. To make the races even more exciting, the cars are equipped with missiles and bombs."[*] Another Super Nintendo game, *Super Smash TV*, takes place on the set of the top-rated twenty-first-century game show in which contestants battle deadly robots to win toasters and sports cars. As you progress from soundstage to soundstage, you graduate from a rifle to spread machine guns, buzz saws, missile launchers, and smart bombs. Along the way, you pick up various keys, and if you have a complete collection of them on the last level, you can kill the announcer and enter the Pleasure Dome, a shining repository of cash and glamorous prizes. Author Neil Postman's critiques of TV have absolutely nothing on *Smash TV*, which delivers a damning indictment of television *and* great graphics. In the world of *Battle Cars* and *Smash TV*, mind-numbing broadcast television is the only force keeping mankind from planet-wide riot. TV makes people stupid, whereas games make them smart (or at least cull dimmer bulbs from the breeding population). Videogames are very snide about TV and entertainment culture in general, even as they feed it. In the future of a postapocalyptic videogame, the media is always the enemy. This is all clearly explained in an ex-

---

[*] Nathan Lockard, *The Good, the Bad, and the Bogus: Nathan Lockard's Complete Guide to Video Games* (Seattle: Adventure Press, 1995), 17.

pensively produced, blockbuster special effects opening sequence at the beginning of the videogame.

These canned expositions are increasingly long, elaborate, and costly. They are meant to imbue the game with narrative depth. Usually, kids just skip past them. Like, yeah yeah yeah, there's a half-hour movie at the beginning of *Wing Commander 3*. When do we get to play the *game?* Just watching video sequences, even if you pace them yourself, is not fun. It's not even really a videogame. It's just stupid remote control tricks. That's why laser disc games never made it past *Dragon's Lair*. The novelty of *Dragon's Lair* was tremendous — it was the summer arcade blockbuster of 1983. Everyone wanted to play it because it looked like a Disney animated feature. It had a traditional movie story: Dirk the Daring rescues the nubile Princess Daphne. But that was just the problem. You had to follow the story. The game was superficially gorgeous, but (like Daphne) it had no depth. In most videogames, certain strategies work better than others, but you have some degree of latitude when it comes to picking up points and dispatching enemies. In *Dragon's Lair*, there was only one real choice in any given situation, and if you didn't hop to it, you got fried. To the mind of a junior high school videogame fan, this is not only fascist but boring. It's like pawing the right rat lever to get your pellet, which in this case was another fifteen seconds of video footage. Once you'd seen someone play *Dragon's Lair* through to the end, there was no real point to it anymore. It was just a television that someone had made really, really difficult to watch by forcing you to punch remote control buttons in a certain order every few seconds just to keep an image on the screen. It was pretty conclusive proof that twitch games did not mix with interactive storytelling.

As arcade games blossomed into hothouse flowers of digital graphics in the late 1970s, another species of entertainment software was evolving in the dark: the text-based adventure game. Hatched on the hulking PDP-10s of academia, prototypes like ADVENT eventually found the light of day in titles like *Wizardry* and *Zork*. The latter, a 1977 mainframe game programmed by Mark Blank and Brian Moriarty at MIT, was originally dubbed *Dungeon*. Accessible through ARPANET (the precursor of the Internet), ADVENT's distinctively wry sense of humor quickly percolated into hacker culture and lore. By 1978, the game had infiltrated virtually every computer lab in the nation. A year later, Blank and Moriarty founded Infocom. And in 1980, the same year that *Pac-Man* and *Defender* took America's arcades by storm, Infocom released *Zork*, the world's first commercially distributed interactive adventure game, for the Radio Shack TRS-80 Model I computer. As *Donkey Kong* hit stateside in 1981, *Zork* slithered from the TRS-80 onto the PC and spawned a successful series of sequels, riding piggyback on the proliferation of personal computers. By 1986, the *Zork* series had sold 750,000 copies — a mountain of floppy disks, even by today's standards.

The key components of *Zork* and its ilk were puzzles, which you had to solve by picking up and using various objects in the course of the game, and rudimentary English commands parsed by a bare-bones syntax program. Instead of manipulating the game with manual devices, like a joystick or a trackball or arrow buttons, you would issue laconic keyboard instructions à la Tonto (Go west. Take lantern). In this fashion, you would make your way on a spelunking treasure hunt through the Great Underground Empire, a subterranean labyrinth of lakes and grottoes, trolls and wild beasts and things that go bump in the night. Because much of the game takes place in unlit caves, you could almost believe that darkness corresponded to the blackness of the screen. The naturally low visibility of a subterranean environment grooved perfectly with the claustrophobic architecture of *Zork*'s underground maze, where descriptive passages illuminated only one step in any given direction, forcing you to grope through a world shrouded in fog. You never knew what kind of puzzle or twist or surprise attack lay around the next dark corner. And so you kept turning corners, just like you would turn the pages of a book. And you kept turning them obsessively for the weeks or months it took to reach the end. Unlike twitch games, which repeated the same half-hour game ad infinitum, computer text adventures were one long string of game play conducted over forty to sixty hours. You didn't start a game like *Zork*. You embarked upon it. You made progress, and you saved your place. And you knew you were going to be on this ride for a long, long time. It was less like picking up a comic book than like cracking *War and Peace*.

In fact, *Zork* was very novelistic. It had a beginning. It had a middle, which was this twisty underground maze. And it had an end. If you talked to two people, both of whom had played the game all the way through, and asked them to write down the story, they would both write down pretty much the same thing. Among game designers, this kind of story world is called a puzzle adventure, and it is trotted out anytime someone uses the term "interactive storytelling," which is supposedly the holy grail of multimedia. We like stories, the reasoning goes. Millions of people go to the movies, and a tiny but dedicated subset of the population even reads books. And we like things that are interactive. Witness the popularity of arcade games, where you can interact with everything on the screen, even if the only way to interact with it is to blow it up. Therefore, an "interactive story" determined by the player should be an exciting design experiment and a sublime game experience, and it should sell like gangbusters.

This is, of course, a myth, from the perspective of both the producer and the player. To make a traditional story truly interactive, a game designer would have to create a branching plot that forks any time the main character has to make a decision. Stay in Hannibal or light out for the territories. Be loyal to Jim or sell him down the river. Act by yourself or team up with Tom Sawyer. At each branching point, the story diverges, creating another set of fictions. The mathematics of this quickly become nightmarish for the designer, who now has the delightful job of writing 256 versions of the same novel. Even if someone tried to do it (and God knows what kind of masochistic soul would undertake this Dickensian task), he'd end up with a narrative sandcastle whose towers and turrets were continually toppling over. Some choices make better stories than others, and constructing a compelling narrative is not a particularly carefree enterprise. It involves a lot of ditchdigging and bridge building and sign posting. And most people don't want to work that hard. That's why they pay authors.

So ultimately, "interactive storytelling" becomes a matter of providing that authorship while giving a player the illusion of choice. In *Zork*'s fictional universe, this meant you could choose your route around territory you already knew — and this world was so idiosyncratic and intricate that it felt very deep, at times unfathomable. And yet the unexplored turf always pointed in one direction, which was the next puzzle (the next expository breadcrumb). You interacted with the puzzles. You didn't interact with the story. Instead, you gradually unlocked a world in which the story took place, and the receding edge of this world carried you through to the story's conclusion.

This tactic is a hallmark of the "free exploration" game, which is sort of a narrative Easter egg hunt using strategically placed characters or puzzles as a way of revealing a predetermined back story. This strategy is instantly recognizable to any murder mystery fan (and why detective fiction lends itself so well to computer games). It's a whodunit, which is to say two stories superimposed. One is the sequence of events that happened in the past, which you can't change but is a very good story. The other is the sequence of events that happens in the present (e.g., you are wandering around trying to solve puzzles), which is a lousy story but is highly interactive. As you hurdle obstacles in the present, you can see a larger picture of the past. This sandwich of interactive and noninteractive stories isn't "interactive storytelling," but the illusion is plausible enough. Piecing together bits of history can feel like an interactive story. This is essentially what happens in *Myst*.

Of course, this is not why *Myst* became the cause célèbre of consumer electronics. *Myst* did not go platinum because it was an intriguing puzzle adventure. The people who bought it were not scratching a heretofore undiscovered itch for phase state logic brain teasers. Many of them never made it past riddle

number one. But that was OK, because they didn't fork over
fifty bucks for a computer game. They paid for the scenery.
Myst was gorgeous — and not just in the sense of being realistically rendered or artistic. At the time, there were dozens of
games with astounding graphics. But they all used very technically impressive artwork to create some kind of hell world filled
with bloodsucking zombies and chain saw–wielding lunatics.
Exciting, yes, but there's only so much time the average person
wants to spend in the rubble of a global holocaust. *Myst* put you
into a world you might actually want to visit, if you only had the
money and time. Its appeal had little to do with problem solving
or some half-buried family drama. It was that you got to take a
vacation on this great island where you could go hiking and
boating and climb trees and be alone as water lapped against a
dock. It was an escape destination, a place where you could fantasize about buying real estate. When all was said and done,
Myst was a grand exercise in virtual tourism. And for lack of
anything better to do with their otherwise useless CD-ROM
drives, a nation of point-and-click armchair travelers made
Myst the killer app of digital multimedia.

A slew of derivative computer getaway adventures followed, relentlessly advertising their scenic attributes in an effort
to out-*Myst* the competition. It's as if interactive entertainment
executives had gotten together and said, "Well, do whatever the
hell you want with the story. Just make sure everyone gets to go
to Cape Cod." Discs like Sierra's *Lighthouse*, for instance, could
have been set on smaller, slightly less fashionable islands in the
same archipelago. Kidnapped father figure — check. Mysterious waterfront property — check. Docks, jetties, lapping tides,
and fog — check.

In a curious burst of synchronicity, Silicon Valley started
pumping out these home computer package vacations right
when "adventure tourism" was becoming a bona fide phenom in
the travel industry. Just as Patagonia, American Express, and
Nike dared you to head for the hills with an arsenal of specialized
outdoor gear, color-soaked ads from Sierra Online, Spectrum
Holobyte, and Bröderbund beckoned you to rappel through the

latest digital dreamscape. They were perfect mirror images: traveling through your computer monitor to some unspoiled natural paradise, or turning the great outdoors into a technical enterprise with a barrage of Gore-tex, Cool-Max, titanium/ molybdenum alloy, graphite casings, and global satellite positioning wristwatches — "Visions of the hills and Souls of lonely places," courtesy of Dow and Dupont. Gearheads sat at their keyboards contemplating Nature, and self-professed outdoorsmen spent hours fussing with their gear.

For a moment, it seemed like the two phenomena would collide, setting off some kind of surreal chain reaction in computer stores and travel agencies. At the height of the CD-ROM-a-rama, a Fodors guide to virtual destinations seemed imminent. Either that or Myst souvenirs (My Dad Went to Myst and All I Got Was This Stupid T-shirt) — or a virtual diorama of every tourist trap on earth stored on optical disc that would let you paste your picture in front of assorted European national monuments, U.S. landmarks, and Mayan rock piles with a custom photoshop application, then print out pictures to show your friends. No one would have to go anywhere anymore. People would just pose amid the seamless virtual scenery.

Now that multimedia producers are over the idea of "interactive storytelling" ("We never really knew what that was, anyway. And besides, it didn't sell"), this kind of elaborate set construction is what the long-form adventure game is about. Rather than building a story, a group of designers and programmers will create a world in which a story can take place. This involves lots of maps and blueprints and three-dimensional renderings and arguments about the lengths of corridors, period furniture, wallpaper patterns, and landscaping. The atmospheric experience of an exploratory adventure world — the prime selling point of CD-ROMs thus far — mostly boils down to style. All the fights a couple might have while restoring a derelict mansion take place among programmers and graphic artists constructing a digital estate from scratch. (The art department wants wrought iron sconces, even though they take twice as long to render on an SGI machine, and the programmers think it's a

complete waste of time. A pitched battle ensues. Insults. Re-
criminations. A teary compromise that satisfies no one.) Instead
of poring over paint catalogs and fabric swatches, virtual world
designers click through screen after screen of pixel palettes and
texture maps. It's a much more elaborate, expensive version of
those virtual home improvements programs that let you map out
your kitchen and see how it would look with different cabinets
and tiles. So while prospective home renovators are rearranging
walls on their home computers, game designers are shuffling
around the furniture in fictional game castles. It's not so much a
storytelling exercise as an architectural undertaking.*

Done badly, this kind of exploratory adventure plays like an
immaculately groomed steeplechase. Done well, it's an atmosphere from which the story seems to emerge and accrete, rather
than pop up piecemeal like ducks in a shooting gallery. These
game worlds are places with stories ground into the dirt and
mixed into the water and bricked into the walls. It's kind of like
what high-tech tinkerers at the Media Lab and Xerox PARC are
doing with flat-panel video screens and computer chips: embed-
ding them into the windowpanes and hallways and doors of intelligent houses. The walls of these future buildings are full of
information, mostly records — voice prints, palm patterns, e-
mail addresses — which suffuse the architecture with digitally
encrypted information. The virtual walls of an adventure game
are also full of information, mostly clues about the past, stories,
secrets, treasure maps, and stuff, which show up as coded mes-
sages in some vaguely Celtic or Mesopotamian script. And you
unlock these indecipherable runes with keys, either literal or fig-

---

* If virtual worlds ever become sufficiently lucrative, electronic publishers will probably try to get famous architects to design them. So you'll be able to play in a world
designed by I. M. Pei or Frank Gehry or Philip Johnson, even if you can't afford to
visit, much less commission, one of their buildings. At some point, Martha Stewart
and Ralph Lauren will put their imprimaturs on CD-ROMs set in insufferably gra-
cious virtual farmhouses and high-beamed seaside bungalows, where at any point in
the game you can take a break from game play to shop — that gnarled wood book-
case may provide important clues, or a lovely accent for your study. Please specify
oak or cherry. Click here to continue *Massacre in the Hamptons*. Click here to order.

urative — other story fragments from other walls. In the futurists' intelligent offices, the code flows through arteries and veins of fiber optics and coaxial cable, carried by the hemoglobin of intelligent agents. In a game, the environment is made of code, so it doesn't need a conduit. Except you. In a game, you're the intelligent agent. Ultimately, these new long-form adventure worlds make the same promise as Ray Bradbury's sentient sci-fi dreamhouse. They respond to you. Depending on the designer's vision, it's either a solipsist dream or a paranoid nightmare: For $39.95, the world really does revolve around you.

"We want a world that reacts to you," says Jeremy Ross, head of game design at Byron Preiss Multimedia, describing his company's *Haunted House* CD-ROM. "So this house, depending on what you do, can get angry at you or it can get spookier and the lights go down, the palette shifts, characters can get more hostile or more friendly."

There are some major advantages to creating the world first and worrying about the characters and plots later — the Old Testament approach to game design. First of all, it's a way around the "Pirates of the Caribbean" syndrome, where you feel like you're on some kind of monorail through the game. You can veer slightly in one direction or another, but you can never go outside the lines. Either the characters push you back into the main lane by implacably parroting the same three lines, or the virtual camera takes you prisoner on a forced march of zooms and dolly shots. That was the annoying thing about *The Seventh Guest,* a best-selling haunted house mystery. You couldn't stop halfway down a hall or up a staircase. It was whoosh! Steadicam up the banister (Care to look around? Too bad. Gotta get to the next plot point. Keep your arms and legs inside the guard rails at all times). Aside from a few designated story objects, you couldn't pick anything up (Don't touch the props, except when the flashing cursor tells you to). It was like being bossed around by a really overbearing invisible director (You wanna get out of this room, you exit around the table, stage right, babe. Or you don't leave at all). If movies are supposed to generate a willing suspension of disbelief, cinematic conventions in an exploratory adventure game do exactly the opposite. They make everything seem like a set. Hotshot digital cinematography doesn't make a digital story immersive.

What makes it immersive is a world where no territory is off-limits, anything you see is fair game, and all your actions have consequences. This is what game designers call a "realtime object-oriented environment," which is to say time moves ahead and the world churns even in places you don't care to look (or haven't found). Characters exist independently. Options shift. Events — some completely beyond your control — unfold in a world that can age. And with this element of passing time, the designer can reclaim a few of the tempo and pacing prerogatives conventional authors take for granted. The volcano explodes at a certain point in time, whether the main character solves the puzzle or not. After pining away, the girl loses patience and marries someone else. With each tick of its internal clock, the fictional world changes. It doesn't cleave to simple story lines. It is a petri dish where complex, semirandom ones incubate, hatch, and grow.

Perhaps the most successful and long-lived of these story worlds is Brittania, the fictional kingdom in Richard Garriott's *Ultima* series. Garriott, the George Lucas of computer role-playing adventure games, has created in *Ultima* a world that people really care about, the same way that they unconditionally adore the world of Star Wars. (Not coincidentally, Garriott now builds new wings onto the Star Wars world by working on Lucas's *Wing Commander* series.) Anyone who's seen the inside of *Ultima* just falls in love with the place and its characters and the sweep of its story. It's great fiction. But it's not written the way a novelist or a screenwriter would write fiction.

"As I've gotten to know more and more fiction authors," says Garriott, "I've compared notes with the process they go through. And a lot of them develop their individual characters in detail, and then say what is their problem in the beginning, and what are they going to grow to learn in the end. That's not the method I've used. Because unlike a piece of linear fiction where the only parts you're going to go through are the parts that are important to the characters' evolution, I have the reverse problem. I have a world. I have a message. And then the characters are there to support the world and the message. They're all parts of the same puzzle, but I have to solve a different set of parts first."

Solving the story-building puzzle from the outside in entails a lot of fictional carpentry and lathe work. But then, Garriott is well accustomed to this, because he didn't train himself to create fiction by writing novels. He cut his teeth making object-oriented environments in a more primitive media. "I grew up playing fantasy role-playing games — *Dungeons & Dragons* and *Tunnels & Trolls* and a whole variety of others. Back when I started playing was the golden era of paper role-playing games. When they began, the people running the games were storytellers primarily, and they were environment creators.

"I was exposed to computers back in 1974, and I began writing games on them immediately. And I would have to type the games in on paper tape and watch them printed out at ten characters per second on a teletype — a typewriter basically. They were very simple. You just wandered around, fought monsters, collected treasures. There was no end to it, no ethical parable or anything of that nature. But it still looked very much like an *Ultima*. You would type in a command like north, south, east, or west, or get a chest, or attack something. And after it would process your command, it would print out a little ten-by-ten grid of asterisks for walls, spaces for corridors, dollar signs for treasure, the letter 'U' and the letter 'D' for up or down letters. So if you just replace that with graphics and speed it up a lot, that's basically what *Ultima*s are today.

"After I got out of high school, my first computer game was called *Alkalabeth*, which was one of these hack-and-slash games but with added graphics. Then *Ultima*s *I*, *II*, and *III* were all mastering BASIC, and then learning assembly language and figuring out how to create a game. I consider that era my 'learning to program' era."

With *Ultima IV*, the twenty-five-year-old Garriott took on another challenge: trying to make his fictional world less violent.

"I had already done three hack-and-slash kind of games and quite frankly, I was bored with that," he says. "Although I never read anything into all the parents complaining that *Dungeons & Dragons* was teaching their children devil worship, I did think that with hundreds of thousands of young people playing my games I had some semblance of personal responsibility. The early *Ultima*s and all of my competitors have what I call standard fantasy role-playing scenario number one, where you're the great hero, and your job is to kill the big bad guy, and what you end up doing is you travel around the world pillaging and plundering, beg-borrow-and-stealing, and doing everything you can until you build up enough magic and power to assault this supposed bad guy, who never did anything to anybody in the game, and you wipe him out and you win. And I thought, there's not much meaning to that.

"At that point, I had mastered the problem of making the game. Anything that I could imagine I now knew I could create. The hardest part of the problem was deciding what is the correct thing to imagine? I wanted to do something with more lasting meaning to it. So I said, OK, the reason why people do good deeds in the world is because it makes sense. If I go around lying and cheating and stealing, nobody is going to help me when I need help. In role-playing games, people generally don't want to feel responsibility for the action a character takes, so they can separate themselves from the person who's going around slaughtering everyone. And that's something I changed in *Ultima IV*. I said, you don't get to be the puppeteer. I want this to be *you*. I don't mean you in the sense of your physique, so if you're this skinny little computer geek, I don't want to mean that in my nice wonderful golden world you have to be a geek. So I'll let you transmute your physical essence any way you want. But the spiritual essence is still you. Your life force is what's driving that character. You are responsible for the actions of that character."

When players returned to *Ultima* in its fourth incarnation, they found that their favorite virtual world had evolved an ethical dimension. It was the same Brittania as before. Only now, everything resonated with moral implications. It wasn't just about slaughtering trolls and pillaging villages anymore. Now you had to roam around trying to become an avatar of honesty, compassion, valor, justice, spirituality, sacrifice, honor, and humility. Of course, if any stray monsters crossed your path, you could massacre them, but the main point of this place was figuring out how to be heroic in a world with ethical consequences. It was really loopy, but hundreds of thousands of kids went along for the ride, mystical spirituality and all, making *Ultima IV* Garriott's first best-selling title.

In a sense, the game grew up with its audience. Every title in the series took the player back to the same place, and everything you remembered was there. Except the fiction had evolved in some respect. Invariably, the visual grain was finer. The sound effects had improved. Still, all the old stories were there, woven into the fabric of the new game as references to earlier *Ultima*s. The game transcended its fictional past, because its fictional past was something that you had personally experienced a few years before as the fictional present. It was as if all the previous *Ultima*s were Russian dolls buried inside the newest and largest one. The world grew by a process of accretion, over itself, until it had acquired an overwhelming sense of place.

This is ironic, considering that computer code is the most ephemeral language on earth, and computers themselves invariably lapse into obsolescence. Any given work of digital fiction has the longevity of a vanishing dialect spoken by a Hutchinson-Gilford victim.* Stories housed on computers are doubly perishable, because their media are obsolescent and also because their craft is still evolving. In this respect, they couldn't be more different from stories stored on paper.

---

* Hutchinson-Gilford syndrome, otherwise known as progeria, is a genetic condition that accelerates the aging process from infancy, turning children into shriveled, toothless, osteoporosed geriatrics by the age of five or six. Progeriacs usually die in their teens of arterial sclerosis or what in an eighty- or ninety-year-old would be called "natural causes."

Nevertheless, Garriott is hopeful about the life expectancy of his world. "Since I'm building off the predecessor to make the next one, you don't really need to go see the predecessor. The predecessor is included. So there's really no need to go back and play many of those earlier games. That's my personal solution to the history problem — just to continue a vein of products for so long that by the time we get to *Ultima 100*, the people playing it will feel a sense of history and craft, and will have an understanding of what came before, all the way back to the beginning, even if those machines and those products have long since disappeared."

Chapter 13
Super^{hero}
Sushi

After walloping her opponent, *Tekken 2*'s heroine, Michelle Chang, swivels within the videogame arena and turns to face the camera, the viewer, the players. And it's a disconcerting moment, because she looks at you intelligently, and there are so many polygons in her face that she almost seems real, and because she is such a confusing mix of signals. She's a slender girl who beats up rippling hypermasculine bruisers. She's computer generated, yet more true-to-life than most of the silicon-enhanced, digitally retouched dreamgirls staring vacantly out from real world magazine racks. She's got an Asian name but ambiguous features — a Western nose, almond-shaped eyes. If you saw her on the street, you'd peg her as Amerasian.

In a way, she is a perfect metaphor for videogames themselves. She's a hybrid, of mixed Asian and American heritage, a creature made possible by the technological innovation of two hemispheres. Videogame characters are a bicontinental crossbreed of American and Japanese pop culture, with elements of Japanese comic books (manga) and animation as well as Western comics and science fiction.

On the Pacific side, videogames' family resemblance to manga and Japanimation are undeniable. In some cases, the games themselves are playable translations of popular Japanese comic books and animated films. In the last decade, hundreds of manga titles have been made into videogames in Japan, crossing over into the United States as manga shifts from cult status to mass acceptance, mostly via MTV. *Dragonball* alone has spawned six arcade games, a dozen titles for the Super Famicon (the Japanese equivalent of the Super NES), and a *Dragonball* Game Boy cartridge.

The salient feature of manga heroes — and the game characters based on them — is a preternatural cuteness and almost freakish babylike quality, which takes the form of oversized heads, tiny noses, and saucerlike, impossibly liquid eyes. This way of drawing characters translated easily into early videogames, which didn't have the graphic resolution to represent characters with adult proportions. Small, cute characters had fewer pixels per inch and were easier to use, and so videogames borrowed, for reasons of expediency, what manga had developed as a matter of convention. Even a character like Mario the Plumber, who's supposed to be an adult, with facial hair no less, is rendered with the roly-poly proportions of a child, like a manga character. You would expect characters to take on mature dimensions as technology enables videogame manufacturers to animate large, complex, realistic forms. But instead, companies like Sega hew even closer to the babyland aesthetic. To paraphrase Gordon Gekko in *Wall Street,* cuteness is good. Cuteness works.

The reason cuteness works, as Scott McCloud notes in *Understanding Comics,*[*] is that abstraction fosters identification. It is only because an animated character is abstract and cartoony that we can project our own expressions onto him. We can't really map ourselves onto truly realistic characters — we see them as objects, separated from us by their details. To use an annoying but useful postmodern term, they read as the Other. The most realistically rendered characters in videogames are

---

[*] Scott McCloud, *Understanding Comics: The Invisible Art* (New York: HarperCollins, 1993).

usually enemies. The good guys are rounded, simplified, and childlike, a puttylike visual glove into which our own hands and faces fit. If anything, early videogames were especially powerful in this sense. The more photorealistic characters become, the less we relate to them. Seeing a cast of TV actors in a full-motion video makes you into more of a spectator or an editor than a part of the story, whereas the polygon people in *Tekken 2* are easy to slide into, and a character like Mario or Sonic is even easier to identify with. A primitive, completely minimal figure like Pac-Man takes this link between pixel and personality to the nth degree. Characters in *Mortal Kombat* have fingers and stubble. You watch them. Pac-Man has one black dot for an eye, and you *become* him.

Videogame companies are well aware of this, which is why their figureheads are all round and minimal and cute, just like, well, jeepers, just like Mickey Mouse. Sega is even working on a version of *Virtua Fighter 2* called *Virtua Fighter Kizu* ("kizu" is Japlish for "kids") where all the adult martial arts characters are rendered with gigantic toddler heads. From a distance, it looks like ferocious dueling lollipops. If you count the height of their hair, the giant toddlers' heads are as tall as the rest of their bodies. The eyes are bigger than their flying fists.

Americans usually read these saucer eyes as Western, as a sign of whiteness. After all, the reasoning goes, Western eyes are bigger and rounder than Asian eyes. This must be the way that they see us. And for some strange reason, they're drawing us all over their comic books. But actually, that's not the case, says Matt Thorn, a doctoral candidate at Columbia University who is writing his dissertation on teen-girl comic books in Japan. "Japanese readers don't think of the characters as white," he says. "Of course, they have these huge eyes. And so to us, the characters do look white, because Westerners expect that the Japanese will represent themselves the way that Westerners represent them. That is, we have these certain standardized ways of indicating to a viewer this character is Asian or this character is black or this character is anything but white, including the slanty eyes and the black hair. And of course, the Japanese don't draw themselves that way. Those characters aren't white, and the readers don't think of them as being white, despite those features. There's a concept in linguistics called the unmarked category. And in the West, which is white-dominated, white is the unmarked category. Everything else is marked and has to be indicated, but white is taken for granted. But in Japan, Japanese is the unmarked category, the one that's taken for granted. They've developed that style with the huge eyes — that's the way that they've developed for drawing people, which means Japanese people. And when they want to indicate that a character is not Japanese, they have different ways of doing it. Like, for white people and black people they use exaggerated features. Like for white people, they'll have big noses or really big bodies or really sharply defined eyelashes."

So within a typical martial arts videogame, the racial continuum is deceptive. It's not a simple matter of ethnic blur. It's a matter of reading the signs in completely different ways. All the indeterminate characters that to Western eyes would read as white look Japanese to kids playing the games in Tokyo. Figuratively speaking, we read these faces left to right. The Japanese read them up and down. This isn't their way of drawing us. It's their way of drawing themselves. Meanwhile, both sets of videogame players look at the screen and think the characters look native. It's counterintuitive. But when you think about it, really, *no one* has eyes that big.

There are characters in videogames that are visibly Asian, the way Westerners would draw Asians. But these characters are never supposed to be from Japan. They are supposed to be from China or Korea or Mongolia or some other part of Asia. "The irony," says Thorn, "is that the techniques that Westerners use to draw Asians are the same techniques the Japanese use when they're drawing Asians other than themselves. So you'll have a manga in which there are Japanese characters, which to us read as white. And then you'll have a Chinese character, and the Chinese character is drawn in such a way as to indicate to the reader that this character is not Japanese but Chinese. And they'll use the same kinds of techniques that we use: the straight black hair, the slanty eyes, etc."

And Americans? Usually, when a videogame character hails from the United States, he's blond. He's broad. He's buff. And he's larger than life, or at least larger than the other videogame characters. He looks more like an American comic book character than a manga hero. And he's not nearly as unassuming and cute. In fact, the more videogames borrow from American comic books, the less cute they get. Whereas Japanese manga characters are generally childlike and unassuming, American cartoon heroes in the Marvel/DC vein are, if anything, hyperadult. "In America," writes comic book historian Fred Schodt, "almost every comic book hero is a 'superhero' with bulging biceps (or breasts, as the case may be), a face and physique that rigidly adhere to the classical traditions, invincibly accompanied by superpowers, and a cloying, moralistic personality."* Like the drawings in a Western superhero comic, American characters in Japanese fighting games have wildly distorted, hyperrealistic, hypersexual bodies. And in American software houses, where Superman takes native precedence over Speed Racer and Astro Boy, the videogames themselves are absolutely devoid of blinking sweetness, offering instead the beloved stateside menagerie of larger-than-life comic book mutants. Capcom's *Marvel Superheroes* arcade cabinet, which is seven feet tall and physically towers over its Japanese counterparts, pumps out sound effects at blockbuster volume and stars veiny, spandex-clad standbys like the Incredible Hulk, Spiderman, and Captain America. The arcade game is, essentially, a moving comic book that replaces Pow! Boom! Zap! bubbles with gut-rattling audio effects. In this way, a Marvel Comics videogame is a more intense comic book experience than the paper it's based on. Comic book characters have always been drawn swooping and swinging and flying through the air. Now they can do it in real time. Comic book videogames are comic

---

* Frederik Schodt, *Manga Manga: The World of Japanese Comics* (Tokyo: Kodansha, 1983), 77–78.

books squared. And with this added dimension the blurry line between comic books and videogames finally dissolves.

This blur between media is epitomized by *Comix Zone,* a videogame for the Sega Saturn. The premise, whose only precedent is Swedish pop group A-Ha's *Take On Me* video, is that your character, Sketch, is trapped in a Marvelesque comic book universe and forced to battle through it, panel by panel, combating enemies drawn by Mortus, an evil comic book artist. Along the way, helper characters yell out from the corner of the screen ("Watch out, Sketch!") in comic book dialogue boxes. The object, ultimately, is to defeat the evil illustrator and rip yourself out of his two-dimensional paper universe. It's like an Escher drawing, where you break out of one trompe l'oeil tableau only to find yourself in another impossible illusion. Beyond the simulated comic book page is a simulated TV cartoon, when, really, there aren't any pages, or any television, for that matter. There are only the conventions of paper and television, twined around each other, to float the action of a videogame.

Of course, to kids playing *Comix Zone* or *Marvel Superheroes* or *Tekken 2,* the distinction between comic book and videogame or Asian and Western is completely irrelevant. The only categories they recognize are "fun" and "not fun." If you walk into an arcade, you don't see white kids choosing white characters and black kids choosing black characters. Kids routinely choose any and all of these options and don't think twice about it, because the only factor in their decision is a given character's repertoire of kick-ass fighting moves. Ironically, all considerations of race, sex, and nationality are shunted aside in the videogame arena, where the only goal is to clobber everyone indiscriminately.

But on a deeper level, the kids playing these games intuitively understand that they're operating in a disembodied environment where your virtual skin doesn't have to match your physical one, and that you can be an Okinawan karate expert, a female Thai kickboxer, a black street fighter from the Bronx, or a six-armed alien from outer space, all within the span of a single game. Members of the previous generation might have a problem with the idea of playing a Japanese schoolgirl in a combat game. At the very least, they would be aware of their decision to choose this character, and maybe even a little smug about being enlightened enough to do so. For kids of the eighties and nineties, shuffling videogame bodies and faces is like playing with a remote control. The game starts, cycles through a bunch of avatars, and you punch the fire button when you see one you like. It's channel surfing.

In this milieu, the classic distinctions between heroes and villains break down. In older videogames, and in all previous media, the good guys look one way and the bad guys look another. It may be as simple as black hats and white hats or as fraught as cowboys and Indians. In movies and TV shows, we know what the hero and the villain are supposed to look like, and those images are very loaded. Heroes talk like midwestern news anchors and own dogs. Bad guys speak with foreign accents and stroke cats. Heroines are slender and blond and adorably helpless. Bad girls have dark hair and red nails and hips and guns they're ready to use. And because of the way these people look, and the way they're lit, it's clear for whom you're supposed to root.

But in an arcade fighting game like *Virtua Fighter 2*, you can't do that, because those categories don't exist at all. You can play any character, and it's every gladiator for himself. This type of videogame doesn't label opposing forces as evil or good, because that would imply a scripted outcome, that the designated "hero" is supposed to win, when really no one is supposed to win. Everyone is supposed to play. It's the skill of the competitors that determines who wins and who loses. In a videogame, unlike in novels or movies or other fictions like history, no one — not even the game designer — knows the outcome of a given contest. And so it's impossible to cast a moral hair light on one character versus another.* There are no heroes

---

* This becomes patently obvious when you play a game like *Tekken 2*, where even the more wholesome characters are monstrously broad-shouldered, earnest, square-jawed, and monumental in the style of socialist realism. This is when you realize that monstrosity is in the eye of the beholder. This is also when you realize that most of the superheroes we hold up for children to admire are freaks.

and villains in a round-robin martial arts game. There are only combatants, each with his or her own special weapons, attributes, and fighting style. In the post–Cold War world, this seems an evenhanded approach. Everyone's a hero. Everyone is also a monster.

Or, to paraphrase the Red Dog beer motto, you are your own monster. Now that the videogame hero is freed from the cosmetic constraints of gallant poster boyhood, you can play a whole menagerie of creatures, from werewolves to ice creatures to dinosaurs. Superhuman strength and/or demonic powers seem to be the only prerequisites for inclusion in the videogame bestiary, which draws from martial arts movies, Arthurian legend, the Greek pantheon, science fiction, Norse mythology, and Jurassic Park. And that's just *Primal Rage,* one of the hotter fighting games of 1996.

Primal Rage is mythic stuff. It's a fight-to-the-death among angry, violent demigods who are also dinosaurs. According to the epic back story, "Before there were humans, gods walked the earth. They embodied the essence of Hunger, Survival, Life, Death, Insanity, Decay, Good, and Evil. They fought countless battles up through the Mesozoic Wars." When these conflicts threatened to destroy the planet, a wiser, more mature deity in another dimension decided to launch a kind of mythological NATO peacekeeping mission to shut them up. "He was not powerful enough to kill the gods," the story goes, "so instead he banished one to a rocky tomb within the moon. This disrupted the fragile balance between the gods; pandemonium ensued, and a great explosion threw clouds of volcanic dust into the atmosphere. The dinosaurs died out, and the surviving gods went into suspended animation. Now, the impact of a huge meteor strikes the Earth. Its destructive force wipes out civilization, rearranges the continents, and frees the imprisoned gods. Get ready to rumble . . ."

The game ensues, throwing you into a kind of fossil fantasy Ragnarok scenario where you choose one of these reptilian gods to fight against all the others. Each of them has its own mythic idiosyncrasies. For instance, the God of Decay has a repertoire of decay-related weapons, most of which involve bodily functions. The God of Survival is a crafty velociraptor lacking in brute strength but incredibly agile and slippery.

In addition to its personal eccentricities, each character also has a coordinated epic backdrop. The fire-breathing Tyrannosaurus rex dukes it out in the Inferno, an active volcanic island oozing lava. The serpentine Goddess of Insanity fights on a Stonehengian knoll under a full moon with petrified enemies planted like lawn sculptures in the background. And, if you make it through all these themed battlegrounds, the final scene of *Primal Rage* is set in a dinosaur graveyard littered with the bones of fallen reptiles. Red cracks split the ground, and a huge vortex swirls in the sky as you leap, bite, and strike as best you can against a very scary-looking, dragonish God of Death. It's a perfect frappé of paleontology and the supernatural, prehistory and the apocalypse. Like the science fiction universe, videogames are where technology melts into the occult. This is a place where missile launchers and mojo are both legitimate weapons. All the old monsters, harpies, dragons, and divinities are excavated from their mythological sediment, sampled, looped, remixed, cross-faded, and digitally recycled. Videogames do to dusty legends what deejays do to vintage vinyl. They weave the old grooves into something accessible to teenagers.

And increasingly, it doesn't matter where those teenagers are. The same way a transcendent house mix leaps from a mixing board in London to sound systems in Tokyo, Los Angeles, and Helsinki, good videogames have a way of becoming popular everywhere. It's all digital. And a certain echelon of global youth all have access to the technology. So if it's fun, it quickly goes transnational. And in the process, it ceases to connote nationality. A successful dance track or videogame doesn't read Japanese or American, German, or British. It's all just pop. And it's yours for fifty cents.

The finest digital architects on the planet have built these playgrounds out of comic books, Hong Kong cinema, scroll paintings and music videos, ancient monsters and digital technology. They pour in their myths and suck out quarters.

And this is what it's about, finally, as the cultural streams of East and West swirl into the Tastee-Freez of global entertainment. Mythic figures resonate, all the more if they're engaged in some kind of combat or action adventure, real or simulated, the most popular forms being basketball and videogames. They resonate for the same reasons mythic figures have always resonated. Only now, the audience numbers in the millions, and the object is not to celebrate ancestors or teach lessons or curry favor with the spirits. It's commerce. And the people transmitting their stories to the next generation aren't priests or poets or medicine women. They're multinational corporations. And they are not trying to appease the gods. They are trying to appease the shareholders. It's not just videogames. It's everything, with the possible exception of the Internet. All the mythic pop stars in Hollywood, the NBA, and MTV are purchasable commodities. Videogames are just the logical extreme, because all the superheroes in them are computer generated for maximum resonance and marketing kick. Unlike sports stars or actors, they don't get addicted, arrested, or petulant. They perform. They may look and act superhuman. They may throw lightning or breathe fire. And when you're in the game, they may really inspire or scare you. But unlike the mythic monsters that preceded them, videogame demons are caged in their arcade cabinets, firmly under the control of their corporate wardens. Demigods used to make people docile. Now it's the other way around. It is Sega and Namco and Capcom and Williams Entertainment, finally, that have tamed the dragons.

Chapter 14
Boys versus Girls

Shortly after videogames became icons, one thing became glaringly obvious: This was a Guy Thing, programmed by and for males. When girls got near an arcade game, they were probably watching their boyfriends or brothers compete. Much to the chagrin of videogame manufacturers, half of the teenage population was conspicuously nonplussed. In an effort to attract girls, game companies tried a variety of stunts, the most successful being Namco's videogame character in drag: Ms. Pac-Man. In 1981, Ms. Pac-Man was the Gloria Steinem of videogames. She could do everything her male counterpart could do, backward, forward, sideways, and wearing a jaunty pink bow. She used the hear-me-roar feminist honorific. And she attracted legions of young women who fantasized about going on a rampage and consuming everything in sight. *Ms. Pac-Man* was an enormously successful game, because it was an oasis for the teenage girls in any arcade. There were a few others: *Centipede, Nibbler, Q*Bert, Burger Time,* and *Frogger*. These games invariably diverged from the standard shoot-and-slay premise and had better-than-average sound effects and usually featured some whimsical, cuddly character. Most of them were as difficult as the panoply of side-scrolling shooters. But were less homicide oriented.

Frogger, for instance, was hugely popular with girls. If you saw a cluster of teenyboppers in a video arcade in the mid-eighties, odds are they were standing in front of a *Frogger* machine. Consider: It is impossible to be aggressive in *Frogger*. The object of this game is to dodge traffic and avoid falling off logs so that you can reach your little frog nest safe and sound. It's a curiously nonconfrontational game. There are no villains to make you feel important and stoke your ego by challenging you to single combat. You're not considered a threat. You're not even acknowledged. Motor vehicles don't veer to run you down. Waves don't sweep up to wash you overboard. None of the obstacles in *Frogger* have anything, personally, against you. They just happen to be deadly. And you just happen to be in the stupid position of dashing through highway traffic and crossing a river with no idea how to swim. You can't kill anything. You can only die. It's like crossing a minefield (*Mine Sweeper*, not coincidentally, was also a hit with girls). This is a game of don't-hurt-anything-but-just-don't-screw-up, just like *Pitfall*. Just like *Tetris*, which is more popular with women than any other game and notoriously addictive among female professionals.

Tetris is a very simple game — an animated puzzle that forces you to rotate and connect geometric shapes at a continually accelerating rate. Essentially, *Tetris* is about coping. It's about imposing order on the chaos. It's about detritus raining down on your head, trash falling into messy piles and piling up until it finally suffocates you. This is a scenario to which many modern women can relate. The challenge is to divide your attention somehow, so that all the runaway fragments fall into neat stacks and *the mess goes away*. The psychological payoff for the player is a state of rapturous relief. "Yes!" she thinks. "Yes! The Mess is vanishing! I can make the Mess disappear!" It's not about blowing things up. It's about cleaning things up. *Tetris* speaks volumes about the difference between women and men vis à vis videogames.

Barbara Lanza, a Byron Preiss game designer and gender-theorist-at-large, has a few ideas about *Tetris*'s popularity with women. In conversation, she is overwhelmingly voluble, staggeringly candid, and cheerfully bossy — a combination of Dr. Ruth Westheimer and Lucy from Charles Schulz's *Peanuts* comic strip. Her videogame gender theories basically boil down to: Boy Games Are From Mars, Girl Games Are From Venus.

"All desires to be politically correct to the contrary," she says, "boys and girls really aren't the same, especially when they're little. They may become more similar as they grow older, but when they're young, they're really not like each other. They're looking for different things. Girls are looking for experiences, and boys are looking for bragging rights. And also, boys are looking for something that they can learn to do that mostly takes perseverance. A guy will say, 'Look what I did — it took me three hours, but I got to level fifteen. Isn't that great?' A girl will look at that and say, 'Let me get this straight: you spent three hours, *three whole hours*, pushing a button so that you could get a phosphorescent glow on the screen. Run that by me again? And you say this is cool?'"

Lanza refers to *Ms. Pac-Man* as a paragon of distaff game design. "What in the world did *Ms. Pac-Man* do that other games of the time didn't do?" she asks. "First of all, the fact that it was called *Ms. Pac-Man* was extremely important. Rule Number One: If you're selling to girls, make it very clear that that's who you're selling to. They're highly socialized. They need permission. One of the cool things about *Ms. Pac-Man* was that it told you right off the bat: This is a female game.

"Now, aside from the fact that it was labeled for girls, *Ms. Pac-Man* has a very interesting game strategy. Notice that in *Ms. Pac-Man* nothing is shooting at you. This is extremely important: the fact that you are not a target. That allows you to cruise around and think about what you want to do. You get to sit back and plan more strategy, because you're not dodging things, because you're not being shot at. Being able to go forward, backward, left, right was extremely important. See, in a normal, typical side-scrolling game, you have to go from left to right. You can retreat if you want to, but it's not going to advance you in the game. It's really not part of the basic strategy. Retreating for a female is like breathing. We're used to the idea that you can win by giving ground. We get into a situation we think is too tight, we back off, we turn around, we find another way to attack it. You can go around it. You can avoid it. You can retreat. You don't have to go straight forward full speed ahead all the time. But too often, in traditional computer games, that's all you're allowed to do. You've got to do it their way. *Ms. Pac-Man* works because you can retreat. You can sneak up on your opponents. We're very big on sneaking up.

"These are the truly big selling points of *Ms. Pac-Man:* the fact that you could retreat, the fact that you could sneak up on your opponent, the fact that nothing was shooting at you but you could go and get *it*. Being chased is not the same as being shot at. Being chased can be exciting. Being shot at can be damned annoying." It's not that women are averse to violence per se. When properly presented, it can be quite appealing — witness the current female vogue for handguns, kickboxing, and *Virtua Cop*. But punching the fire button 380 times a minute is not a twelve-year-old girl's idea of fun.

The problem is, videogame designers, being mostly male, can't seem to figure out what girls want in a videogame.* Even if, at some point, a topflight videogame company in Japan or Silicon Valley decided to woo would-be female gamers, it's doubtful that a bunch of guys who've spent their lives clutching a joystick could design something that resonates in the mind of a fourteen-year-old girl. And it's a dubious assumption that they would even try — this is not the kind of swaggering, high-status project that traditionally attracts hot-shot designers. Like, oh yeah, what are you working on? *"Doom 5*. What are you working on?" Cough, mumble. *Sassy: The Game*.

Catering to boys is much more fun. Videogame companies are very good at it, and it makes them rich. And they don't want

* This is an industry where "Females and Adults" is a categorical descriptor, used in the kind of automatic way that "women and children" is used aboard sinking ships or to describe wartime casualties.

to mess with a winning formula. At this point,
Christian Slater in *True Romance,* the indus
toward females is motivated by two things: f
There's a lot of money to be made if you can sel
On the other hand, there's a fear of developing
Because if you make a game that looks like it's too friendly to girls, the boys will ditch it in one hot minute, because boys don't want to play girl games. Stereotypes congeal at a tender age.

According to Justine Cassell, a cognitive psychologist at MIT's Media Lab, kids of both sexes make sweeping generalizations about gender just as soon as they can pronounce the word "cootie." "By age three," she says, "children are sex-typing games. Little girls will say, 'Oh no, that's a boy toy.' At three they start to do that with household objects like brooms and hammers. Those gender stereotypes are pretty fixed, and we know that you can get gender stereotyping for objects, professions, and traits — they can do all that by age five. We know that those girls who want to be girl-girls are going to stay away from aggressive activities because they would be betraying their gender alignment."

This begs the question, what type of game would actually appeal to girls without making them traitors to the prepubescent idea of femininity? The consensus (among people who don't make videogames) is that storytelling is a key element in what girls do for kicks. "Girls are very interested in narrative play," says Cassell. "There are patternists and dramatists. Patternists are people who enjoy numbers for their own sake, or putting puzzle pieces together. And dramatists are people who enjoy telling stories. Technology toys can also be divided into pattern toys and drama toys. And girls like drama toys. They like telling stories. Girls will tell stories about anything. I remember doing a biology assignment when I was in fifth grade about hydrogen and oxygen falling in love and setting up house together. And that's a very common girl approach to science."

The irony is that all this story-oriented play requires more sophisticated engineering than the most brilliant twitch response games. It's much easier to create a spatial dimension ɦan a social dimension. Computers were designed with spatial logic in mind. They were not designed to deal with interpersonal interaction and storytelling. Making a game based on social logic presents some incredibly thorny code problems and may not be possible with today's technology, which is mostly good at making pretty pictures spin around in complicated ways. For boys, this is wonderfully satisfying. Girls are quickly bored by it and demand breakthroughs in artificial intelligence.

This does not imply that girl games are necessarily gentle or friendly. Girl games can be just as ruthless — in some ways, more ruthless — as a round of *Mortal Kombat*. But there aren't as many open gunshot wounds and gushing bodily fluids. It's much more abstract. It's more subtle. It involves volleys of deftly inflicted psychic trauma. Science fiction writer Orson Scott Card said it best: "For those of you who think that girls are immune, remember that playing with dolls is another manifestation of power fantasies: all those lovely little people, always doing *exactly* what you want."*

In this spirit, Mattel has recently decided that what girls want in an interactive entertainment product is — you guessed it — Barbie! For $44.99, the *Barbie Fashion Designer* CD-ROM lets girls six and up mix and match Barbie's wardrobe and then force her to model these kicky vacation outfits and wedding gowns ad nauseam in virtual reality. You are the art director. You are the fashion police. You are the pint-sized image consultant who sends Barbie's 3D polygon avatar vamping down the perfect plane of a cartoon catwalk, hips swaying, her newly composed fashion statement swinging in the viscous Silicon Graphics atmosphere. She does a little swivel at the end of the runway, tips her chin, and smiles the quintessential Barbie smile — a flawless cheesecake come-on designed to spark girlish yearning for these fabulous computer-generated clothes. But not to worry, they can be yours! You *can* conflate fantasy and reality. Because *Barbie Fashion Designer* lets you print these ensembles on special ink-jet-compatible sheets of white fabric,

---

* Orson Scott Card, "Power Fantasies, Moral Responsibility, and Game Design," *Compute*, May 1989, 10.

cut them out, and tape them onto the real live plastic Barbie dolls you already own (the average girl apparently owns eight). This is what girls are supposed to want from Pentium PCs circa 1997.

But then, it's only fair that girls should get to see Barbie dolls on computer monitors, because boys have been seeing them for years. Until very recently, videogame heroines have been ornamental and completely incapable of any action — "window dressing," in industry parlance. They were scrumptious, partly because they were used as some kind of Cracker Jack prize — if you made it to the end of the game, the kidnapped princess appeared as a reward. But they were also scrumptious because they were part of a superhero universe where all the men have lantern jaws and broad shoulders and all the women are busty and nippy waisted. Videogames are like comic books that way. They drive visual ideas of femininity and masculinity to opposite poles of hyperreality.

That's just the nature of the beast — the beast being videogame designers rather than the medium itself. "It's an unspoken thing" says Brenda Garno, who designs role-playing adventures for Sir-Tech Software and is one of the few female veterans of the industry. "If a guy says, listen, there's two characters in this scene, Mary and Bob. Do me a 3D rendering of them. Mary, ten times out of ten, is going to have a big chest, tiny waist, and blond long hair or brown long hair. It's just accepted, because there aren't women in the industry right now. I don't think necessarily the male role in games has been that defined. Well I did, in a way, with this *Druid* guy. I actually sent a fax to our artists saying, 'I want him to look this way: Well-defined chest. Well-defined arms. Stomach blocks. Great ass. I'm definitely guilty of reverse sexism there, no question. This guy is exactly what I would like to look at when I get up every morning."

She sighs. "Maybe we need more female designers. We need people to start saying, listen, we're sick of being window dressing. Can you tone down the chest? Can you tone down the hips on that lady? Can you present us as just a little bit real?"

Female videogame characters may not be getting any more

real, but they are becoming increasingly dangerous and, in some cases, damn scary. With the rise of fighting games as the preeminent videogame genre, female characters have become players. They are not window dressing. They are lethal. And in games that take their cue from Marvel comics, they are flamboyantly lethal, in a distinctively female way. If videogames are a bastion of death-mongering hypermasculinity, these are the digital Valkyries. *FX Fighter,* for instance, has two female gladiators, one of whom, stylishly decked out in a vinyl v-kini, thigh-high boots, and opera-length gloves, delivers a crushing knee-to-groin attack. The other, a hellion with Mandarin talons, has a list of martial arts combinations such as Claw Charge, Swipe Claw, and Face Rake. *Mortal Kombat 3* has comic-book she-demons in abundance, including a white-haired harpy who shrieks her opponents into stunned helplessness and has the choice of two Fatality Moves: "Screamer of the Week," which leaves her foe windblown and skinless, and "Hair Spin." The latter involves a whiplike action of her silver 'do, which cocoons a hapless opponent, then retracts, spinning him into an explosion of limbs and blood. And lest *Mortal Kombat 3* fall short on racial diversity, the roster also features an eight-foot black female bodybuilder from Hell (literally) who bleeds green and wears heavy metal cuffs on all four arms. Alternating Fatality Moves, she'll either punch your head off with a strong uppercut or literally skin you alive. Both of these pumped-up, anabolic gorgons have a very obvious adult sexuality that's incredibly intimidating, especially to adolescent boys. I mean, what could be more frightening to a thirteen-year-old than a fire-breathing monster with triple-D breasts?

In videogames that draw from Japanese cartoons, the women are more proportionate and less threatening. That wide-eyed Japanese cuteness makes them more approachable. They'll still pummel you in combat. They'll still humiliate you. But they're sort of girlish about it. In *Street Fighter 2,* there's a Mary Lou Rettonesque character named Chun Li who wears miniature Princess Leia hair buns. And when she wins a fight, she jumps up and squeals. Another Sega game, *Fighting Vipers,* is a

veritable United Colors of Benetton ad: a Zapatista butch goddess in combat pants and dog tag earrings, a black martial
artist/inline skater whose retractable razors give the phrase
"roller blades" new meaning, an Asian schoolgirl whose lace pet-
ticoat, white angel wings, puff sleeves, and pigtails belie her fear-
some force, and Picky, a skateboarding gamine who proves that
this slacker stunt vehicle can also be used as an effective
weapon.*

Not surprisingly, this latest crop of winsome female videogame ninjas have become pinups for the discerning readers of
Electronic Gaming Monthly. And every year, they become more
important to an arcade game's success. The unveiling (so to
speak) of a new chick gladiator is a major event — they are to
videogames what future model dream cars are to automotive
trade shows. Guys are crazy about them. And why not? A martial arts superbabe is the girl next door who'll also trounce you
with a heart-melting smile. Case in point: Sarah Bryant, the
reigning queen of 3D polygon fighting game characters. She's a
Jeet Kune Do expert built like an Olympic swimmer.† She's not
delicate or curvy. She's not even particularly thin. This woman
has powerful shoulders and strong legs, and she's tall — usually
taller than her male opponents. All in all, she's considerably
more realistic than Pamela Anderson.

And there she is in the pages of *Next Generation* magazine,
lounging, poolside, seen from below against blue sky, as if some
virtual cameraman had crawled up to her deck chair on his belly,
as well he should. She's a monumental babe. And so casual! A
few stray polygon hairs flying away from her blond ponytail (not
too neat, nice touch), sunglasses on top of head, a tropical drink
in red-fingernailed hand, eyes closed, soaking up the sun, confi-

---

* Not to miss a cross-marketing opportunity, Sega has also designated Picky as a shill
for the Pepsi Corporation. The Pepsi logo is texture-mapped onto her skateboard,
and a Pepsi billboard and truck are in the background of all her fights. Score one for
product placement.

† And a rather modestly attired one at that — blue head-to-toe halter bodysuit, black
boots, black gloves. You can see her arms, basically. This woman is dressed for business, not for show.

dently buff. There's even a vital stats sheet, à la *Playboy*, but quelle différence: "Height: 5'10". Bust: You wish . . . Waist: you in 30 seconds. Weight: You'll know when I body *slam* you! Ambitions: To kick everyone's butt and achieve world peace." All of this on a seventeen-by-twenty-one pullout poster under the headline "Sarah Bryant — She'll break your heart, then kick your butt." This is a wonderful message for the adolescent boys of North America. And they lap it up.

In the videogame industry, what teenage boys want, teenage boys get. And if they want pixillated distaff superheroes, boom, hundreds of millions of dollars are spent to flood raster monitors with female mercenaries. At the Electronics Entertainment Expo (E3), the numero uno videogame showcase in North America, 1996 was the Year of the Woman.* The EEOC couldn't have laid down a more messianic affirmative action policy. In Namco's new fighting game, *Soul Edge,* half of the characters are female, and so very multicultural — the Viking warrior princess with flying blond braids and the deadly Thunder Strike, the ninja assassin armed with windmill kicks and shooting stars, and an Asian highland nomad with combination moves like "Sparrow's Rush," "Spinning Sparrow," and "Mountain Crusher." In the space of an hour, dozens of guys line up to play this game, and every single one of them plays a chick fighter.

At the Capcom pavilion, a herd of fifty-five die-hard male game fans cheer as Chun Li fights a mirror image of herself on a twelve-foot screen overhead. The players controlling these dueling cupcakes are both guys, Capcom employees at the con-

---

* The notable exception to E3's femme fever is a GT Interactive title, *Gender Wars,* a combat strategy game set in the future, when men and women have decided that they can't even bother living together anymore and are instead engaged in commando warfare. At the beginning of the game, you get to choose your gender (this is, after all, the nineties) and conduct a guerrilla campaign against the opposite sex. So if you choose female, for instance, you have to select your squad leaders and troops and then accomplish missions like planting a listening device in the male central computer, killing off the military leader, blowing up the ammo supply, and stealing sperm samples from the enemy compound (why men would leave sperm samples hanging around the barracks is anybody's guess).

trols of a *Street Fighter 2 Alpha* cabinet. Initially, their enthusiasm seems to be fueled by the same impulse that makes men tune in to *Foxy Boxing* and the female segment of *American Gladiators*, that kind of let's-see-the-girls-get-all-greased-up-and-sweaty leer-o-rama. But no. When one Chun Li hits the mat and disappears, her doppelgänger squares off against an outsized martial arts ogre and wins, and the audience goes absolutely nuts. These are straight, white, middle-aged men screaming at the top of their lungs, "You go, girl!" And after the demo ends, they all line up at the machine so that they can play Chun Li, too.

At the Viacom booth, the trophy game is *Aeonflux*, starring MTV's favorite jackbooted female assassin kicking, diving, ducking, and pistol-whipping her way through a combat strategy game for the PC and Sony Playstation. A short distance away, Acclaim is showcasing a mystery adventure game, *D*. In this game, you play a young woman whose physician father has gone on a murderous rampage in Los Angeles National Hospital, and you have to wend your way through a labyrinth of blacked-out medical wards to track him down. (Spoiler: It turns out doctor dad is a vampire who at one point tries to convert you, and you have to decide in the end whether to kill or join him. Try *that* for psychodrama.)

But for aesthetic violence, these titles pale in comparison to the gothic fantasy world that is *Meat Puppets*. Part H. R. Giger, part Frank Herbert, part *Terminator 2*, the demo for this game begins with white letters on a pitch-black screen: "One girl. One gun. One game."

"Once upon a time . . .

"Someone gave an angry young woman . . .

"A beautiful, beautiful gun . . .

"(The gun was friend) . . .

"So Lotos Abstraction, as she was known, went out to play."

And then we see the hero of this game, this female Terminator character — sharp and angular and vaguely metallic — go ballistic. She sneaks up behind an effete enemy officer, puts a chain gun to his head, and pulls the trigger. She kicks over a large glass vat containing a hyperencephalic alien, which flops helplessly as its amniotic bath traces rivulets through shattered glass. At which point, she kicks down hard on its grotesque exposed brain, releasing a torrent of black goo.

It's tempting to think that, at last, someone understands.

But alas, these games aren't designed for girls. These are the same brilliant boy games in drag, and 95 percent of the people playing them are guys. While girls are busy playing *Barbie Fashion Designer,* guys are jostling to play female kickboxing champs and action adventure heroines. They're playing these empowered women, kicking ass and taking names while their sisters concentrate on making computerized mannequins look glamorous. When it comes to videogames, *teenage boys* are the ones with positive female role models. It's painful to say this, but boys' games have the only female characters worth playing.

They *always* get the cool stuff first.

Chapter 15
Moral Kombat

Of course, *Doom* was far from the first violent videogame. By the time it became a phenomenon, videogames had been incorporating some degree of violence for more than a decade. Given the technology, violence was the obvious first choice for a videogame premise: put a target in front of the player and have him shoot in its general direction. At some point the target shoots back until one of them dies. It's self-explanatory, interactive, and highly entertaining. It's also damned easy to program. After twenty years, we've got bigger and faster machines to make the whole production more sophisticated and realistic. But arguably, videogames haven't gotten much more violent since we started blowing apart Space Invaders. They've just acquired more graphic resolution. Not as much as television cop shows. Not as much as the latest Stallone, Schwarzenegger, or Bruce Willis vehicle, all of which feature more blood, bigger explosions, and higher body counts. Videogames are closer to Wile E. Coyote than Quentin Tarantino. They're a cartoonish parody of real-world violence.

But even at their most abstract, videogames have the power to shape behavior — the behavior of social guardians. Videogames inspire unstinting hysteria among adults in positions of bureaucratic authority. In the heyday of arcades, no less than the redoubtable surgeon general, C. Everett Koop, felt compelled to rail against the subversive impact of videogames on the nation's youth. "Children," he warned, "are into the games body and soul — everything is zapping the enemy. Children get to the point where they see another child being molested by a third child, they just sit back.* This official fear and loathing came in the absence of any conclusive research on the psychological impact of videogames. There was none.† There still isn't. There were, however, a bunch of suburban kids loitering after school, ditching classes occasionally, and pouring loose change into newfangled machines for a form of entertainment their parents didn't understand. It wasn't jukeboxes in 1953. It was arcade machines in 1983. But it was still adults freaking out about their precious darlings being driven to new heights of deviancy by popular media.

---

* Koop delivered this jeremiad at a meeting of the Western Psychiatric Institute and Clinic. Cited in the *Journal of Applied Social Psychology* 16, no. 8, 1986, 726.

† Egli and Myers (1983) argued that videogames are a social activity "and not as 'addictive' or 'compulsive' as it might at first appear," citing data from a large survey of L.A. arcade teenagers — 68 percent of them had an academic average of C or above, over 50 percent had full- or part-time jobs, and 39 percent participated in extracurricular activities in school. The majority played less than half the time they were inside arcades, spending the rest of the time watching other kids play or talking to their friends ("The Role of Video Game Playing in Adolescent Life: Is There a Reason to Be Concerned?" *Bulletin of the Psychonomic Society* 22, no. 4, 1984, 309–12). McClure and Mears (1986) found that high-frequency videogame playing does not correlate to neuroses, conduct disorders, drug use, school problems, unstable, abusive family life, psychopathology, or speeding tickets, for that matter ("Videogame Playing and Psychopathology," *Psychological Reports* 59, 1986, 59–62). G. D. Gibb et al. (1983) concluded that there is "no evidence to indicate that the games encourage social isolation, anger, antisocial behavior, and compulsivity. The data clearly show, for both males and females, that there were no significant differences between high- and low-frequency videogame users along the personality dimensions of social withdrawal, self-esteem, and social deviancy. . . . Both males and females also scored significantly lower on the personality dimensions of obsessive-compulsiveness than the norms established in this measure" ("Personality Differences Between High and Low Electronic Video Game Users," *Journal of Psychology* 114, 1983, 159–65). Kestenbaum and Weinstein (1988) went one step further, arguing that videogames are actually a release, rather than a trigger of teen aggression ("Personality, Psychopathology and Development Issues in Male Adolescent Video Game Use," *Journal of American Academic Child Psychiatry* 24, 1988, 329–33).

After all, videogames elicited primal, heart-pounding endocrine reactions, *clearly* anomalous in junior high school boys.
(Not coincidentally, the first wave of baby-boomer offspring
was hitting its teens right around this time.) Suddenly, little
Johnny wasn't a well-behaved grade-schooler anymore. His
bloodstream was awash in adrenaline and testosterone, and he
wanted to smash things. Obviously, videogames were making
him violent. Not only that, but videogames were also insidiously
luring him away from home, to the video arcade, a horrible,
dangerous place where he might come into contact with all sorts
of social undesirables, blue-collar kids, maybe even blacks and
Hispanics. Clearly, videogames were a first-class ticket to delinquency.

With this in mind, town fathers across the country embarked on a crusade to banish the evil games from their communities, or at least protect minors from their corrupting
influence. "Children are putting their book fees, lunch money,
and all the quarters they can get their hands on into these machines," said the mayor of Bradley, Illinois, who reported seeing
"hundreds of teenagers smoking marijuana in a video arcade in
a nearby town."* To safeguard the pubescents of Bradley, the
city had just passed an ordinance shutting kids under sixteen
out of videogame arcades. Towns like Snellville, Georgia,
banned videogames outright.† And even large cities passed laws
restricting arcade hours for minors. It's amazing, in retrospect,
to think about the prospect of having to present ID to get into a
video arcade. But yes, we were actually carded at the door (of
course, this only made the arcade a more attractive teen destination and prompted thousands of adolescents to acquire the
fake driver's licenses they would later use to buy alcohol).
Videogames were actually classed with cigarettes and liquor as
purchases that required legal proof of age.

But then, to listen to cultural critics (many of whom had

---

* "Videogames — Fun or Serious Threat," *US News & World Report*, February 22,
1982, 7.
† "Video Game Fever — Peril or Payoff for the Computer Generation?" *Current
Health*, September 1983, 24–25.

never played a videogame before writing diatribes on the subject — or played three games of *Robotron*, only to be humiliated
by a nine-year-old), you would have thought that arcade consoles came equipped with some hidden intravenous device. Just
as the Reagan administration was charging full throttle into the
War on Drugs, op-ed pieces about videogames ran inky with language of addiction. America's youth were being "hopelessly
hooked" on videogames, falling from straight-A grace into arcade junkiedom. Descriptions of *Donkey Kong* contenders at the
local mall read like World War I era portraits of morphine
addicts fixing in opium dens of the Far East. The glazed eyes.
The slack jaws. The telling unresponsiveness to reporters — a
sure sign of minds blown beyond recognition.* Eventually,
videogames were blamed for destroying the minds of a generation and generally sending society on a toboggan ride straight to
hell.

The crusade against these demonic, lurid entertainments
reached fever pitch in 1991 with a book by Eugene Provenzo,
professor of education at the University of Miami. Entitled
Video Kids, its basic argument is that videogames are driving
children insane and irreparably eroding the moral fiber and
team spirit of America's youth. "There are no conscientious ob-
jectives in the world of video games; there is no sense of community; there are no team players," he writes. "Each person is
out for himself. One must shoot or be shot, consume or be con-
sumed, fight or lose."† He also deplores the fact that popular
videogames are "based on themes of the autonomous individual
acting against the forces of evil."‡

But these themes are hardly new — they'd already hard-
ened and dried when John Wayne swaggered onto the silver
screen. That's what we do in America: glorify autonomous indi-

---

* This, despite the fact that anyone who's ever actually watched kids play
videogames knows that they squirm, grimace, and yell like fully grown sports fans.
† Eugene Provenzo Jr., *Video Kids: Making Sense of Nintendo* (Cambridge, Mass.: Harvard University Press, 1991), 118–19.
‡ Ibid., 126.

vidualists. What else would we possibly glorify? The autonomous collective? One can only imagine the kind of arcade game that would pass muster with the leather-elbow-patch set (leap over the running dogs of capitalism, liberate the oppressed proletariat, and accumulate enough petition power points to defeat the evil Murdoch). And as for this nasty, brutish social reality fostered by videogames, let us examine, for a moment, the social reality based on timeworn childhood golden oldies like, say, *Monopoly.* What is the social reality based on *Monopoly?* Hmmm . . . it seems to be a pretty ruthless everyman-for-himself, eat-or-be-eaten contest. Sense of community? Absolutely none. What little team play there is consists of cutthroat antitrust tactics undertaken with the express purpose of throttling a third party.

But, argue the critics, a videogame provides no legroom for a child's imagination to soar. A child must strictly conform to the rules of the electronic microworld or be defeated by it. It's not open-ended like, say, *Parcheesi.* Videogames are supposed to be rat mazes, training children to "run the program" in a matrix where freedom of choice is illusory; they are unlike classic games such as *Chutes and Ladders, Candyland, Backgammon,* and *Life* (a best-selling board game modeled on utopian Eisenhower-era family values, where the only way to win is to go to college and graduate school, get a corporate job, marry, buy a house, fill it with children, and retire with a million dollars. It's a race to see who can be the best suburban lemming).

Then there is the criticism that because violence is the prime operative function of videogames, they undermine our traditional values. But consider dodgeball. Dodgeball is a game played by every schoolchild in America, and its main operative function is violence. The object of this game is to throw a rubber ball as hard as you can, hoping it will hit another kid, thus eliminating a member of the opposite team. Meanwhile, you are ducking projectiles from the other side that are aimed squarely, with a maximum force, at your head. Kids take very real pleasure in hurting each other this way. They enjoy seeing their classmates limp out of the arena with round, red rubber ball prints on their arms and legs. The stakes are high. Hence the thrill. This is not abstract violence. This is not theoretical fantasy violence. This is very real violence that involves targeted aggression resulting in physical pain. Kids get injured playing dodgeball. Aside from the occasional case of carpal tunnel syndrome, kids do not get hurt playing *Mortal Kombat.* But a great hue and cry would ring out if any legislator tried to ban dodgeball, because it is an American institution. And it is a simply fantastic game.

So is *Mortal Kombat.* But *Mortal Kombat,* the most hyperbolically graphic and wildly successful martial arts game of 1992, sparked a congressional fracas. As a prequel to their crusade on rap music, legislative alarmists on Capitol Hill singled out a couple of videogames as scapegoats for the rising tide of crime, drugs, and social unrest. Thus, *Mortal Kombat* and *Night Trap,* a Sega CD game, became the Snoop Doggy Dog and Nine Inch Nails of a federal videogame witch hunt. In *Kombat,* the object is a pretty straightforward fight to the finish featuring the usual punches, kicks, and leaping strikes, as well as now notorious fatality moves like ripping your opponent's still-beating heart out of his chest or tearing off his head and holding it aloft, spinal cord dangling — antics ripped off from *Indiana Jones and the Temple of Doom* and *Clash of the Titans,* respectively, with a dash of *The Highlander* thrown in for good measure. There was no resulting increase in the number of decapitations or ritual heart removals on the national crime blotter. There was, however, an egregiously written movie adaptation of *Mortal Kombat* starring Christopher Lambert. *Night Trap,* possibly the cheesiest game ever burned onto optical disc, was a spoof of z-grade vampire flicks of the 1950s, using full-motion video footage of embarrassingly bad actors to stage a vampire hunt in a sorority house.* The object of the game was to trap the vampires before they sunk their teeth into the girls. If you played it successfully, you actually prevented violence. If you failed, you were subject

---

* *Night Trap*'s marquee draw was Dana Plato, the erstwhile teenage star of *Diff'rent Strokes,* who graduated from sitcomville to a career in armed robbery.

to campy horror scenes worthy of Ed Wood — the loudest groans of pain were your own.

On December 1, 1993 — just as the 1993 Christmas shopping season kicked into high gear, Senator Herbert Kohl of Wisconsin threw down the gauntlet in a press release that smacked of *Reefer Madness:* "The days of Lincoln Logs and Matchbox cars are gone for a lot of kids. Some of these interactive video games, complete with screams of pain, are enough to give adults nightmares." Meanwhile, his senatorial compatriot, Senator Joe Lieberman of Connecticut (who later spearheaded the Time Warner rap confrontation with C. Dolores Tucker), held a press conference, flanked by Bob Keeshan, the erstwhile Captain Kangaroo. "After watching these violent video games," Lieberman growled, "I personally believe it is irresponsible for some in the video game industry to produce them. I wish we could ban them constitutionally, or that the industry would stop making them." Shortly thereafter, Captain Kangaroo added that it takes a village to raise a child and cast biblical aspersions. "The lessons learned by a child as an active participant in violence-oriented video games will be lessons the thinking parent would shun like a plague," he said. "Indeed it could become a plague upon their house."

A week later, the U.S. Senate Committee on Governmental Affairs' Subcommittee on Regulation and Government Information and the Judiciary Committee's Subcommittee on Juvenile Justice convened to discuss *Mortal Kombat* fatality moves and the screaming sorority girls in *Night Trap.* Lieberman kicked off the proceedings by narrating a *Mortal Kombat* video clip. "In the first segment, which is Sega's version, blood spatters from the contestants' heads. When a player wins, the so-called death sequence begins. The game narrator instructs the player to, and I quote, 'finish' his opponent. The player may then choose a method of murder ranging from ripping the heart out to pulling off the head of the opponent with spinal cord attached. The second version, made by Nintendo, leaves out the blood and decapitation, but as you will see, it is still a violent game." After a brief pause due to technical difficulties with the audiovisual system, he continued. "The second game is *Night*

Trap, which is a game set in a sorority house. The object is to keep hooded men from hanging the young woman from a hook or drilling her neck with a tool designed to drain her blood. *Night Trap* uses actual actors and achieves an unprecedented level of realism. What is particularly troubling about the scene in this film that we have an extract of is a graphic depiction of the violence against women, with strong overtones of sexual violence. I find this segment deeply offensive, and believe that it simply should be taken off the market."

"It ought to be taken off the market entirely," Kohl agreed, "or at the very least its most objectionable scenes should be removed."

"Shame on the people who produce that trash," added another senator. "It is child abuse, in my judgment." The heaping of shame upon Sega seemed to be the dominant theme of the session, as a schoolteacher from Farmington Hills, Michigan, took the floor to rebuke the company. "The only words you can say to the manufacturers and the shareholders of the company," she said, "is shame on you. I think they really should stop and think about what they are doing. I mean, how would you like to have a teenage daughter go out on a date with someone who has just watched or played three hours of that game?"

William White, Sega's vice president of marketing, pointed out that the average Sega CD user is almost twenty-two years old, and that Sega Genesis owners were old enough to be in college. But to no avail. After Nintendo president Howard Lincoln declared that his company would never dream of releasing such a horrific game (a moot point, considering that Nintendo had no CD player on the market),* White was firmly planted in the

---

* Lincoln's statement was also disingenuous when you consider that Nintendo's core customer base is still in elementary school, unlike Sega's teens and twentysomethings. Publishing hardcore fighting games for older kids isn't part of Nintendo's business plan, and banning such games would only hurt their competition. As if to underscore Nintendo's family values agenda, Lincoln also submitted Nintendo's *Video Game Content Guidelines,* a pamphlet with pictures of Mario the Plumber next to circular slash symbol bullet points: No sexist language or depictions. No random gratuitous or excessive violence. No excessive force in sports games. No profanity or obscenity. No use of illegal drugs, smoking materials, and/or alcohol. Anyone who's ever ridden a school bus has seen these rules prominently displayed.

congressional hot seat. "Mr. Lincoln just a few minutes ago, as president of the other leading company in this field, Nintendo, said, and I quote, 'This game simply has no place in our society.' Why don't you agree?" asked Senator Lieberman, raising the flame under White to a steady broil. "Why doesn't Sega just pull *Night Trap* off the market?" White tried to explain that more research was necessary.

"Well," said Lieberman, "why don't you pull it off the market until the research is done?"

Eventually, *Night Trap* was pulled off the market, only to resurface as a PC CD-ROM, advertised in *Wired* magazine with a double-paged American flag and a government-bashing retort: "Some members of Congress tried to ban *Night Trap* for being sexist and offensive to women (Hey. They ought to know.)." When the dust had settled, the whole controversy only generated valuable publicity for this admittedly mediocre game. As for *Mortal Kombat,* it had already sold 3 million copies by the time it drew congressional fire, and the legislative ruckus only augmented its bad-assed cachet. Both sequels became best-sellers, generating a tide of action figures, trading cards, and other paraphernalia. It also prompted a host of imitators, including a game called *Killer Instinct,* featuring *Mortal Kombat*–esque Humiliation Moves (your opponent is forced to dance a little jig before he keels over and croaks) and No Mercy Moves (snapping necks, sans dangling spinal cords, slicing and dicing with a broadsword, and literally freezing your opponent). *Killer Instinct* did pretty well, for a Nintendo game.

But in the end, the worst possible outcome of the congressional hearings — a government ratings system — was averted. Taking their cue from Hollywood, the leading lights in the videogame industry formed the Interactive Digital Software Association (IDSA),* modeled after the Motion Picture Association of America. The IDSA was given a year to impose an industry rat-

* The IDSA's founding members were Acclaim (of *Mortal Kombat* fame), Atari, Capcom, Crystal Dynamics, Electronic Arts, Konami, Nintendo, Philips, Sega, Sony Electronic Publishing, Viacom New Media, and Virgin Interactive.

ings system to Congress's satisfaction before the government would step in with a labeling scheme of its own. The industry's ratings board would be responsible for classifying all cartridges and CD-ROMs into age-appropriate categories and enforcing these ratings among a boisterous field of rival game producers, all of whom distrusted each other as much as they feared the prospect of federal regulation. Nobody wanted to slaughter cash cows like *Mortal Kombat*. And yet no one could afford to piss off Congress again. The IDSA needed an objective yardstick for videogames and a way to protect the testing process from both under-the-table lobbying shenanigans and conservative political pressure.

The result was a kind of blind trust, namely the Entertainment Software Ratings Board (ESRB), under the direction of Dr. Arthur Pober, a former elementary school principal and vice president of the Children's Advertising Review of the Council of Better Business Bureaus. Basically, Pober is the key to the whole process, because he is the only one with the authority to hire and fire raters and the only one who knows their identities. Essentially, he oversees a kind of witness protection program for over a hundred videogame raters, three of whom evaluate each game.

"They range in age all the way from twenty years of age all the way up to sixty-five, seventy," he says, a paragon of circumspection. "They're married, some of them are single. We try to create what we call a reading triad — a triad is made up of somebody who's young, old, married, single, et cetera, so we get a fairly good perspective of what the game is like. For security, each submission is logged into a central computer, raters are assigned, demographically balanced, and then the ratings are entered into the computer, reviewed, and validated by a staffer." To make sure the companies don't slip an extra decapitation into the mix after an early version passes ESRB inspection, the games are retested ten or fifteen days before shipping to make sure the packaged product correlates with the test copy.

The final rating falls into one of five categories: Early Childhood (EC), Kids to Adults (which may include Mild Animated

Violence, Comic Mischief, and Animated Violence), Teen (all of the above plus Realistic Violence, Suggestive Sexual Themes, Mild Profanity, and Gaming), Mature (all of the above plus Animated Blood and Gore, Realistic Blood and Gore, Mature Sexual Themes, Profanity, and Use of Tobacco and Alcohol), and Adults Only. These categories correspond to G, PG, PG-13, R, and NC-17 movie ratings, respectively, and impose the same age limits on potential customers.

"We don't dictate taste," says Pober, shying away from even a hint of social activism, "nor do we make judgments. All we do is labeling. Based upon that labeling, we generate what the rating should be. If two out of three people look at a game and say that somebody's decapitating a head and there's blood and there's guts and there's gore or whatever, well that would certainly get it a mature category." And unlike the MPAA ratings board, the ESRB is pretty explicit about what it takes to change a rating. "If it's one particular scene, then the publisher gets a report. If they're willing to eliminate those scenes, then that's how the rating can be either brought down or appealed."

Of course, as with R-rated movies, sometimes a zesty rating is what producers want. Looking safe and parentally approved does not exactly score points with adolescent die-hard videogamers. Games stamped Mature tend to play it up. And sometimes even games that fall short of the notorious M rating will drown their tamer Teen or KA ratings in a maelstrom of macho advertising. An ad for Acclaim's T-rated *Resurrection Rise 2*, for instance, was a pulp sci-fi painting of your character's fist ripping the arm off a cyborg, printed next to an adrenal videogame epiphany that read, "It's that moment just after you rip it off, when the circuits are still pumping 'cause they don't know what hit 'em, and they've got that expression on their face like 'Hey, that's my arm!'. . . the first gush of oil from the open socket . . . the lights in their eyes going dim . . . yeah, that's when I know . . . I'm alive." Crystal Dynamics put it more succinctly in their ad for *Total Eclipse Turbo:* "Screw the Prime Directive. If it's on radar, it's toast." Videogame players love this stuff. And it's not because Sega has turned us into atavistic little zombies. It's not because we see the same attitude flaunted by celebrity athletes on a daily basis. It's not even because of TV cop shows and warmongering special effects movies. It's because as long as we've been consuming narrative entertainment, we've thrilled to the exploits of blood-streaked warriors who hack limbs off their opponents. In the past, this entailed listening to someone recite epic verse about the Trojan War or reading *Beowulf*. Now it means singing the praises of particularly ruthless arcade characters in Internet discussion groups ("Why?" asks a fan of *Fatal Fury 2*'s Krauser character. "Because anyone who fights in a cathedral with a full orchestra playing Mozart as a stage, and that starts out the match by literally saying 'I'll chisel your grave stone. Sleep well.' is just redefining badass.") If you look at fictional violence with a sense of perspective, videogame blood spatters aren't particularly new or disturbing.

Ultimately, the really disturbing thing about videogame violence is the question of whether it's really all that transgressive. It's easy to look at a first-person gunslinger game and leap to the conclusion that it fosters anarchy. There's a guy with a gun, shooting people (aliens, monsters, demons from hell, whatever) — he must be a criminal on the rampage, right? But if you look closely, you'll see that this character you're playing in these bang-up blast-fests is most likely wearing a uniform or carrying a badge. This guy is never a criminal, a punk, or a leftist insurgent. He's either some kind of military commando or else a cop. These are *police* that are supposed to be blowing everyone away. In games like *Narc* or *Virtua Cop*, you're a SWAT team member sharpshooting drug thugs in a hostage situation. In *Technocop*, the hero is a postapocalyptic highway patrolman blasting enemy cars off the road, racing to the crime scene to apprehend radar-monitored miscreants, and gunning them down with an .88 Magnum, whereupon they immediately collapse into piles of bloody bones. That defines due process in the videogame regime. Miranda rights? Forget it. Habeas corpus? Dream on. Law 'n' order social conservatives should love this stuff. If anything, it teaches kids to be shit-scared of cops. Or, more frightening still, these videogames might inspire the really nasty, power-hungry kids to *become* cops because, judging from the game play, the police, the narcs, the riot troopers, and the U.S. armed forces can blow away pretty much anything that crosses their path with total impunity and all the latest toys. The NRA, the Christian Coalition, and the Contract With America folks shouldn't leave it to granola-head free speechers to defend violent videogames. They should run with this stuff. It wouldn't be very much work to say, code a special Operation Rescue level of *Doom,* where you gun down abortion doctors, or navigate the subterranean corridors of Capitol Hill as a freshman Republican pulverizing gridlock with a tank-caliber chain gun and an endless supply of ammunition. You could turn all-out, full-scale armed conflict into a gigantic, expensive weeklong videogame.

But then, been there, played that. Gulf War.

Chapter 16
The Military-
Entertainment
Complex

On February 27, 1991, General Norman Schwarzkopf held a Gulf War press conference to explain that, despite all appearances to the contrary, "This is not a Nintendo game." He felt the need to clarify this issue, perhaps because every tank driver in Kuwait had been trained in a virtual reality pod, and once the Gulf War was under way, many of its armored skirmishes were considerably shorter than a typical after-school session of *Donkey Kong Country*. The Battle of 73 Easting, for example, which saw one U.S. tank troop decimate an entire Iraqi armored brigade with no American casualties, took less than twenty-three minutes. The army was so proud of this that later they took all the black boxes and satellite images and reconstructed the whole engagement, second for second, as a high-resolution 3D videogame, so that now, tank driver trainees at Fort Knox can clamber into soundproofed SIMNET cockpits and play the battle again. When a virtual tank is hit, the screen goes black, and a sheepfaced, buzz-cut recruit climbs out to debrief before his commanding officer hits the restart button. According to the Defense Department, training soldiers to fight on Sun workstations and networked PowerMacs is extremely effective, since most modern warfare takes place behind the screen anyway, via satellite surveillance, radar, infrared sights, and spook-proofed computer monitors.

By the age of twenty, most military personnel have been playing videogames for a dozen years, so this works out perfectly. Today's joystick jockeys, as Ronald Reagan liked to argue, are tomorrow's high-tech soldiers. The Discovery Channel hammered this point home in the wake of Operation Desert Storm by showing *Mortal Kombat* battle sequences illuminating shiny-faced Latino adolescents while a baritone voice-over boomed, "These are the warriors of tomorrow. Their strategic sense, rapid responses to continually changing threat environments, and their thirst for the kill, combined with their ease with computers, makes them ideally qualified to fight the wars of the future. *Years* of high-speed opponents have prepared them for modern war, where the body heat of distant enemies is spotted in video screens and flesh is seared from bone by remote control." Aside from being great family fare, this episode of *Fields of Armor* highlights the appeal of videogames as a strategic asset. It's an exquisite intuitive leap, cleansing away the arcade's taint of wasted time and teenage delinquency. Concerned mothers can now rest assured that their children have a mandate, if not a moral obligation, to play as much *Virtua Fighter 3* as possible. It's in the interest of national security.

The U.S. military has been using videogames to simulate the nuts and bolts of war for quite some time. At first, computers were used merely as scorekeeping devices in conventional war games. Instead of using, say, clipboards and pushpins to track a field exercise, game-meisters at the Army's National Training Center in Fort Irwin began using computer screens upon which they could squiggle red and blue lines in a high-tech military version of *Monday Night Football* sportscasting. (American infantry units were blue. Commies were red.) While real tanks rolled around on the field, computers would track their positions and render an overhead view with Lucky Charms icons: squares for tanks, diamonds for armored personnel carriers, crosses for artillery, umbrellas for radar, and stick figures for infantry units.

As computers pervaded every nook and cranny of the armed forces, they quickly transcended their original use as electronic scorecards and subsumed the games themselves. As the arcade craze boomed from mall to mall in 1978, Atari was building a souped-up version of *Battlezone* for the Defense Department's Advanced Research Project Agency (ARPA). While consumer flight simulators proliferated as home computer games, Air Force materiel managers programmed their computers to spin variables (fuel levels, weapons load, radar profile, what the pilot had for breakfast that day, etc.) into a supersonic airborne battle with snazzy color graphics. The Navy's Enhanced Warfare Gaming System allowed an omniscient game director to generate scenarios from SimNorthSeaSkirmish to SimGlobalTorpedothon while opposing ensigns peered into their separate sets of screens. These simulators could get especially stressful, considering that all submarine battles, in or out of the water, take place on screens. Unlike the experience of an artillery volley or an air raid, there's no illusion of manual control in a sub battle. In a submarine, all information is mediated by electronics, whether it's a training exercise or World War III. The more tanks and planes and other military equipment rely on computer interfaces — the closer they get to being airborne submarines — the more they resemble their simulators. As the training games approach reality and the actual war becomes more of a media experience, the membrane between the two, from the soldier's perspective, begins to evaporate.

This may explain why virtual reality has become the holy grail of Defense Department research in the 1990s. A World Wide Web search turns up thirty-six separate military agencies, offices, and programs devoted to modeling and simulation, or "M&S," as the Pentagon likes to call it (one can only imagine the lively boardroom banter were the letters reversed), which encompasses everything from the Defense Mapping Agency's conversion of the planet's surface into a VR soundstage to the virtual missiles flown over this high-fidelity synthetic battlefield by the Smart Weapons Management Office. According to the Army's M&S Master Plan (their term, not mine), "To get the job done, the Force XXI Army will depend on advanced simulations, powerful computer workstations, realistic computer images, multimedia digital transmission and global networking to generate information, to share knowledge and to operate on a plateau never possible before. Simulators, constructive simulations and the synthetic battlefield will be central and essential features of this Army."

Once every conceivable military conflict has been converted into a programmable, playable, superrealistic videogame, the final phase of this process consists of converting this fabulous videogame interface into a real war tool. And this is already being done. When a modern fighter pilot straps himself into the so-called "supercockpit," he sees sheets of visual information projected onto a heads-up display so he never has to look down at the controls. All he has to do is look ahead to see his current altitude, airspeed, remaining firepower, and infrared camera pictures of enemy aircraft projected at infinite distance, so his eyes don't need to refocus. As helmet and glove sensors track motion back to a central computer, yellow and green grid lines on the display indicate topography and three-sided boxes outline an optimal flight path. As in most videogames, the kind of weapon you select lights up in red, and target icons vanish from the display when enemy planes are dispatched. The purpose of these arcade conventions is to superimpose the virtual airspace onto the real one, and the end result is a pretty good approximation of *Wing Commander.* Ironically, the technology used to project these images onto glass is a nineteenth-century vaudeville magic trick called Pepper's Ghost, which is also used to project ghouls into the bumper cars of Disney's Haunted Mansion.

A hundred years after this vaudeville innovation, the military has come full circle. Now military contractors are getting into the entertainment industry. In 1993 Kaiser Electro-Optics, the contractor that builds displays for the Apache helicopter, licensed that technology to Visions of Reality, a company that builds large, expensive networked flight simulators for arcades, enabling dozens of teenage boys to engage in epic space battle via headmounted LCD helmets (all the thrills of the Gulf War, without the nasty chemical rash). In his fondest dreams, Ronald Reagan could only have hoped that someday virtual reality videogames would join the list that includes Tang, Velcro, and Ray Bans. These are your tax dollars at work.

At the center of what can now be safely called the military-entertainment complex sits Lockheed Martin, the largest defense contractor in America, which is conveniently located in Orlando. Now that military contracts are drying up, the reasoning goes, why not put all that cool technology to work as entertainment? This is the kind of synergy that can only take place in a city where the U.S. Army Simulation Training and Instrumentation Command, the Naval Training Systems Center, and the University of Central Florida operate in the shadow of Disneyland. The entire local economy is maintained by imagineers.

Lockheed Martin's foray into the magical world of digital special effects can be traced back to GE Aerospace, which did a series of tank and fighter jet training programs that cost the Department of Defense (DOD) between $2 million and $5 million apiece. In due time, GE Aerospace was acquired by Martin Marietta, and Martin Marietta merged with Lockheed, making the new company, Lockheed Martin, not only a great white shark in the goldfish bowl of defense contractors but also, retroactively, one of the founding players in the military videogame industry. With Lockheed Martin's acquisition of SIMNET manufacturer Loral in 1996, the empire was complete. As Brian Jameson, the director of Lockheed Martin's entertainment division, puts it, "Now, we're one big happy family."

After assembling half a dozen simulation and graphics companies, Lockheed Martin consolidated all the new siblings into a company called Real 3D and started (to use Jameson's favorite transitive verb) "transitioning" Lockheed's military patents into low-cost commercial products. "The first application that we developed was for ship bridge trainers," he says. "This trains captains that drive, like, the Exxon *Valdez*. They need a lot of help, right?"

"He didn't say that," interjects Lockheed's jocular good ol' boy press wrangler, Carlton Caldwell, who is babysitting Jameson via speakerphone.

"That was a joke," says Jameson. "Thanks, Carlton. See, that's why Carlton's here, so I don't get the company in trouble, But, yeah, we have large customers in Europe that are buying many of these low-cost simulators to support driver training applications and bridge training." Initially, shipping magnates were the only entities outside the U.S. military who could afford these simulators. But inevitably, Moore's Law (which states that chip speed doubles every eighteen months) kicked in, and the technology started shrinking and getting cheaper, to the extent that programs the Defense Department had bought for millions of dollars could be purchased off the shelf for a hundred grand and change.

At that point, Sega started sniffing around the fire hydrant and, after months of negotiation, gave Lockheed Martin a contract to design components for an arcade platform for games like *Daytona, Virtua Fighter, Virtua Cop,* and *Desert Tank.* "We design the special purpose chips that house our real-time simulation technology," says Jameson, "and we sell that technology to Sega. And the next generation of arcade hardware, which we call Model 3, will be the next level of graphics for the arcade. So our technology, our hardware, is driving the graphics in those arcade games — our simulation technology. That's how we got from $5 million DOD simulators down to these arcade platforms in terms of the silicon. Sega does the bulk of the software development. We've done one game for them, and we're working on several additional titles for home videogame platforms as well as PC."

One of these computer products is a low-cost 3D graphics chip based on Sega's arcade board, which will shift PC graphics applications into warp speed. The add-in graphics cards that incorporate these chips will not be manufactured by Lockheed Martin and will probably not run advertisements boasting "Lockheed Martin Inside." But, says Caldwell, "In 1997, you'll be seeing computers running Lockheed Martin chips on somebody's card." He makes a halfhearted attempt to cast this chip as a productivity boon to CAD/CAM programmers, architects, and graphic designers before admitting that most people will use it to play a meaner game of *Doom*. That's the ironic thing about videogames. They are the most demanding applications you can run on a PC — far more of a drain on your computer's speed and memory than any database or word processor or electronic check-writing program. All the sensible things that justify buying a computer don't require the hottest turbo-charged high-performance processor on the market, which can run all of them simultaneously at a mere trot. It's the leisure programs that strain silicon components into a galloping lather.

At the 1996 Electronics Entertainment Expo, Lockheed's Model 3 arcade board is on display as the engine driving *Virtua Fighter 3*, Sega's new showcase for polygon gladiators. The demo is pitched onto a fifty-inch television screen and opens in a virtual forest. In the muted light of a winter afternoon, a girl wearing a pink kimono is performing a Chinese fan dance in the snow. And in every subtlety of human movement, in all the twists and shifts of wrists and shoulders and knees, she's real. Or rather, surreal, because at times she's even more finely articulated, physiologically, than a physical person. And as this fluid, Zen fan tracery metamorphoses into a martial arts display, her eyes follow you — and she blinks. And it takes more sophisticated technology to make this girl blink than to animate all the virtual tanks in Fort Knox. The pixellated platoons don't begin to approach this level of detail. But then, that's probably for the best. As these characters become more and more human, it gets progressively more difficult to blow them up. Sega will likely arrest their development soon, not because of technological constraints, but because in a very short while, they're going to cross the threshold from abstract pixel puppets to three-dimensional people. And at that point, it becomes much less fun to brutalize them, which makes the game less profitable. By the same token, simulated Iraqis in the Army's tank training programs will no doubt remain featureless blockheads, even when technology can give them faces. You can't humanize the enemy, even in sim. That would defeat the whole purpose of the exercise. These decisions have nothing to do with hardware. These are software design issues. In any case, Lockheed Martin makes money off the chips.

Granted, next to contracts for tank simulators and fighter jets, videogames are small potatoes. But entertainment is the site of Lockheed Martin's most intensely concentrated growth. Not only does Real 3D generate cash from hardware sales to Sega, but research in the entertainment division actually defies the absurd gravity of Reaganomics and trickles up to the Pentagon. "As we downsize the technology to support entertainment applications, we're learning more," Caldwell explains. "We're getting better. And the beauty of it is that we can spin that technology back up and sell it right back to the government again at a lower cost. One thing that we're talking about with the Army now is chip technology — the same sort of chips that we do for games — reinserting them back into live platforms that will allow people out in the field to play simulation in their tanks. If you remember Desert Storm, we put all those forces out there, and they were deployed out there for months before they actually did anything, right? So if you had cheap simulators built into the platforms, they could practice daily out in the field. Make-believe battles in real tanks. The technical term is "embedded simulation." And it is all economically feasible, he says, because Lockheed Martin has had so much practice making small, cheap simulations for Sega.

"From the entertainment side, we're bringing product back into the military. Now the entertainment research is funding the government stuff. For example, human animations, which you see a lot in games — people jumping, fighting, running. Well, if you dress these human animations up in military uniforms and have them running in single file in formation and you feed that back into a DOD military simulation training scenario, now you've brought entertainment into a military training product.

In a way, this repurposing of entertainment R&D for national defense brings videogames full cycle. Lockheed Martin may be beating digital ploughshares into swords, but most of the technology that's now used in videogames had its origins in military research. When you trace back the patents, it's virtually impossible to find an arcade or console component that evolved in the absence of a Defense Department grant. It's very easy to forget, when you're contentedly playing with say, a Game Boy, that the twenty-year-old technology in its silicon guts was originally financed by the Pentagon. The artists and animators who render videogames on Silicon Graphics workstations can only afford to do so because SGI's largest customers, until recently, were companies like Boeing and Lockheed that needed computational Clydesdales for military projects. If they hadn't bought thousands of these machines, it wouldn't be economically possible to develop *Donkey Kong Country 2* or *Battle Arena Toshinden* or *Toy Story*. Online gaming? The Internet was hatched and incubated by DARPA.

These factoids are cracked over my head like raw eggs by Michael Wahrman, a forty-one-year-old veteran of the Rand Corporation who now runs a digital production and special effects lab for Viacom. After a series of ill-fated deals with Hollywood producers and multimedia moguls, Wahrman is just a smidge bitter about the entertainment industry and is all too ready to glorify the military-industrial complex at its expense. "The technology people I've worked with and the entertainment people I've worked with, their ethics are *below whore* relative to the people in the defense industry who finance new and interesting technology and reward and cultivate talent," he hisses. "When we talk about ethics, give me a nuclear strategist any day of the week over a Hollywood executive. Any day of the week." In the mahogany half-light of a Manhattan bar, the red-haired former wunderkind seems to seethe with a kind of nervous, rabbitty angst. Thin and bespectacled, he surveys the room with constant, searching vigilance, as if to spot undercover Los Angelinos secretly plotting against him.

"Anyway," he says, "pretty much everything you're seeing in videogames — computer animation production, and networks — is financed by the military. It's all Department of the Air Force and ARPA. There is some NSF as well, but I sometimes call the NSF a convenient front for people who can't take checks from Lawrence Livermore. They take checks from Lawrence Berkeley and think it's different. But I'm not so sure. If you examine different technologies and find out whose fingerprints are on it, you always see the same groups of people. Follow the grants. Computer graphics was 100 percent financed by the Department of Defense in its early days. Jim Clark [the founder of Silicon Graphics, and later Netscape] was financed at Stanford to create geometry engines using VLSI technology by Carver-Meade. They took it to prototype and then he went out and got financing. In graphics, you will see big Department of the Air Force fingerprints. Then there's all the simulation technology that depends on those fundamental technologies to execute. Then on top of that, there's a variety of distributed networking experiments."

Wahrman is practically rattling with the kind of volatile, you-don't-know-how-far-it-goes intensity you only see in Oliver Stone movies. "Everyone you know in the media industry was funded by the Defense Department," he sneers. "It's only the wankers who came later, using other people's ideas, who weren't."

Much to Wahrman's chagrin, the wankers are succeeding, because unlike the military engineers who invented the technology, Hollywood types place entertainment value above rock-ribbed realism when designing simulations for the consumer market. Despite the uncanny resemblance between the Army training simulators and the latest batch of arcade games, their raisons d'être do not entirely overlap. One game has to be strategically significant, at all costs. The other just has to be a yee-haw entertainment experience, with an eye toward the bottom line. "The videogame people need to make something that's fun at incredibly low cost margins," he says, "way below what TV commercials cost every day of the week in this country. The military has a different problem. Their problem is: You are charged with simulating a scenario. If you fuck it up, people die. You're not going to fuck it up. So you build a system that really works like those goddamned tanks do. Ultimately, there's two different businesses going on, and one business is national defense, and the other business is entertainment, and ultimately, there's different criteria for success."

If anything, extreme realism compromises a videogame's play-through and hobbles its pacing. Lockheed Martin's first draft of *Desert Tank* was a lousy arcade experience, because it was too much like a real tank. The vehicle dynamics were great — you could practically feel the terrain rolling underfoot. When you fired the cannon, there was a great force feedback effect. But you had to wait forever to fire again, because real missiles generate so much heat that you have to pause while the cannons cool down. This stuff is really key when you're training tank pilots. They have to know all this stuff. But it doesn't make for the greatest gaming experience. Taking a minute and a half to reload kind of kills the buzz. Needless to say, Sega put Lockheed's *Desert Tank* code through the equivalent of a Hollywood rewrite, forcing the contractor to "transition" a meticulously wrought tank simulation into an arcade blockbuster ("Tone down the realism, babe. Speed up that cannon. More ammunition. This isn't rocket science. This is show biz").

It's oddly appropriate that a military-industrial juggernaut would be forced into the role of junior scriptwriter for the entertainment industry, seeing as how the Gulf War itself was quickly converted from Pentagon press releases and CNN footage into a slew of videogames. Nintendo and Sega consoles needed ammunition for their multibillion-dollar cartridge war, and CD-ROM drives were just breaking into mainstream use. Operation Desert Storm was just the ticket. It was the greatest thing to happen to the interactive entertainment industry since Sonic the Hedgehog. Everyone in America had seen missile footage through laser-guided sights on television. Now they could play the war on their very own home computers. Within a year of the Gulf War, Spectrum Holobyte released a tank game based on the Army's SIMNET land combat training program. Shortly thereafter, Absolute's *Super Battletank* put you in the cockpit of an M-1A1 Abrams tank in Kuwait, where, in a curious reversal of America's Gulf War odds, you got to play the U.S. Armed Forces as underdog. In *Super Battletank*, it's just you and your 115 millimeter cannon against all of Saddam Hussein's SCUD launchers, mines, helicopters, tanks, and the entire Iraqi army. And after you have successfully thrashed the Republican Guard into submission, you can play *Super Battletank 2*, in which Saddam (like Jason in *Friday the 13th*) is back with more hardware and human cannon fodder, and you, a single tank operator in the Twenty-fourth Mechanized Infantry, have to kick his army's ass yet again.

Electronic Arts had its own version of this black-is-white, day-is-night David and Goliath scenario called *M1 Abrams Battletank*, in which not only do you have to single-handedly fight the Gulf War, but you have to do so as the driver, gunner, commander, and cupola of a bigfoot monster tank, simultaneously steering, firing, surveying the enemy, receiving radio signals, and mapping as you switch between four different views and job descriptions. You don't just drive the tank. You *are* the tank. Gamers flocked. And as competing developers raised the bar of verisimilitude, players' expectations of an authentic military hardware experience only escalated, until the obsession with combat dashboards reached the level of pure fetish and product descriptions transmogrified into vehicle porn.

The most successful vehicle pin-up from the Persian Gulf was unquestionably the Apache helicopter, originally designed by McDonnell Douglas and glorified in a dozen Gulf War simulations like Electronic Arts' *Desert Strike,* an arcade-style blast-fest for Super Nintendo and Sega Genesis in which you pilot the fabled chopper on a mission to blow up mobile SCUD launchers, destroy nuclear and chemical weapons factories, free POWs, and trawl the Gulf for a Mad Dictator's personal yacht. As with most Manichean special effects epics, there was a sequel, *Jungle Strike,* for Sega, because even though you blew the Mad Dictator's yacht to smithereens in the first game, his son escaped and promptly started selling high-tech weapons to Central American drug lords and inundating Washington, D.C., with terrorists. Your mission: Stop the swarthy, non–Judeo-Christian Bad Guys from bombing our national monuments and save the President of a kinder, gentler America with your kick-ass Apache helicopter, motorcycle, hovercraft, and stealth fighter.

Upping the political ante one notch further, Electronic Arts' other helicopter opera for Sega, *LHX Attack Chopper*, takes place in a not-so-distant future, when every country in the world has become democratic except Libya. Libya is still on an unrecalcitrant kidnapping, bombing, and hijacking spree, forcing the U.S. into the inevitable (God, we hate to do this, but . . .) declaration of war. The Air Cavalry, starring you as ace chopper pilot, storms in to prime Libya for our ground forces. The specificity of this game is fantastic. You don't just get generic weapons. You get a detailed roster of U.S. munitions circa 1990. And this isn't some videogame à clef set in a fictional north African dictatorship. It's Libya. When you think about it, *LHX Attack Chopper* is a digital, apple pie version of radio Tripoli. After a few sessions on the Sega Genesis, American kids may not be able to locate Libya on a map, but they know we should bomb the hell out of it. This is what Libyan kids hear over the PA system all day. Destroy the infidels. It's the same basic message. We just have better toys.

In some games, the toys are actually an end in themselves. The thrill is not so much sheer artillery discharge as the illusion that mastering the game is equivalent to actually flying a multi-million-dollar aircraft. In a top-of-the-line consumer simulation, the level of detail has to be high enough to convince military hardware nuts that, yeah, they could stroll from the rec-room PC straight into the cockpit of an Apache helicopter and do just fine, and that playing with a very realistic pretend plane will put you on par with a real live pilot. For these connoisseurs of vehicular verité, there is *Apache,* a meticulously crafted digital helicopter produced by Interactive Magic in the heart of North Carolina contractor country, right down the road from Fort Bragg.

What you see when you load this CD-ROM is, for all intents and purposes, what an Apache pilot sees, down to the last knob, switch, and dial. This is no surprise, given the *Apache*'s developer was in bed with McDonnell Douglas for the duration of the project and lifted technical specs straight from the shop floor. The designers then assembled a squad of erstwhile Apache pilots to test and tweak the game and generally drive the code till it creaked. After the program had passed top gun muster, Interactive Magic invited active duty chopper jocks over for videogames, and assumably for milk and cookies as well. "The base is right down the road from us," says Interactive Magic's spokeswoman, Gina Waluk, sounding every bit the Boy Scout den mother. "They had about twenty-five of their Apache pilots stationed across the road from our offices here. A few of them had gone out and even bought the game. But they came over and flew the aircraft and said how cool it was. They loved the game. In fact, they're trying to get the army to use *Apache* to train some of their pilots, as an initial weeding-out tool, because it's a lot cheaper to have these guys play the computer game than fly the helicopters."

This may sound like a marketing maven's pipe dream. But commercial computer games have been nipping at the heels of military flight simulators for years. "Computer games were better than most of the simulators for a long time," says Interactive Magic's chairman, J. W. "Wild Bill" Stealey, an Air Force Academy graduate and retired military pilot whose voice booms with the gravelly bombast of a former flight jock. "I was still flying old Link trainers in the Air National Guard — no motion no visuals no nothing — and I had 3D visuals on my computer games. So we were ahead in terms of low-cost 3D. I remember one company got a contract with the U.S. Air Force, and the whole deal was they didn't charge enough for their product. So they had to find a way to put some seats on it and put some stuff around it so they could write a spec for it and charge $250,000 for it, because the military wasn't used to buying a fifty-dollar computer game. The issue is, I always thought I could do a military simulation, and it would take me $1 million to get it done 95 percent. It would take me another $19 million to get through all the nitpicks of the process of doing military simulation. You know, this accounting, that minority hiring, this tool. I'd never get through it. That's why I always avoided it."

Instead, Stealey concentrated on pure entertainment as the chairman of Microprose, which he cofounded in 1982 with code-meister Sid Meier (of *Civilization* fame). Microprose virtually invented the genre of commercial flight simulation, mostly because Wild Bill Stealey wanted to become Top Gun of the Pennsylvania Air National Guard. When Stealey wanted to practice his strafing, Sid wrote a souped-up version of *Hellcat Ace*. "And I was, for three months, the Top Gun," he recalls, with the requisite braggadocio. "And that was an *Atari 800 game* that I practiced my strafing on, and Sid wrote it for me in his basement. And the Army paid me $10,000 to take my original gunship product and use it to screen new helicopter pilots."

Likewise, when Stealey wanted to fire up the F-15 he never got to fly in the Air Force, Microprose software engineers went to work on *F-15 Strike Eagle*. "That's what I wanted to do at the Air Force, and I didn't get to, and I knew a lot of other people who wanted to fly the F-15 and never got to," he says. "So we did it, and gave 'em all a chance. Most everybody thinks they can be cooler than they are — it's just a matter of luck and timing. You go down and spend your fifty bucks and timing doesn't matter. You're now in the middle of World War II or you're in the twenty-third century."

As it happens, a good chunk of Stealey's clientele fought in World War II the first time around. Compared to most videogame players, flight sim enthusiasts are positively geriatric. They are out of the market for Nintendo cartridges, or "joystick wigglers," as he likes to call them. The virtual planes of the flight sim world, like the most complicated and expensive model train sets, are designed for boys who are edging toward retirement. "We target adults," says Ms. Waluk, flatly. "We're looking for the kid's father. We're one hundred percent male, and we go from age twenty-five all the way up. There's a lot of older retired people that are getting into this as computers become more prolific. All the retired military types want it. We have a lot of World War II retired military guys in Florida calling all the time — they were psyched about *Apache* and they're looking forward to the World War II simulation we're releasing in September."

Basically, Interactive Magic can count every Air Force vet and cammy-clad poseur with a home PC as a core customer for life. Military history buffs. Guys who've read all of Tom Clancy's novels. The wired segment of the militia movement. "All the military board game guys have come out of the woods," chuckles Stealey. "They're a pretty big market now, but almost an underground market. They're the guys that know everything about everything on every tank and every armored personnel carrier. They're into the details. They argue about how many shots an APC can get off with its Gatling gun. They argue about that stuff and write us nasty letters on the Net telling us why we're not exactly right."

This isn't about combat. It's about the American Top Gun fantasy of what a military mission is like. People don't want to experience war. They want to experience life as a Tom Cruise character. So they go out and buy Spectrum Holobyte's *Top Gun: Fire at Will* for the Sony Playstation, so they can play the role for a little while. Get a goofy nickname. Train on an F-14 Tomcat at the Top Gun academy. Bomb Libya.

As Stealey says, "It's about doin' something cool when the rest of your job is interesting but you perceive it as cooler to drive submarines, fly airplanes, be General Patton. It's something that we've all had a fascination with for a lot of years. A lot of people thought they could've been Top Gun or had the Right Stuff, or whatever it is, and they've got boring jobs like lawyers and bankers and authors. There's no real excitement in that. But flying is exciting, and it's even more exciting when you're in no real danger. You can just go out and be cool."

You may even learn something valuable (flight, like sports, being one of those Great Metaphors For Life). Suddenly serious, he recites the gospel of flight sim according to Wild Bill: "Flying is about thinking. It's about knowing how to use your energy. It's about knowing how to use your gas. It's about knowing how to use your weapons. It's about knowing when to fight and to not. What's the whole situation. You better know everything, not just a little bit. And that's what life is all about. You play these games as a kid, you grow up understanding the risks and rewards of making decisions in real life. And the best part is, if you crash into the sea, you turn it off and start over again. So now you know not only the risks and rewards of this action, you see that there are some significant consequences, some of which you don't like."

Ultimately, the most surprising thing about Stealey is that, for all his military jargon and flight jock bravado, he's a dove in hawk's feathers. He'd just as soon resolve international conflicts with computer games as watch opposing forces duke it out on CNN. "I was on CNN a couple times during the Gulf War," he recalls. "And they said, 'Can you really use these to train pilots?' And I said absolutely you can use these to train pilots. I mean, I was trained on these things, and ones that were a lot worse than the games we're putting out right now. But the best thing would be to put a couple of those leaders in a room and let them go at it on these things, then nobody gets killed. And we could figure out the same things. We'd use all the weapons. They'd just sit there and push them buttons, and we'll have a simulation on this, and nobody'll die. And we'll just live by the results."

This is Stealey's grand vision, this sprawling electronic playground for forty-five-year-old boys, and how great it would be if we could just let them all loose in there to annihilate each other's toy soldiers. He even has a prototype fired up on a network server somewhere in northern Virginia. So as the Defense Department and the U.S. intelligence community hover around their terminals fighting simulated wars and trying to protect the Pentagon from foreign hackers, Stealey and hundreds of his corporate pals and military buddies are playing this huge, twenty-four-hour videogame where they all get to pilot digital fighter jets and tanks and helicopters and command armies online. "We're hoping that we'll get thousands and thousands of people playing this," he says, "and it'll be one magnificent virtual war."

Chapter 17

Sim Society

People are often attracted to a simulation
of reality because it allows for the
creation of a manageable version of the
complex realities of real life. This ability
to model options without interfering with
the real world has attracted the attention
of corporations and government organizations wanting to "imagineer" new direc-
tions.

— Gareth Branwyn

Having converted conventional warfare into a series of videogames for training purposes, Pentagon brass quickly realized
that the computer could be used to create all kinds of fantasy scenarios. Of course, software was great for simulating fighter jets,
submarines, and tanks. But why stop there, when you could
wage a full-blown make-believe nuclear war? And so geopoliti-
cal strategists at the Rand Corporation started playing computer
games to see whether we could actually win a war with nuclear

weapons.* The largest and most complex of these games was a comprehensive mock-up of World War III called the Rand Strategy Assessment. The way it was set up, the player would define all the initial conditions: how many missiles, ships, and tanks were on each side, the fervor of Soviet expansionism, congressional belligerence, and the probability of nuclear attack. And then the computer would play itself on land, sea, and air, weighing the balance with political factors. The applied math division of the Rand Corporation played this game with every conceivable configuration of diplomacy and firepower, trying to determine a winning strategy that didn't end in nuclear holocaust. And they couldn't do it. The result of these marathon gaming sessions was the theory of mutually assured destruction, and it successfully convinced a bunch of generals in underground bunkers that launching warheads wasn't such a hot idea.

But as simulation, nuclear standoff was pretty thrilling. It had all the ingredients of a great computer game: challenging strategy, epic scale, and a dramatic conclusion. So it didn't take long to trickle down from the military. By Reagan's second term, the personal computer had become a yuppie status symbol, dueling superpowers were all over the headlines, and simulated nuclear war was selling briskly on floppy disk. Chris Crawford's *Balance of Power* was the ultimate power trip for type-A personalities. Play Leader of the Free World in your own living room. Decide which leaders to coddle with military aid, which puppet states to bully, and where to foment covert insurgencies. Rack up international prestige points and single-handedly save the world from nuclear apocalypse. Even though there were no mushroom clouds and flying body parts to punctuate the worst-case scenario, *Balance of Power* acquired a cult following among corporate lawyers and Wall Street traders and spawned a string of successful sequels. After nuclear standoff, there was Crawford's oil

---

* One of the Rand Corporation's earliest cognitive psychology experiments was an ICBM simulation to determine how many missiles an air defense tracker could track before becoming overwhelmed. Years later, a virtually identical game was mass-marketed as Atari's *Missile Command*.

crisis simulation, *Energy Czar*, then *Guns & Butter*, in which the player assumes the macroeconomic responsibilities of benevolent dictator — mining natural resources, managing the peasant labor force, maximizing agricultural efficiency, and winning an arms race with a neighboring banana republic. So here you had, on your desktop, this opportunity to rule thousands of fictional people by totalitarian fiat. It was a hit.

By the decade's end, there were a dozen of these Sun King simulations that gave you undisputed authority over some computer-generated country. And lest the player waste mental energy on questions of political legitimacy rather than, you know, squeezing labor out of the serfs, these games all subscribed to a kind of digital divine right of kings. Because in most of them you were not just an absolute monarch. You were also God. Sometimes, this was meant quite literally. In Electronic Arts' *Populous*, for instance, you are an actual deity with all kinds of impressive sky god powers, and your mission is to jostle aside other religions by making sure your followers out-worship and out-breed members of opposing faiths. Of course, this entails a lot of celestial micromanagement — sending your worshipers on crusades, making sure they build enough temples and tend their crops properly, picking an opportune moment for a strategic natural disaster, and so on. The idea is that God is some kind of overworked supernatural comptroller or chief executive, and that different religions are really competing players in the worship industry.

In this respect, these so-called "god games" bore an uncanny resemblance to corporate capitalism simulations, which were also best-sellers at the time. In these supply-side empire-building games, you did all the same things that God did, but you did them as a bank president, Wall Street raider, commodities broker, railroad baron, or real estate speculator. Instead of starting out with some hardscrabble Mesopotamian tribe of hunter-gatherers, you start out with, say, a small shipping company. And instead of creating a world religion, you build a monopolistic railroad empire. But the strategy elements are all the same. It's all about expansion.

Hundreds of thousands of these gray flannel dreamworlds were sold in the 1980s — there was something about them that captured the spirit of the times. There, on the screen of a brand-new IBM computer, was this epic vision of the monumental corporation, led by an omniscient and omnipotent executive, that could just grow and grow and grow until it took over the world. Even in the current climate of lean management and downsizing, there's this industrial-strength fantasy attached to corporate role-playing operas, which have been updated to reflect global business conditions. Instead of driving one company to the top of an industry, now you get to synergize behind the wheel of a multinational conglomerate. *Capitalism,* a 1996 business simulation (programmed in Hong Kong) boasts, "Over six different industries to dominate. Nearly every aspect of the economic world is here, and now you can control things your way. . . . Execute a merger and double your market share overnight. Stalk the PC market with secret R&D projects and strike with products that are light years ahead of the competition. Strengthen your profit-making potential by streamlining production and re-organizing retail outlets. Become one of the nation's few power mongers and top the list of the world's billionaires. . . . Test your ability to compete, raise prices, cut supply, create demand, play the stock market and control the world!" The player logs off, flushed, pulse racing, dials into his Schwab One account, shuffles his mutual fund portfolio from Income to Aggressive Growth, and goes back to his freelance, zero-benefits, post-layoff home-office consultancy.

But that's the great thing about sim. It reduces all kinds of messy, uncontrollable, and chaotic situations to manageable proportions. These programs promise to simplify, as much as to simulate, reality — a prospect that grows all the more appealing in the face of information overload. Simulations chop reality up into bite-sized pieces. In a game like Wil Wright's *SimCity,* for instance, all the headaches of an urban mayor are simplified and structured so that your mind can parse them. You have to deal with property values and tax rates and crime statistics and pollution. But all the variables are well-defined. Things fit into nice, neat categories. This is residential. That's commercial. There's no in between. The system is complex enough to give you a sense of reality. It smells real. But you don't feel helpless, because you know the range of possibilities. There are no random forces of destruction lurking around the corner. And girding the whole experience is an implicit promise that you will be able to cope with this world. If you do things right, everything will work out, and pretty soon your little city will be pumping along pretty well, growing and prospering in an environmentally sound, politically popular way. And if all falls apart, you can start over and do things differently. And there's a kind of security in that, a sense of control and containment that's hard to find in a nonvirtual environment.

And this premise scales seamlessly from *SimCity* all the way up to *SimEarth* and all the way down to *SimAnt*, a model anthill based on E. O. Wilson's lifetime of entomological research. It's all of a piece: building urban infrastructure, fortifying the mound, fighting crime, fending off the red ants, developing a healthy agrarian society, feeding the larvae. Each volume of Wright's SimSeries pushed the same buttons, spurring thousands of people to create a self-contained, fully functioning, personal microworld. The software was designed, Wright says, as a kind of mental homestead or digital terrarium. "You've created something that's yours. It's unique. Nobody created one just like it. So you tend to empathize with it. You tend to identify and say, oh look what happened to my city, you know, or my planet, or my ant colony. And the more time you spend with it, the greater that ownership is." At its core, *SimCity* isn't about conquering the universe. It's gardening. It's a digital window box for people who spend their lives staring at computer screens and lack the patience for real-time horticulture. In a simulation, you can watch things grow at an accelerated rate, like a time-lapse film of plant seeds splitting their shells, writhing with vegetal growth, and exploding into bloom. In sim, you can do all sorts of interesting things with time. You can speed it up, slow it down, make it stop, rewind, replay, and skip forward to the parts you like. On a computer, time is just another parameter, subject to arbitrary control.

And ultimately, this feels a lot more godlike than redrawing boundary lines on a map. People can already do that. They already build all kinds of simulated environments with metal and paint and balsa wood and glue. But they can't play with time. "When I was a kid," says Wright, "I used to build a lot of models — plastic models, wood models, little electric models that did things. So I always enjoyed the idea of modeling reality. But it wasn't until I came across the computer that all of a sudden I was able to take my models from being static structural models to dynamic process models. It was like modeling different things all of a sudden. If I'm modeling a city out of, say, wood, it's entirely structural. It's the buildings, it's the roads, it's the trees, it's the hills. If I'm dealing with the computer, all of a sudden I'm dealing with time and the way these structures change through time. So now I'm modeling things like decay, growth, population shifts — I'm actually modeling processes rather than structures. Those are the components that I'm building the model out of, which, really, is a huge leap. I mean, it's the difference between still cameras and film."

So what you have, in the end, isn't a set of digital Lincoln Logs. It's a set of four-dimensional building blocks that you can stack up and then see what happens. It's not about circumstances. It's about the forces that produce them, which operate regardless of particular decisions. Making decisions doesn't change the system. It just allows you to see how it responds. Making choices doesn't entirely determine the outcome. It just pushes the envelope of outcomes to see how far it will stretch before the system pushes you back. If a course of events is a line, and a branching story is area, this is volume. And the way you understand things in this solution space is very different than the way you understand things from books. Because books can illustrate a process, but sim can animate it. And certain things that are incredibly abstract and confusing in two dimensions can seem intuitive in three.

In college ecology classes, for instance, students are generally given a bunch of multivariable calculus equations to explain how animal populations fluctuate in the wild. And after taking a bunch of derivatives and drawing graphs, they can answer word problems on an exam. But it doesn't seem to relate to anything. If, on the other hand, you put them in front of a computer simulation, the same concepts become intuitively obvious. Personally, I learned population dynamics on a program called *Pop-Dyn* that a graduate student had written in his spare time. It was a minimalist affair, a simple ecosystem that only had two animals: bobcats and bunnies. And each of these animals had its own set of vital statistics. And by playing with different rates of reproduction and mortality and predatory success, you could see that the bunny and bobcat populations would fall into distinct cycles that varied according to the numbers you plugged in. And you could see that this worked in a systematic way. And just being able to play with the system showed you what happened, so that you instinctively understood the process at work. It was, to say the least, an attractive alternative to endless derivative equations. As sim-meister Wright observes, "Humans, on an instinctive level, can do calculus without thinking, if you present the information in the right way."

For that matter, so can dogs, if you throw a Frisbee at them.

Perhaps it is for this reason that sims have become such a widespread training tool for bureaucrats, politicians, and corporate executives. In civics classes and urban planning seminars, *SimCity* is regularly used to give budding policy wonks a preview of their chosen career. Even established players are using sim as a soundboard these days. In fact, at the 1994 Mayors Conference in Portland, Oregon, more than a hundred city mayors gathered to demonstrate their bureaucratic chops in a marathon SimCity session conducted between panel discussions. After attracting SimBusiness, constructing public SimTransportation, and building pretty SimGreenBelts, contestants emerged as born-again point-and-click public officials, muttering, "Every day, in every way, I'm becoming a better SimMayor."

In the realm of SimForeignAffairs, a 1990 sim called *Hidden Agenda*, set in a fictional composite of Nicaragua, El Salvador, and Haiti, made a splash with the State Department. In this game, you play the president of a Central American country after the overthrow of an unpopular dictator. Your mission: Select a cabinet from the ranks of far-right, centrist, and left-wing political parties, finesse the superpowers, and stave off invasion, counterrevolution, riots, death threats, inflation, and a bloody coup. *Hidden Agenda* was used as a training device for diplomats, as well as new recruits to the FBI, CIA, and Drug Enforcement Agency.

And ever since the phrase "electronic town meeting" bobbed to the surface of American political consciousness, no national campaign is complete without a sheaf of simulations from competing parties trying to imagineer the federal budget. Of course, the idea of a budget itself is a kind of simulation, but it has only recently been made available to the voters as an actual videogame. In 1989, it began with *Hard Object,* an aptly titled budget sim from the National Economic Commission that challenged you to eliminate the budget deficit by 1994 solely by restraining Congress, without cutting Social Security or interest payments on the national debt. It's a sort of liberal Skinnerian box that demonstrates why taxes must be raised. Predictably, *Hard Object* provoked the righteous ire of conservatives in the National Chamber of Commerce, who released a competing budget game called the *Fair Freeze Simulation,* which let you tweak the rate of economic growth, so that you could see how, if everyone in America started taking amphetamines at work, the budget would balance just fine. On the World Wide Web, there are now scores of macroeconomic simulations that let you role-play some hapless staffer at the federal or state level. ("Want to see how your ideas on government spending will affect the budget? This site gives you the chance." Click. "Like to take a crack at drafting your own electronic version of Texas's biennial state budget? A program designed by students at the Lyndon B. Johnson School of Public Affairs lets you." Click. "Budget Battle Home Page by Citizens for an Alternative Tax System." Click. "Washington GOP Balanced Budget Web Site." Click.)

The one thing these political simulations all share is the insistence that you, the player, are in control. You adjust the dials, right? It's all up to you. And it's really easy to get that impression, because you're taking such an active role, and because the system works in this pseudomechanical way that seems transparent. But of course, this transparency is sim's first and greatest illusion. Sim is not neutral. You can gain or lose weight, but you can't get away from gravity. Every sim has a set of embedded biases and assumptions. For instance, *SimCity* favors public transportation because Wil Wright is a proponent of public transportation. Which is great, but it necessarily limits the range of winning strategies (i.e., Wright's little simcitizens will only commute so far in automobiles, but if you build subways they'll go all over the place). And of course, there are always factors that are significantly absent. You can build something that looks like Detroit without building in racial tension.

And so, really, it boils down to a kind of social contract. That sense of security in sim, that feeling that everything can work out, that you can win, is only possible because you have discovered, by trial and error, what the rules are, and you have agreed to live by them. You have accepted the designer's values and assumptions, at least for the duration of the game. And that's fine, as long as you realize what you're doing. But often, especially if the sim is lavishly produced, people don't twig. That's what makes sim so effective at convincing people that certain types of political behavior are appropriate. Once you're in the game, you've agreed to let someone else define the parameters. And so the question is who defines the parameters. Who has created this environment, and what do they want you to believe? And as politicians, media conglomerates, public relations firms, and management consultants churn out more simulations, this question becomes proportionately more important. Because if you're going to buy stocks on a simulated trading floor or work in a virtual office or fight a computer-mediated war — if you're going to play these games — it's a good idea to know who's making up the rules.

Acknowledgments

Thanks to:

Sloan Harris, for guiding me through the maze.
Michael Pietsch, for giving me the quarter.
Carl Goodman, for telling me where to find the Easter eggs.
David Cole, Rudy Naarvas, and Tony Seideman, for research power-ups.
Gary Susman, for bonus points of wit at the eleventh hour.
Ann, David, and Stacy, for life-extending sanity and advice.
My professors in the Harvard Biology Department: A little knowledge is a dangerous thing.

For color, sound, and inspiration, thanks to the American Museum of the Moving Image, Carlton Caldwell, David Cole, Walt Freitag, Brenda Garno, Richard Garriott, Rob Hubbard, the International Council of Shopping Centers, Eugene Jarvis, Henry Jenkins, Al Kahn, Jeff Kitts, Barbara Lanza, Todd Lappin, George McAuliffe, Andrew Nelson and the crüe at Cyberflix, Spencer Nilson, Alexey Pajitnov, Jonathan Rheingold, Jeremy Ross, Steve Russell, George Alistair Sanger, Hilton Sessel, Kaile Shilling, Tommy Tallarico, Eileen Tanner and Karyl Levinson at Golin Harris, Matt Thorn, Michael Wahrman, and Wil Wright.

Index

[]

Interactive Digital Software Association (IDSA), 191–192
Interactive Magic, 209–212
Internet, 58, 69–72, 83–85

Jameson, Brian, 201–202
Jarvis, Eugene, 77–80
Jenkins, Henry, 142, 144
Jobs, Steve, 37
Joust, 19
Jump Raven, 92
Jungle Strike, 208–209

Kahn, Al, 134–137
Kashiro, Yuzo, 110
Keeshan, Bob, 189
Killer Instinct, 81, 191
Kingdom, 9
kingdom-building strategy games, 9
Kohl, Herbert, 189, 190
Koop, C. Everett, 184
Kotick, Bobby, 73

Lambert, Christopher, 141
Lanza, Barbara, 172–174
laser disc games, 20, 147
Latham, Mark, 118–120
Legend of Zelda, 27
LHX Attack Chopper, 209
licensed products, 131–137
Lieberman, Joe, 189–190, 191
Lighthouse, 151
Lincoln, Howard, 190
Lockheed Martin, 201–204, 207
Lunar Lander, 8–9
Lunicus, 92

M1 Abrams Battletank, 208
Macintosh apple puzzle game, 28
Magnavox Odyssey games, 14, 15, 33–34, 37, 39
Main, Peter, 132–134
manga characters, 161–165
Mario games. *See Super Mario* games
martial arts games, 163–164
Marvel Superheroes arcade game, 165
Mattel, 20, 35
  Aquarius project, 38, 39
  Intellivision, 16
McAuliffe, George, 49, 50, 52–53

McCloud, Scott, 162
Meat Puppets, 181–182
Meier, Sid, 211
Microprose, 211
Microsoft classic games reissues, 74–75
Milton Bradley
  Microvision, 36
  Vectrex, 18, 38, 66
Mine Sweeper, 172
Missile Command, 16–17, 64–65
modeling and simulation (M&S), 199–200
Moriarty, Brian, 148
Mortal Kombat: The Movie, 140–141
Mortal Kombat games, 22, 80, 121, 163, 178, 188, 189, 191
Motorola microchips, 36
movies
  games based on, 26, 137
  Mortal Kombat: The Movie, 140–141
Ms. Pac-Man, 171, 173–174
Myst, 11, 98, 150–151

Narc, 77–78, 80–81, 194
National Economic Commission, 222
National Semiconductor, 35
NBA Jam, 22
NEC
  Turbo Express, 21
  Turbo-Grafx 16, 21
Netscape, 90
New England Journal of Medicine, 17
Next Generation, 179
Nibbler, 171
Night Trap, 188–191
Nilson, Spencer, 106–111
Nintendo, 17, 22, 39, 105, 190, 191
  customer service, 128–130
  game balancing by, 119
  licensing of products, 132–137
  marketing, 121
  North Bend Distribution Center, 113–116
Nintendo 13, 23, 64, 117
Nintendo Entertainment System (NES), 13, 20, 21, 23, 71–72, 116
Nintendo Game Boy, 13, 21
Nintendo Power, 124, 126–129, 130
Nintendo Ultra 64, 41